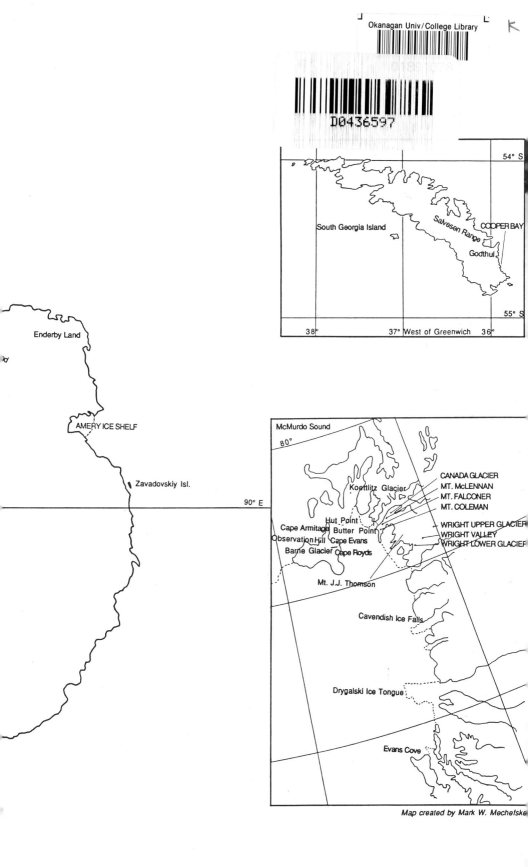

54° S

South Georgia Island

Salvesen Range

COOPER BAY

Godthul

55° S

38° 37° West of Greenwich 36°

Enderby Land

AMERY ICE SHELF

Zavadovskiy Isl.

90° E

McMurdo Sound

80°

Koettlitz Glacier

CANADA GLACIER
MT. McLENNAN
MT. FALCONER
MT. COLEMAN

Hut Point
Cape Armitage Butter Point
Observation Hill Cape Evans
Barne Glacier Cape Royds

WRIGHT UPPER GLACIER
WRIGHT VALLEY
WRIGHT LOWER GLACIER

Mt. J.J. Thomson

Cavendish Ice Falls

Drygalski Ice Tongue

Evans Cove

Map created by Mark W. Mechelske

IN A CRYSTAL LAND

DATE DUE

APR 1 8 2001	

BRODART   Cat. No. 23-221

DEAN BEEBY

In a Crystal Land
CANADIAN EXPLORERS
IN ANTARCTICA

UNIVERSITY OF TORONTO PRESS
Toronto Buffalo London

© University of Toronto Press Incorporated 1994
Toronto Buffalo London
Printed in Canada

ISBN 0-8020-0362-1

Printed on acid-free paper

Canadian Cataloguing in Publication Data

Beeby, Dean, 1954–
  In a crystal land : Canadian explorers in Antarctica

  Includes bibliographical references and index.
  ISBN 0-8020-0362-1

  1. Antarctic regions – Discovery and exploration –
  Canadian. I. Title.

  G870.B44 1944   919.8'904   C93-095229-4

This book has been published with assistance from the
Canada Council and the Ontario Arts Council under their
block grant programs.

For Nikolai and Josef,
fearless adventurers

Contents

Acknowledgments

THESE STORIES are based wherever possible on unpublished diaries, journals, logbooks, and letters. Published accounts of the expeditions, including books, newspaper clippings, magazine and journal articles, provided essential background and occasionally useful material on Canadian expedition members. I was able to interview three of the survivors. 'Red' Lymburner (now deceased), Andrew Taylor, and Fred Roots were living links to that golden era in Antarctic exploration, though they would chafe at any suggestion that their deeds were heroic. Gareth Wood, a 'modern' Antarctic adventurer, also gamely agreed to an interview. Some who have since died were interviewed by the Ontario Educational Communications Authority (now TVOntario) in the early 1970s for a series on Antarctica. Thanks to the prescience of Paul Marquardt, producer of the series, the material was deposited at the National Archives of Canada. Family members have been the most enthusiastic sources of information and supporters of this project, especially Dr Ken Cheesman, Eleanor

Davies, Patrick Douglas, Eleanor Evans, Tim Hollick-Kenyon, and Marjorie Howard.

The following also provided research assistance; some likely have moved on to other jobs and postings, so the affiliation and locations below were at the time of my original enquiries: Patricia Beeby, Rimbey, Alberta; Colin Bull, Rolling Bay, Washington; Douglas E. Cass, Glenbow Museum Archives, Calgary; Phebe Chartrand, archivist, McGill University, Montreal; Keturah Cheesman, West Vancouver, British Columbia; Marjorie H. Ciarlante, Civil Reference Branch, National Archives, Washington, DC; the late Alan Cooke, Montreal; Philip Cronenwett, Dartmouth College Library, Hanover, New Hampshire; Diane Duguay, National Archives of Canada, Ottawa; M. Eisenberg, College of Physicians and Surgeons of Ontario, Toronto; Stan Fox, TVOntario, Toronto; Mrs M.R. Gemie, Dumfries, Scotland; Linda Harris, Canada's Aviation Hall of Fame, Edmonton; R.K. Headland, Scott Polar Research Institute, Cambridge, England; Raymond Hebert, National Archives of Canada, Ottawa; Eileen Herman, Qu'Appelle, Saskatchewan; Richard Holden, Canada Council, Ottawa; Margaret Hollick-Kenyon, Vancouver; Joy Houston, National Photography Collection, Ottawa; Barry Hyman, Manitoba Provincial Archives, Winnipeg; Elizabeth Innes-Taylor, Whitehorse, Yukon; A.G.E. Jones, Tunbridge Wells, Kent; David Kenyon, Sherman Oaks, California; Andris Kesteris, National Film, Television and Sound Archives, Ottawa; James F. Kidd, National Archives of Canada, Ottawa; Esme Langer, Winnipeg Free Press, Winnipeg; R.M. Laws, British Antarctic Survey, Cambridge, England; the late Jessie Lymburner, Orange Park, Florida; Keith Lymburner, Guelph, Ontario; Lynn McPherson and Charles Maier, archivists, Yukon Government; Barbara Malcolm, Saint John Regional Library, Saint John, New Brunswick; Paul Marquardt, Toronto; Ken Molson, Toronto; Judith Murnaghan, Veterans Affairs Canada, Charlottetown; Roger de C. Nantel, Rideau Hall, Ottawa; Roger Nickerson, Ontario Archives, Toronto; Claudia M. Oakes, National Air and Space Museum, Smithsonian Institution, Washington, DC; John H. Paveling, Personnel Records Centre, National Archives of Canada; Alfred Petrie, London, Ontario; Madeleine Proulx, Rideau Hall, Ottawa; Joanna Rae, British Antarctic Survey, Cambridge, England; Sylvie Robitaille, National Film, Television and Sound Archives, Ottawa; Eugene Rodgers, Midlothian, Virginia; Walter Roots, Galiano Island, British Columbia; Peter Borden St Louis, Ottawa; Lord Shackleton, London; Pauline Stubbs, Vermilion, Alberta; Alice Gibson Sutherland, Ottawa; Charles Swithinbank, British Antarctic Survey, Cambridge, England; Kathlyn Szalasznyj, Saskatchewan Archives Board, Saskatoon, Saskatchewan; Laraine Tapak, Thunder Bay Public Library, Thunder Bay, Ontario; Mrs Glenna Tisshaw, Toronto; Anne Todd, British Antarctic Survey, Cambridge, England; Peter Wadhams, Director, Scott Polar Research Institute, Cambridge, England; Larry Weiler, Ontario Archives; Mrs F.L. Wells, CP Air, Vancouver; Ian Whillans, Ohio State University, Columbus; Carol White, National Archives of Canada; Alison Wilson, National Archives, Washington, DC; Louise Wuorinen, assistant city clerk, Thunder Bay, Ontario; and the staffs of the Library of Parliament, the Ottawa Public Library, the Halifax Public Library, the Killam Library, Dalhousie University, Halifax, and the McLennan Library, McGill University, Montreal.

I did not write this book for academics, but hope they will find the endnotes useful. No government grants or other direct aid from taxpayers was used in the preparation of the manuscript, though I did much of the research in publicly supported libraries. All research materials are being deposited with the University of Toronto Archives.

This work owes much to groundwork laid by Patricia Wright. In the 1970s, she received a small grant from the Canada Council to prepare for publication the Antarctic diaries kept by her father, Sir Charles, who died in 1975. She did a superb job, though her own work did not find its way into print. (The diaries were later published in a volume she jointly edited with

Colin Bull.) As a related project, Wright began to collect material about other Canadian explorers in the Antarctic. When I contacted her in the 1980s, she generously opened her files and sent me letters sketching out some of the detailed work that remained. Later she provided copies of key documents and articles. My queries to her over the years arrived at inopportune moments, yet she always found time for a response. Her help, generously given, has been invaluable.

Gerry Hallowell, history editor with the University of Toronto Press, was the first to read the entire manuscript and his enthusiasm never waned. His support and encouragement far outweighed the occasional frustrations of ushering this book into print. Diane Mew was a knowledgeable and thoroughly professional copy editor; an Antarctic buff herself, she saved me from many a crevasse. Special thanks to Mark Mechefske, who took time from his studies to produce the maps. My wife, Irina, and our children, Nikolai and Josef, have accepted my Antarctic obsession with good cheer these many years; indeed, Irina has since succumbed to the polar passion. My sons, though, are obsessed with other frontiers in the far reaches of time and space. Their flights of imagination often leave me trailing and breathless.

DEAN BEEBY
Halifax
May 1993

Note on Weights, Measures, and Place Names

The expeditions discussed here relied primarily on the imperial system of weights and measures; these have been retained throughout. Miles are statute miles. Antarctic place names are from Fred. G. Alberts, comp. and ed., *Geographic Names of the Antarctic* (Washington, DC 1981).

IN A CRYSTAL LAND

He giveth snow like wool:
    and scattereth the hoar-frost like ashes.
He casteth forth his ice like morsels:
    Who is able to abide by his frost?

Book of Common Prayer, 1662

Introduction

THE GOLDEN AGE of Antarctic exploration came to an end on 4 October 1957, when a 184-pound sphere called *Sputnik* soared into orbit. The sixty-year struggle to conquer the last unexplored region of the earth's surface had withered into scientific routine, and the world turned its attention to the superpower race to conquer a new frontier. The challenge to be first to step on the moon's airless plains recalled the quest at the turn of the century to plant a flag at the South Pole. The cycle of exploration had begun anew.

Men and women continued to live and work in Antarctica, but technology and bureaucracy drained their enterprises of dash, adventure, and heroism. Governments, armed forces, and scientific committees now directed the minute dissection of the continent, notably during the International Geophysical Year in 1957–8, when more than a dozen countries established about fifty outposts, including an American station at the South Pole. This storming of the bottom of the planet inaugurated a new Antarctic age, in which giant transport planes, snow-tractors, icebreakers, and corrugated steel dwellings largely replaced the sledges, tents, wooden ships and plank huts of old. The few remaining blank spots on the map were sketched in, and the babel of names for new features was standardized and made systematic. Antarctica's first tourists arrived in 1956–7, and an international treaty signed in 1959 soon imposed restraints on what had been the last terrestrial free-for-all. In the 1960s some of that first generation of explorers, men such as Sir Charles Wright, flew in comfort to the pole that half a century earlier had beckoned them across the killing ice and taken the lives of comrades.

Canada's contributions to the era of space exploration are numerous, beginning in 1962 when *Alouette I* separated from its American booster to glide into orbit. Canada thus became the third country in space, and this early expertise in satellite communications earned Canadian scientists a reputation for excellence. The space shuttle's Canadarm, the Anik satellite series, an astronaut training program, and a project to build a mobile servicing system for the American space station – all these demonstrated Canada's continuing commitment to the space sciences. Canada's first man in space, Marc Garneau, became an overnight celebrity before he had even stepped inside the cabin of a space shuttle. Roberta Bondar's voyage on a space shuttle in 1992 offered welcome relief for Canadians weary of constitutional bickering and economic uncertainty.

The achievements of Canadian explorers in Antarctica, on the other hand, rarely received headlines during the first half of this century. Canada has never mounted a national expedition to Antarctica,[1] but, just as in the exploration of space, many Canadians have joined teams from other countries and have earned their share of records. A Canadian was a member of the first expedition to winter on the Antarctic continent and in 1900 stood closer to the pole than any explorer had yet travelled. A Canadian pilot was at the controls for the first flight across the continent in 1935. A Canadian soldier headed a British expedition that established the first permanent base in Antarctica in 1944–6. A geologist from British Columbia completed the longest unsupported field trip in Antarctica in 1951–2. And like the icebergs that ring the continent, these are only the peaks. Underneath lie stories of dogged scientific observation, back-breaking labour, hunger, and frostbite. The Antarctic map is dotted with the names of a dozen Canadians who tested their mettle against the ice.

Canadians today continue to make forays to the south polar regions. A Canadian geophysicist, for example, was scientific leader at the US South Pole station in 1984. And each year, up to ten Canadian researchers are stationed at various Antarctic bases. Some hardy Canadian adventurers today even make headlines, such as Gareth Wood, who in 1985–6 retraced Captain Robert Scott's doomed march on the pole, and climber Pat Morrow, who in 1985 completed his quest to scale the tallest mountains on the seven continents with an assault on Antarctica's Vinson Massif.

The federal government has never seriously considered organizing a south polar expedition. Canada's vast north soaks up the few dollars available for the polar sciences. Policy advisers in the Department of External Affairs urged the government in the 1980s to support a small expedition if only to enable Canada to become a full member of the Antarctic Treaty.[2] This international accord, open to any nation supporting scientific work in Antarctica, protects the fragile environment with restrictions on resource development while encouraging the exchange of scientific information.

As a full treaty member, Canada would have a say in the protection of Antarctic ecosystems and in the distribution of resources. The continent is likely a storehouse of minerals and there is an abundant supply of protein offshore in the form of a shrimp-like creature called krill. The Antarctic waters may also guard vast reserves of oil. In an era of dwindling resources and rising populations, it is claimed that Antarctica's food could help Third World countries escape grinding poverty. Policy advisers have argued that Canada, as a middle power with no direct interests at stake, could act as a broker between the haves and the have-nots. And with growing expertise in the protection of vulnerable polar habitats, Canada could credibly adopt a role as environmental watchdog.

Scientists add another argument in support of Canadian funding of Antarctic research. Given that polar sciences figure prominently in Canadian research, there is a need for observation and analysis at both ends of the earth. A March 1987 federal study, *Canada and Polar Science*, noted that 'Canadian research on arctic problems is incomplete or made more difficult without complementary or supportive studies in southern polar regions ... In some subjects, such as ionospheric or planetary magnetic phenomena, the research is genuinely bi-polar, with simultaneous observations in Antarctica and at the geophysical counterpart or "conjugate" point in northern Canada.'[3] A Canadian glaciologist, thus, could hardly ignore the world's largest continental ice sheet and hope to develop an understanding of arctic ice masses. As custodian of the North Magnetic Pole, Canada has an obligation to support geomagnetic studies, which require observations in both the north and the south. There are some scientific questions raised in the Arctic that can be answered only in the Antarctic. The discovery in 1984 of an ozone hole in the atmosphere above Antarctica and, later, of its counterpart in the Canadian Arctic was a chilling reminder of the links between north and south.

There is a purely political argument as well, inspired by the Antarctic Treaty. Signed by a dozen countries in 1959 and effective in 1961, the agreement set aside competing national claims on territory. The treaty has proved remarkably durable. The Soviet Union and the United States, for example, developed a regime of mutual aid and support in Antarctica that was impervious to the vagaries of the Cold War. The continent can be a crucible for mutually supportive international relations. Some polar experts believe Canadian scientists have become too closely identified with their American counterparts because Canadian polar scientists most often join us programs.

By signing the treaty, Canada would demonstrate its independence and join an exciting experiment in extra-national peaceful cooperation.[4]

Given the enormous expense of operating in Antarctica's bleak environment, however, these and other arguments are unlikely to coax money from the federal treasury. But Ottawa did take a half-measure in May 1988 by becoming a 'non-consultative' member of the Antarctic fraternity. This is a form of second-class treaty membership, shared by about a dozen other nations, that requires no continuing Antarctic research. But it also prevents Canada from casting a vote when the treaty terms are being revised. Canada has merely agreed to abide by the terms of the Antarctic Treaty and can sit as an observer at regular meetings of the inner group of consultative members.

'Canada wishes to endorse a treaty that has created the world's sole, effective non-militarized zone,' Joe Clark, then external affairs minister, said in announcing the 1988 decision to sign. 'Canada is acutely aware of the uniqueness of Antarctica and will, through accession to the Treaty, be better able to work for the protection of its sensitive environment and dependent ecosystems.'[5] Canada thus became the last major Arctic country to sign the Antarctic Treaty, with Iceland the only holdout. To underscore this broader outlook, the federal government in September 1991 established the Canadian Polar Commission, with responsibilities to coordinate and support polar study. And on 5 October 1991 the federal government put its signature to the most important protocol of the Antarctic Treaty since its creation – an agreement to ban mining and oil exploration on the continent for at least fifty years.[6]

The following chapters are written in a way I hope Canada's earliest Antarctic explorers would have approved, as stories of young men burning for adventure and finding it at the bottom of the world. These fifteen Canadians – soldiers, scientists, dog-drivers, and aviators – threw themselves into gruelling work under extreme conditions, usually with humour, good grace, and tenacity. Many were the first humans to set eyes on the last unknown features of the earth's surface, the continent's mountains, valleys, glaciers and ice plains. Many who returned to Canada used their Antarctic experiences as a springboard for further study of Canada's own polar regions. For some, unveiling the continent was the most intense and wistfully recalled experience of their lives, despite the punishing conditions – much as some veterans remember the battlefield, despite its horrors. Antarctica maimed and killed comrades, but those who survived were bound in lifelong fellowship.

The expeditions discussed here are also a representative selection from the golden era of Antarctic exploration, though this was by chance rather than design. Carsten Borchgrevink's 1899–1900 wintering party, the first on the continent, generally marks the beginning of mainland exploration in Antarctica.[7] A Canadian, Hugh Evans, was there. Captain Robert Scott's tragic assault on the South Pole in 1910–12 is perhaps the most widely known Antarctic narrative. A Canadian, Charles Wright, was there. And so on, through the expeditions of Ernest Shackleton, George Hubert Wilkins, Richard Byrd, and Lincoln Ellsworth. For readers not yet exposed to the rich and abundant literature on early Antarctic exploration, this collection can serve as an outline from which the novice can make field trips. For Antarctiphiles, these pages will offer fresh perspectives on savoured adventures.

Many of these fifteen men wore their Canadian identity with a quiet pride. Most wrestled with bitter Canadian winters during their youths and this acted as a kind of calling card when they applied to join Antarctic expeditions. Certainly the bush pilots Silas Cheesman, Herbert Hollick-Kenyon, and J.H. 'Red' Lymburner were sought out for their skills in flying and maintaining aircraft in frigid climes. Most developed a taste for outdoor work early in their careers, whether as surveyors, civil engineers, mountain climbers, or geologists, and were temperamentally suited to the demands of Antarctic field-work.

They did not conceal their origins. During the long winter

night of 1899 at Cape Adare, Hugh Evans regaled his fellow expedition members with inflated tales about his adventures in the Canadian Northwest. Charles Wright hoisted sledging flags displaying a beaver and a maple leaf during ceremonial occasions on Scott's expedition. Herbert Hollick-Kenyon christened a lonely, windswept encampment in the middle of Antarctica 'Camp Winnipeg,' after his home base in Canada. On Byrd's 1933–5 expedition, dog-driver Alan Innes-Taylor dubbed his personal farthest south 'Camp Yukon' after his spiritual home.

In other contexts, these young Canadians who tagged along on great British or American enterprises might have felt like poor cousins. But in Antarctica, where the struggle against ice, wind and snow counted for everything, Canadians were accorded respect simply for having been born or raised in conditions similar to those in the south. Many with rugged outdoor skills – dog-driving, mountaineering, snowshoeing, or surveying, for example – became teachers on these expeditions. In the 1944–6 British wartime expedition known as Operation Tabarin, Canadian Andrew Taylor was given command. He reported no reluctance on the part of his British underlings to accept his position. On another expedition, that of Lincoln Ellsworth in 1935–6, three of the five principals were Canadians, including Herbert Hollick-Kenyon, who defied Ellsworth during one flight of exploration and turned back because he judged the weather too unreliable. There was no lack of confidence among men accustomed to dealing decisively with harsh climates and rough terrain.

The Antarctic exploits of these men also resonate with the 'outpost' mentality that stamped the early Canadian character. Just as Hudson's Bay posts bravely kept the lamp of civilization flickering against the wilderness, so too these explorers huddled inside their wooden huts and canvas tents staving off the killing cold, the insanity, and the creeping erosion of compassion. Such experiences demanded rigorous mental discipline, strong bonds with comrades, on whom one's life might depend, and a studied cautiousness about every proposed action. Canadians adapted to these conditions with an ease born of familiarity.

And there wasn't a deadbeat in the lot. Many Antarctic expeditions were vexed by personnel problems, some severe enough to place lives at risk. Drunkards, grumblers, thieves, and layabouts plagued wintering parties, but the troublemakers were never Canadian. Virtually all of the men in these chapters were professionals, and many were natural leaders. They occasionally vented their disappointments and frustrations, a few sometimes drank too much, and they sometimes made mistakes. But without exception, they were regarded by their colleagues as genial, hard-working, and competent. Their reasons for coming to Antarctica were mixed and varied, whether it was scientific curiosity, career advancement, or even to escape a bad relationship. The common thread, though, was adventure. All of them caught its scent and followed, despite terrible risks. For that reason alone, their stories deserve a place in Canadian history alongside the fur traders, the Arctic explorers, the Métis, and all others who burned to know what lay beyond the next bend in the river.

ONE

Winter at Cape Adare

WHEN THE WIND RISES at Cape Adare, at the west entrance to the Ross Sea, anything nailed or tied down rattles furiously, and everything loose is scooped up by the gusts and hurled against everything else. When the wind rises at Cape Adare, the pelting snow crystals blind you, the roar deafens you, the cold steals your touch, the gusts stop your breath. Your legs are yanked to horizontal, you have to crawl to stop the fury from getting underneath. When the wind rises at Cape Adare, it smashes the sea ice in Robertson Bay and churns ice boulders in the spray-tipped waves. But worst of all, the winds at Cape Adare pick up tiny pebbles from the beach and sling them staccato against your chest, arms, legs, against your stinging face.

On 25 May 1899 Hugh Evans stepped into this maelstrom, a hurricane lantern clutched in one hand.[1] He was an ox of a man, twenty-four years old, tall with broad shoulders and a big chest. It was his turn to cross the three hundred yards from the wooden hut to the meteorological screen to take the reading. The gusts fused his clothing to his body, and each step was laboured and short, only as far as the wind and the small circle of light from the lantern would permit. It was early winter. The sun had disappeared below the northern horizon ten days before and would not appear again for more than two months. Only the stars and the moon offered respite from the black void, and the frequent gales blotted out even this weak illumination. The pale arc cast by the hurricane lantern was the only defence against blindness.

Evans had not gone far when a blast snuffed out the flame. A curse, a meticulous 180-degree turn, and Evans held to a course he hoped would take him back to the hut. In a few minutes, he could see the glow from the windows but had to drop onto all fours as he approached because of the whirlwinds that swarmed around the structures. Back inside, he held a match to the lamp wick, hardly noticed by his nine companions. He tugged at the door again and stepped back into the storm. This time he successfully struggled all the way to the meteorological screen, hung the lamp, opened the small hatch, took the readings, closed the hatch, stuffed his pencil and paper into a pocket, grabbed the lamp, and had not gone more than a few paces when the wind snuffed the damn flame out again. Another gust knocked him flat and by the time got to his knees he had lost all sense of direction.

Although the gale was generally from the southeast, the gusts were coming from all quarters. One simply could not deduce direction in the confusion of wind. Still clutching the lantern, which was smashed in his fall, Evans began to stumble around in hope of finding the hut. Shouting was useless in the howl of the storm and tracks survived no more than a second or two. Frostbite began to stab at his face and fingers, and ice built up over his eyebrows. He lurched on, one hour, then two, becoming bone-tired but knowing that rest meant sleep and certain death. Finally he came to the base of a cliff and sat in the shelter of some rocks. All this time, flying pebbles pelted his face and body.

Back in the rattling hut, Louis Bernacchi grew uneasy when

after half an hour Evans had not returned. He poked his head out the door, but could not see beyond a few inches in the whirling snow and dark. He announced to everyone that something clearly had happened to Evans, and soon they were all pulling on windproof garments. Bernacchi, the expedition physicist, tied a rope around his belly while William Colbeck, a navigator and magnetician, knotted the other end around his. They stepped out into the gale.

'The shrieking storm which dashed one repeatedly to the ground, the blinding snow which cut one's face like a knife, the dense obscurity, the cold and dreadful chaos everywhere constituted a scene not easily forgotten,' Bernacchi wrote later.[2] The pair started to zigzag across the beach, back and forth, in the hope of stumbling upon Evans or at least catching him in their rope. They shouted, but their words were whipped away by the wind. The cold began to stiffen their limbs and ice began to shroud their faces. They found it difficult to breath and stooped low to avoid being knocked on their backs. Soon they were lost.

The expedition leader, Carsten Borchgrevink, also headed out and after a few minutes passed a dog kennel made from empty packing crates that had been lashed down with ropes and stakes. He noticed two very human legs jutting out of the entrance and assumed he had found Evans taking emergency shelter. On closer inspection, he saw the limbs belonged to one of his fellow searchers, a Finn named Per Savio. Borchgrevink angrily demanded an explanation for this apparent act of cowardice. Savio explained that if the violent gusts had flattened Evans, he, being half Evans's size, was likely to be carried away bodily. No sense losing two expedition members.

A third group, led by Anton Fougner, finally happened upon the half-frozen Evans, who was just about played out. They helped him limp back to the hut, only a few dozen yards away, and there he began to vomit uncontrollably. Bernacchi and Colbeck, on all fours, dragged themselves inside a few minutes after the others. Miraculously, they had stumbled onto the huts. Evans, frost-bitten and badly weakened, was bedridden for two days before he could get back on his feet.

Hugh Blackwall Evans was a Canadian by choice. He was born 19 November 1874 in Aylburton, Gloucestershire, from which his father, the Reverend Edward Evans, soon moved the family to Gloucester.[3] Young Evans attended the King's School and was a member of the Gloucester Cathedral choir but, to his father's disappointment, developed no desire to pursue a clerical or even a business career. If young Evans had any native interest it was to learn about the natural environment. His father heard about a new agricultural college at Qu'Appelle, in Canada's wild northwest, run by the Anglican church. St John's College, founded in 1885, was primarily a theological institution but also taught agriculture to a small number of students. The college, with its 640-acre farm, ran into financial difficulties and by 1890 was calling on church members in England to donate money and find new students.[4] Reverend Evans thought it a good opportunity for his aimless son.

So in 1890 Evans was given a boat ticket and enough money to get to Qu'Appelle Station, a Canadian Pacific Railway stop in the Assiniboia district of the Northwest Territories (now southern Saskatchewan). His father also paid the $300 tuition for a one-year course in agriculture. Evans completed the training, then faced two years of apprenticeship on a local farm before he would be deemed able to homestead. He worked as a hand on a farm at Indian Head, just ten miles east of Qu'Appelle Station along the railway line, and found the work dispiriting.

Evans next moved to a cattle ranch about forty miles north of Indian Head, in the heavy bush between the Beaver and Touchwood Hills. When not tending to the two hundred head of cattle, he would hunt and trap, picking up tips from local Indians, with whom he maintained good relations. He liked to tell of the night he gave shelter to the young Cree, Almighty Voice. He learned later his visitor was a fugitive from the North

West Mounted Police for having killed a sergeant in October 1895. (Almighty Voice was eventually killed in a shootout in which six died.)

For three years Evans and his boss, Jack Salter, lived in a log hut struggling to make the ranch a success. In 1896, apparently at his father's bidding, Evans returned to England, although for what purpose remains unclear. He was soon at loose ends again. The following year he accepted an invitation from his cousin Charles Rowlands to join a sealing expedition to Antarctica's Kerguelen Islands.[5] Rowlands was underwriting the venture, and asked his unemployed cousin to look after his interests on the voyage. Evans was to be paid £100 and all expenses, and would share the officers' cabin. His contract stipulated he was to assist an ornithologist on the trip, who taught him taxidermy.

Evans joined the crew at Melbourne, Australia. The ship was a Norwegian brig, the *Edward*, built more than ninety years earlier but still in fine condition. The vessel sailed on 28 October 1897 and arrived at the Kerguelens in early December. From the sea, the islands looked lush, though in fact they were barren, covered only with a low mossy plant. The islands had been discovered in 1772 by a French expedition led by Yves-Joseph de Kerguélen-Trémarec. The rocky coast, fog, and rough waters prevented a landing by the French explorer, but on his return Kerguélen reported he had found a verdant continent. In 1773, with King Louis xv's blessing, he led a vain attempt to colonize the islands. A landing was made but, blaming everyone but himself, Kerguélen abandoned the venture and returned to France in 1774. He was sent to prison for his folly.

The crew of the *Edward* spent eleven weeks among the islands, hunting and skinning elephant seals and boiling down the blubber for oil. The harvest was large as the islands had been virtually ignored by sealers for the previous two decades. About nine hundred skins were brought back along with nineteen thousand gallons of oil, providing the investors with a handsome profit. Evans spent much of his time collecting and preparing bird specimens obtained from landings on the islands.

The ship arrived back in Melbourne in March, 1898, after a rough passage. Evans returned to England, one of a select group of young British men who knew some science and had survived an expedition to Antarctic waters. Evans and his father soon met the wealthy magazine publisher Sir George Newnes, who had been an investor in the Kerguélen expedition, and the younger Evans described the voyage of the *Edward* in some detail. Newnes mentioned he was backing another Antarctic expedition, a purely scientific voyage led by Carsten Borchgrevink and departing in the fall of 1898. Evans immediately approached Borchgrevink for a position.[6] It was not the first time he had spoken with the Norwegian explorer. Before Evans left England for the Kerguélen trip, Borchgrevink asked him to look up Louis Bernacchi in Melbourne and convey an invitation to join the south polar expedition just then being planned. Bernacchi, whose father had made a fortune in Tasmanian vineyards, was a young physicist at the Melbourne Observatory. On receiving this message, Bernacchi immediately sailed for England to prepare for Borchgrevink's expedition. Evans thus unwittingly met two of the nine men he was to winter with in such cramped quarters at Cape Adare eighteen months later.

Borchgrevink was born in Christiana (now Oslo) in 1864, the son of a Norwegian father and English mother.[7] He went to Australia in 1888 and for the next six years was a teacher and government surveyor. By 1894 Borchgrevink had settled on polar exploration as his path to fame and learned that a whaling expedition was headed that September for Antarctic waters. As luck would have it, a scientist and an Arctic specialist failed to arrive in time for the departure and so Borchgrevink was accepted as a common seaman. The ship, the *Antarctic*, came within viewing distance of Cape Adare on 16 January 1895. Seven days later a launch was put out from the ship and a landing made at the cape – the first landing on the Antarctic mainland.

Just whose foot touched the shore at Cape Adare first remains in dispute. No fewer than three of the seven men in the launch claimed the honour, among them Borchgrevink, who insisted he jumped off the boat and waded ashore in part to chase a jellyfish and in part to relieve the boat of some weight to allow it closer to the shore. True or not, the account illustrated Borchgrevink's penchant for self-aggrandizement, which many in the Antarctic fraternity found uncouth.

Following the return of the *Antarctic* to Melbourne on 12 March 1895, Borchgrevink set about in lectures and articles to magnify his role as an explorer and to seek funding for another expedition that he would lead. Although money was already being raised for the British Antarctic party that Robert Scott would lead between 1901 and 1904, Borchgrevink persuaded Sir George Newnes to part with £40,000 in support of his ambitious proposal. The brash Norwegian this time planned to land a party at McMurdo Sound, overwinter, and sledge to both the South Pole and the South Magnetic Pole.

Evans met Borchgrevink in London in 1898 and after a fifteen-minute interview signed on as assistant zoologist at a salary of £100 for the entire trip – modest pay, but Evans was after adventure.[8] He soon met fellow expedition member William Colbeck, a twenty-six-year-old mariner from Hull. The two became chums. Borchgrevink had hired Colbeck for his experience as a navigator and sent him for a crash course at the Kew Gardens Observatory so he could also become the expedition's magnetic observer during the winter on the ice.

The expedition ship was christened the *Southern Cross* after the cluster of stars in the southern sky. It was designed by Colin Archer, the same man who built the *Fram*, the vessel Roald Amundsen took to Antarctica for his assault on the pole in 1910–12. Originally called the *Pollux*, the *Southern Cross* was built in Norway in 1886. Rigged as a barque, she was 522 tons and 147 feet long, with two decks and a quarterdeck; engines rated at 100 horsepower supplemented her sails.

The Norwegian zoologist Nicolai Hanson and Bernacchi, the physicist, were to oversee the expedition's scientific program. Anton Fougner, a whaler from Australia, and Dr Herlof Klovstad, a Norwegian physician, also signed on, as did two Finns, Ole Must and Per Savio, who were in charge of the expedition's ninety Siberian and Greenland dogs. At the last moment Colbein Ellefsen, a crew member from the *Southern Cross*, was taken ashore at Cape Adare as cook. Everybody but Must and Savio was fluent in English, and despite the range of nationalities, the expedition was self-consciously British.

The ship, docked at London, was the focus of public curiosity during the weeks of preparation. On departure day, 22 August 1898, St Katharine's Dock was jammed with thousands of well-wishers. Members of the Royal Geographical Society, though, were conspicuous by their absence. While civil in their public utterances, society members had a generally low opinion of Borchgrevink, partly because he had drawn away money that might otherwise have gone to the large British Antarctic expedition then in its planning stages.

After a coaling stop at St Vincent, Hanson became seriously ill with a fever for three weeks. Passing through the tropics, the ship was threatened on occasion by waterspouts that sometimes rose hundreds of feet and carried tons of sea water. The crew, fearful that one of these columns would smash into the ship, reportedly fired their rifles into the whirlwind to collapse the spouts. The ship finally arrived in Hobart, Tasmania, on 28 November 1898, ninety-eight days after leaving London. There, the crew spent almost three weeks outfitting, loading supplies, and attending social functions in honour of the expedition. At one reception the main speaker concluded his remarks with a morbid exhortation: 'Take a good look at these men for they will never be seen again.'[9]

The ship left on 19 December, encountered the pack ice about ten days later, and spent the next forty-three days a prisoner of the ice. The loss of valuable time dashed every hope of landing at McMurdo Sound, the most promising spot to launch a bid for the South Pole. When a route through the ice was finally found, the transit took just six hours.

With winter approaching, Borchgrevink had no leisure to scout out a site for his base. Cape Adare was a known quantity, so he had the captain make for Robertson Bay with all speed. On 15 February they sighted the cape, black cliffs of basalt capped with snow. The weather prevented them from entering the bay, northwest of the cape, until 17 February, when they finally dropped anchor. A small party including Evans made for the 180-acre beach at the base of the cliffs. On landing the men immediately became nauseous from the odour of guano – penguin droppings – which was four inches thick in most spots but several feet deep in others. The highest part of the triangular pebble beach was about twenty feet above sea level. The area was littered with the bleached remains of thousands of penguins, and skuas swooped and dived at their heads. It was a desolate, almost repulsive, first home for man on the continent.

Evans and Bernacchi scrambled to the top of the cape, an hour's climb of about 950 feet. 'The silence and immobility of the scene was impressive,' Bernacchi wrote later, 'not the slightest animation or vitality anywhere. It was like a mental image of our globe in its primitive state – a spectacle of Chaos.'[10] The next day the unloading of supplies began. First ashore were the sledge dogs, who immediately tore into penguins waddling on the beach, creating a bloody, feathery mess. The crew had to stand in the icy water up to their knees to unload the small boats that ferried supplies from the *Southern Cross*. A site was selected for the two wooden huts, and construction began.

A great storm blew up without warning on 21 February during the unloading and the ship was nearly lost. Its moorings snapped, pebbles rained down upon the deck, and the wind sent it drifting out to the open sea. With engines fired, the crew struggled through the night to keep the ship in the bay. Evans, Bernacchi, and two or three others were caught on the beach during the gale. The huts were just skeletons still, so they put up a tent to get out of the weather, its sides weighed down with boulders. Many of the ninety or so dogs squirmed inside as well, their body heat and thick hair preventing their masters underneath from freezing to death.

The storm passed without serious damage, and attention turned to completing the pine huts. Each measured fifteen feet square and had been prefabricated in Norway. On the windward side, the roof dipped to the ground and was covered with seal skin. Papier mâche, wool, and fur were used to insulate the walls and floor and the area between the two huts was covered over with lumber to serve as an unheated porch. The smell of guano permeated the interior. Each of the ten men staying through the winter had an enclosed bunk that afforded some privacy. Borchgrevink wrote: 'It was by special recommendation from the doctor that I made this [bunk] arrangement and found that it answered well ... To work at the table with nine hungry minds, starved by the monotony of the Antarctic night, glaring at you through nine pairs of eyes at once indescribably vacant and intense, was impossible.'[11]

The ship finally set sail for New Zealand on 1 March, leaving the shore party to face the approaching Antarctic winter uncertain precisely when – or even if – they would be picked up again. The ship might be lost in a storm, or fail to negotiate the pack in the Antarctic spring. Worse, the sunless winter in a too-small hut might infect them all with madness. It had happened before. In 1898–9 the crew of a Belgian Antarctic expedition endured an austral winter in their ship the *Belgica* when it unexpectedly froze in the pack ice. Minds snapped. One crew member, who knew little French, became convinced the words 'quelque chose' in fact meant 'kill.' In self defence, he would attack whoever used it.[12]

Evans was by far the strongest, tallest, and heaviest man of the shore party. He weighed in at 185 pounds, and was just over 5 foot 11, with a barrel chest. As the expedition taxidermist he was given a small insulated room to carry out his work. He was also given charge of the fuel, ammunition, and guns, and acted as Hanson's zoological assistant and Bernacchi's photography assistant. (A movie camera taken along proved useless when it was discovered the film for it did not fit the machine.) All members of the expedition took turns taking readings from the meteorological observatory and as the autumn slipped away and the sun appeared for shorter and shorter stretches, it became clear the cape was one of the windiest places on earth. On at least two occasions the weather vane and anemometer were smashed to bits by the gusts that poured down off the Antarctic plateau. On 15 May the sun disappeared altogether and would not return for another seventy-two days.

Earlier, on 19 March, Borchgrevink had led a three-man party on a short reconnaissance trip into the interior. They took dogs, a sledge, and food for ten days. All of the men helped the party get their supplies to the top of Cape Adare, a difficult ascent that demonstrated how badly situated were the huts. Even after getting onto the cape heights, the party faced a treacherous traverse of the Admiralty Mountains, whose peaks average seven thousand feet. Evans nearly got killed as he headed back to the huts once Borchgrevink's sledging team was on its way. He, Bernacchi, and Hanson came upon a long snow-filled ravine that extended to the beach and offered a short-cut home. The trio trudged down until they suddenly came upon slick ice. All three lost their footing and began to accelerate on their backsides towards certain death below. Hanson and Bernacchi managed to grab an outcrop of rock soon after tumbling. But Evans, not far behind, skidded out of control. Hanson lay across the rock full-length, grabbed Evans's clothing as he sped by, and hauled him to safety.[13]

Further exploratory sledging trips had to be put off until the spring, so the men sought ways to cope with life in a cramped hut. Cards, books, chess, and a phonograph helped to dispel some of the boredom. Routine duties – washing, cooking, fetching ice for water, taking meteorological readings – also kept idle minds occupied. Although whisky and other spirits were available, these were brought out only for special occasions, such as birthdays. Rarely did anyone rise before eleven in the morning in this life of 'bovine repose,' as Bernacchi put it. Borchgrevink was less poetic: 'We were getting sick of one another's company; we knew each line in each other's faces. Each one knew what the other one had to say. Our whole repertoire was exhausted, but knowing the fact, all kept cheerful.'[14]

Unlike the *Belgica*'s crew, expedition members found the long winter tolerable. 'We got along excellently,' Evans recalled in an interview in 1971. 'We had no trouble amongst ourselves at all. We were all good fellows. Of course, naturally we had lots of arguments but they were all pleasant arguments, there was no acerbity about them at all. We just argued for the sake of arguing.'[15] One such argument focused on the precise moment the new century would begin, a timely subject in 1899. Some argued for 1 January 1900, others for 1 January 1901. 'With the utmost care I invented fresh arguments in favour of the losing side,' Borchgrevink wrote, 'only for the purpose of keeping a desirable dispute going.' He did not record the winner.[16]

Evans also regaled his mates with tall tales about his ranching days in Canada's rugged northwest. Borchgrevink related one of them:

Once upon a time, he told us, he was driving cattle in Canada. It was on a big plain; and he and a bosom friend had charge of some 500 cattle; they were riding leisurely along behind the tails of the oxen, enjoying an evening pipe under their broad-brimmed hats. It was just getting dusk when up rides a highwayman, pointing his revolver at them and demanding their money, watches, and, if I do not remember wrongly, their pipes also.

'It was hard luck,' Mr. Evans said, but they had to give up all as they had no weapons themselves, and resistance would have been useless. However, when the robber was about to depart, Mr. Evans conceived a bright idea. He drew out a pack of cards and invited the departing robber to make a third in a game which he consented to do. Mr. Evans and his mate showed themselves as great experts in handling cards as their savage visitor in the handling of his revolver; they stuck to cards until, by the help of them, they had regained not only their watches and money, but also their pipes, and, in addition, became the possessors of the watch, money and revolver, horse and saddle, of the unfortunate thief. 'Poor fellow,' Mr. Evans remarked with intense compassion, 'he was fairly done, and when he told me he had not enough money to get back to the nearest town, I lent him a dollar out of his own purse!'

For some minutes profound silence reigned around the table, then Mr. Bernacchi, who had heard similar stories in the Australian bush, had to remark, 'Come, come, Mr. Evans, you do not mean to say that you were mean enough to pay him out of his own purse?' 'Well, you see,' Mr. Evans replied, 'it was a fair game.'[17]

Everyone in the hut enjoyed a pipe but soon after the ship departed the shore party learned that the packing crate supposed to contain fine English pipe tobacco in fact contained coal-black plugs of sailors' chewing tobacco. The discovery was greeted with alarm since meagre personal supplies of pipe tobacco would soon run out. Some of the men diced a plug with a knife, put the bits in their pipes and took a few puffs. It was wretched strong but in a few days all got to enjoy it. After returning to civilization, Evans found he simply could not taste pipe tobacco any more and for years continued to smoke chewing plugs.[18]

The health of everyone remained good throughout the winter, with the sad exception of Nicolai Hanson, the Norwegian zoologist. Hanson needed three weeks to recover from whatever malady had attacked him in the tropics but seemed fine after that. While unloading the ship at Cape Adare, however, he pulled something inside and was not able to do much work. In July, the middle of winter, he took a turn for the worse. Headaches plagued him and he lost all sensation in his legs, which soon swelled badly. He could walk only with help and soon came to spend all his time in his bunk. Some took the symptoms to be the onset of scurvy, although no one else had them and lime juice was a regular part of the diet. Dr Klovstad, unable to consult with colleagues, could offer little medical help. He applied an electric current to Hanson's legs with no results. Hanson, ever cheerful, continued to direct Evans in the expedition's zoological studies and kept copious notes of his observations.

'On the 27th July a fiery segment of the sun appeared above the purple horizon,' Bernacchi wrote, 'and one felt like an anchorite catching a glimpse of the seventh heaven.'[19] With the return of the sun, sledging trips were begun anew. These were short sallies across the now-frozen Robertson Bay to explore the coast; Borchgrevink had abandoned all attempt to probe the interior because of the difficulty of getting beyond the Admiralty Mountains. Evans and Colbeck spent two or three weeks exploring a nearby glacier. One morning during this trip, while Evans was in the tent preparing breakfast, Colbeck noticed that the sea ice had disappeared from Robertson Bay, which was now open water. They now had no way to return to the huts. Evans came out and saw the same scene but, perplexed, could hear no sound of waves. The image – a shared mirage – then faded and the sea ice returned.[20]

On the same trip, a very real crevasse nearly meant the end of Evans. They were examining a medial moraine, the heap of boulders, sand, and rocks formed at the point where two inland glaciers meet. They had removed their skis and Alpine ropes as they examined a level area of the moraine, Colbeck about fifty yards ahead of Evans. Suddenly the ground disappeared from under Evans as he slipped into a crevasse hundreds of feet deep. He couldn't get a foothold but his ski pole jammed into the ice on one side and rested on a boulder on the other while he dangled between. Colbeck came rushing up and using ropes managed to extricate Evans. All the while they could hear rocks tumbling hundreds of feet to the sea below.[21]

Back at the hut, Hanson's condition worsened. By 4 October he could no longer retain food and became extremely weak. Nine days later everyone except the doctor moved to a tent out-

side to improve the air of the hut. They were awakened at two
o'clock in the morning on the 14th with word that Hanson was
about to die and wanted to shake everyone's hand and bid farewell. Each man came alone to his bedside. Hanson's last wish
was to be buried atop Cape Adare in the lee of a boulder he had
visited several times earlier in the year to gaze north toward his
native Norway. Half an hour before he died, the first penguin of
the spring arrived at Cape Adare. Evans brought the bird inside
and Hanson examined it from his bedside, dictating notes.
Death came shortly after three in the afternoon. His illness
remains a mystery to this day.

Getting Hanson's swollen body and the heavy wooden coffin
to the cape heights was a back-breaking business. Even more
difficult was the chore of chiselling out a grave. One day's work
with pickaxes produced a four-inch depression, so the next day
they used dynamite – and soon had their hole. Hanson's wife
had sent him some dried flowers in her last letter. These were
placed on his chest. Borchgrevink read the Anglican last rites
and the coffin, bedecked with a British flag, was lowered into
the grave. 'It was a terrible time for all of us,' Evans said in 1971,
'as we were all cut off, we didn't know when the ship would
come back or anything ... we cut out a place for his coffin to lie
in the solid ice and I expect he's just the same now as when we
buried him.'[22] The first tiny community in Antarctica reluctantly gave the continent its first grave.

The return of the penguins brought a welcome change in the
expedition diet. After some failed experiments, the men
learned how to roast and broil penguin breasts and got to enjoy
the meat immensely. Roasted penguin hearts were a delicacy
reserved for Sundays, as well as penguin eggnogs made with
their precious store of rum. And as it was getting late in the season, they began to collect penguin eggs by the hundreds to boil
and salt as emergency supplies in case the ship did not return.
By December they had packed away four thousand of them.

The ship was expected by Christmas and there was unspo-
ken worry when the day passed without a sighting. The men

took turns climbing to the top of Cape Adare with a telescope to scan the horizon. Robertson Bay had been fully explored and there was little to do but watch and wait. On 28 January one of the men, Colbein Ellefsen, went outside to fetch a bag of coal while everyone else slept. He saw a large figure in the distance, larger than even an Emperor penguin. Was this a new species? he thought. As the figure drew closer he recognized Bernard Jensen, captain of the *Southern Cross*, a mail bag slung over his shoulder. After a few quiet words with Ellefsen, Jensen opened the hut door, threw the bag down on the table and shouted 'Post!' A few seconds of groggy confusion ensued, then everyone was shaking Jensen's hand and digging into the mail bag.

The *Southern Cross* pulled out of Robertson Bay on 2 February and headed south for about a month of ship-based exploration. First stop was Possession Island on 3 February, where the party located a wooden marker erected by the crew of the *Antarctic* in January 1895 during Borchgrevink's first visit south. The ship's advance was soon halted by the enormous Ross Ice Shelf, a giant ice sheet fronting the sea for about 450 miles and extending south up to 500 miles. Colbeck calculated the highest latitude reached by the *Southern Cross* as 78° 34′ 37″. This broke the farthest-south record set by Capt. James Clark Ross, who discovered the ice shelf in the British ships *Erebus* and *Terror* in the summer of 1840–1. The *Southern Cross* found a harbour and the expedition made man's first landing on the ice shelf, which had apparently receded some thirty miles since Ross's visit sixty years earlier. With Colbeck and Savio, Borchgrevink made a five-hour trip south by sledge on 16 February. He estimated they had travelled to latitude 78° 50′ south – the farthest south yet reached by man.

Borchgrevink carefully recorded the accomplishment in his published account of the sledge trip,[23] but neglected to mention a rival claim. On 19 February, Evans, Bernacchi, Fougner and crew member Axel Johansen also skied south for about eight hours and estimated they had travelled ten miles, to a point between 78° 50′ and 78° 45′ south. Bernacchi faithfully recorded this trip in his published account of the expedition and left out any mention of Borchgrevink's claim.[24]

The ship headed back to civilization on 19 February and reached Hobart about six weeks later, more than fifteen months after the shore party had set out. Expedition members sailed on the RMS *Ortona* for England in May 1900 and for the next few years Borchgrevink lectured and wrote articles about his achievement. He was received coolly in England and Scotland, where public interest was focused on Captain Robert Scott's planned expedition to the south. Some in the scientific community, annoyed that Borchgrevink had siphoned funds away from the Scott expedition, claimed he produced little scientific information for the pounds spent. Others found the scientific and geographical results shoddily presented. Evans, for instance, had turned over his and Hanson's notes and specimens to Borchgrevink for delivery to scientific authorities in England. For reasons still unexplained, most of the material disappeared while in Borchgrevink's care.[25]

Eleven years after it had been abandoned, Borchgrevink's hut became the locale for the most southerly boxing match in the world. In one corner, Raymond Priestley, a geologist from Britain. In the other, George Abbott, a petty officer with the Royal Navy. Each wore improvised boxing gloves made from two pairs of woollen mitts padded with seaweed. The wool, being abrasive, was an added reason to duck the blows of the opponent. Three flickering candles cast a yellow glow on walls which, because there was no heat, were coated with hoarfrost. The pair had stripped down to their underwear and as they sparred, great clouds of vapour rose from their bodies. Towards the end of a three-minute round, neither could see the other for the fog. More than once Priestley landed a punch on a door or post, thinking he saw Abbott's form take shape through the mist. They would call a halt and sit on the edges of the old bunks while the fog cleared.[26]

Priestley and Abbott were members of a six-man exploration team with Scott's *Terra Nova* expedition. Plans called for them to erect a hut in King Edward VII Land (now Edward VII Peninsula) to the east of the Ross Ice Shelf. There they were to spend the winter, surveying and mapping this virtually unknown sector of Antarctica. However, the *Terra Nova* had difficulty finding a suitable landing spot and as they back-tracked they came unexpectedly upon Roald Amundsen's ship, the *Fram*, at the Bay of Whales, the only harbour along the ice shelf. They met Amundsen and learned his men had erected a hut just to the south from which he intended to make his dash to the pole the next summer.

The discovery immediately ruled out a base in this vicinity for what until then had been called Scott's 'Eastern Party.' The *Terra Nova* returned to the main base at Cape Evans and passed on word of Amundsen's location, then headed north to find a wintering spot for the Priestley's party along the barren shore of Victoria Land. As with Borchgrevink's party, the lateness of the season and the rugged coast forced the team to land at Cape Adare: it was either that or return to New Zealand with no work accomplished. And so this guano beach was the scene of yet another expedition, even though the area had been excessively explored by Borchgrevink and offered no access to the interior.

The six-man party found Borchgrevink's huts still standing, although the storage hut had lost its roof in a gale. As they brought their supplies ashore, a seaman began to restore the old stove left behind by the *Southern Cross* expedition and had a hot lunch ready by the time the soaked landing crew needed a respite from the cold. A tarpaulin was roped onto the unroofed hut, which again became a storage shed, and for two weeks the other hut became a sleeping and living quarters while a new dwelling was raised.

There was plenty to scavenge from the supplies abandoned a decade earlier by Borchgrevink's men: coal, charcoal, cloth, rope, bottles, ammunition. There was also some food, including thousands of chocolates flavoured with lime juice and something ingloriously dubbed 'glue jam.' It was a 'stiff, brown paste stored in large stone jars and tasting of greengage and malt extract,' Priestley wrote.[27] No one knew quite what it was but everyone loved it. During a sledging trip, expedition members located a food cache left by the earlier team. They also found a mummified penguin carcass with a string on its leg stretched towards the sea, obviously captured alive ten years earlier and carelessly forgotten.

The achievements of the *Southern Cross* expedition, which had been obscured by Borchgrevink's self-aggrandizement, were rehabilitated somewhat after the northern party's winter at Cape Adare. Priestley confessed he was 'sceptical of the accuracy of the reports which laid stress upon the fact that men were constantly being struck by flying pebbles. In the light of after events, I can only place on record an apology for ever having doubted the accounts of our predecessors.'[28] And to the suggestion that Borchgrevink had not done enough exploring in the vicinity, Priestley countered that Cape Adare 'proved a very poor centre for sledging operations; the country all round, as can be seen from our own narrative, proved to be very impenetrable, and the work of the expedition was, therefore, very much restricted. Nevertheless Borchgrevink did good pioneer work in opening up a new field of exploration, and in the opinion of those of us who have followed his footsteps, he has not received his fair share of credit for his achievements.'[29]

This benign assessment of the work carried out by the *Southern Cross* expedition helped persuade the Royal Geographical Society in 1930 to award Borchgrevink its patron's medal. Three decades had softened earlier harsh judgments. Even so, Borchgrevink never again led a polar expedition, and died in Oslo in 1934 after years of illness and financial difficulties.

Evans faded quickly into obscurity after the expedition. He considered applying to join Scott's *Discovery* expedition (1901–4) but changed his mind after a discussion with Sir Joseph Hooker, an eminent British scientist. Hooker, a friend of Evans' maternal grandfather, had been a biologist with Sir James Clark Ross's expedition of 1839–43. The elderly scientist told Evans in

1900 that the proposed *Discovery* expedition was likely to fall apart for lack of funds. Under some pressure to settle down, Evans returned to the Canadian northwest with two friends and began farming and cattle ranching in the unsurveyed Vermilion River Valley, east of Edmonton, where he built a log cabin.[30]

In 1901 Evans was formally offered a post with Scott's first expedition to the Antarctic but had to turn it down because of the demands of establishing his new farm. He was also asked by fellow Cape Adare veteran William Colbeck to sail on the *Morning*, which in 1902 had been commissioned with Colbeck as captain to relieve Scott's expedition. Again, Evans had to decline because of the responsibilities of his farm.[31] In 1908 he married Douella Jack, born and raised in Dublin, and together they worked the land. Colbeck became godfather to Evans' first child, Eleanor, born in 1909. Until the age of seventy, Evans ran the valley farm and helped establish the school and Anglican church in Vermilion. He was also a founding member of the Alberta Wheat Pool when it was organized in 1923.[32]

Evans's connection with the Antarctic was virtually unknown until he was 'rediscovered' in the early 1970s. Antarctic historians, reporters, and film crews trooped out to Vermilion to interview this curious survival from another era. At least three film presentations resulted and his slides and negatives from the *Southern Cross* expedition were donated to the Scott Polar Research Institute in Cambridge, England. Tragically, Evans's personal papers from the expedition were lost in the mail shortly after his return to Canada. When traced they were found to have been auctioned off in Toronto as lost property.[33] Evans had a keen memory and intellect, though, even beyond his hundredth year, and in 1973 and 1974 he produced three scholarly articles about his Antarctic experiences.[34] He also kept some reminders of the *Southern Cross* expedition, including an ancient plug of chewing tobacco. He carried a lifelong sensitivity in his fingers and face to the cold, the result of his three hours lost in a blizzard at Cape Adare. He came down with pneumonia and died at Vermilion on 8 February 1975.

TWO

Shackleton's
Broken Doctor

A MYSTERY hangs about the figure of Dr William Arthur Rupert Michell, ship's surgeon of the *Nimrod*, the vessel that took Ernest Shackleton and his men to the Antarctic in 1908 and returned for them in 1909. Much has been written about Shackleton's famed expedition, which discovered the South Magnetic Pole and put four men just 112 miles from the elusive geographical pole. Shackleton had proved himself an extraordinary leader, able to conjure superhuman efforts from his men under adverse conditions. After the expedition, the once obscure Shackleton returned to acclaim and knighthood in Britain. At least two exhaustive biographies and dozens of other works attempted to sum up the accomplishments of this extraordinary Anglo-Irishman, including a fat volume about the *Nimrod* expedition by Shackleton himself.[1]

Michell, a native of Perth, Ontario, is mentioned only in passing through all this literature and he never sought publicity for his role in the expedition. From scattered scraps of information it is possible to reconstruct most of his career and some of his personal experiences from the *Nimrod*'s voyages. But there is also evidence suggesting Michell held a secret he guarded carefully until his death in 1966. Two forays into the Antarctic apparently broke Michell's health, rendered him a lifelong semi-invalid, and embittered him about the experience. And two personal diaries Michell kept while in the south were suppressed because they chronicled the terrible deprivations he underwent.

Michell was born in 1880, the second child of Francis Lambton Michell and his wife, Margaret Helen Bell.[2] Francis Michell, a University of Toronto graduate in classics and mathematics, became principal of the Perth high school in 1875, in charge of about forty students. In 1881 he became public school inspector for the County of Lanark, a position he held until retirement in 1922. His son William, named for his grandfather William Henry, who had emigrated to Canada from England in 1832, was known simply as Rupert.

In the late 1890s Rupert was sent to the University of Toronto, where he studied medicine, graduating in 1902. He was licensed as a doctor in July 1903 and practised in Ontario's Muskoka region and in Peterborough, Ontario, until 1906, when he went to Britain for postgraduate training in Edinburgh, Glasgow and London. Believing his health had deteriorated from working in a stuffy London hospital, Michell signed on as surgeon on the steamer *Sekondi*, which plied between Liverpool and the west coast of Africa.

After two voyages, during which he conducted some research on malaria, Michell in 1907 returned to London. There he met Rupert England, who had been first officer on the *Morning*, the ship sent to Antarctica in 1902–4 to relieve Captain Robert Scott's first expedition. England had also worked on a British government vessel in West Africa, but was invalided home with sunstroke. The pair became fast friends, swapping African seafaring tales. England had recently been hired as captain of the *Nimrod* and told Michell about Shackleton's grand plan to sledge to the South Pole. Michell became one of about four hundred men who applied to join, and in June 1907 he was accepted – on England's recommendation – as the *Nimrod*'s surgeon at a salary of £200.

'When I saw the ship she looked rather small and very dirty, as she had been in the Newfoundland sealing trade about forty years,' Michell wrote years later. 'However, a few weeks of hard work changed her appearance, and she looked very fit for the work.'[3] Shackleton had bought the three-hundred-ton vessel, built in Dundee in 1866, for £5,000. That almost depleted his meagre funds, leaving just enough to refit the vessel. Its schooner rigging was soon traded for barquentine and the worn engines overhauled.

Shackleton's first choice as captain had been William Colbeck, who had wintered at Cape Adare with Hugh Evans. Colbeck was also captain of the *Morning* during its 1902–4 *Discovery* relief voyage. Shackleton himself had been a member of that expedition, during which he joined Scott and Dr Edward Wilson in an abortive dash to the pole. To Shackleton's bitter regret, he become seriously ill during the march back, sometimes spitting blood. At one point he had to be dragged on a sledge. The experience was humiliating and left Shackleton with a profound desire to redeem himself.

Colbeck had evacuated the ailing Shackleton in the *Morning*, where they quickly got to know and like one another. Shackleton now offered him a good salary to come south again in command of the *Nimrod*. While Colbeck had a secure job with a passenger line and turned down the invitation, he did recommend his former first officer from the *Morning*, Rupert England. England had never commanded a ship, but Shackleton had no time for quibbling. He had to get the *Nimrod* out to sea by early August if she was to arrive for the beginning of the Antarctic summer. England, one of a handful of British seamen with experience navigating the south pack ice, was duly hired.

The *Nimrod* was much too small for the supplies and equipment – not to mention men – that Shackleton proposed taking
south. 'We lived in small, not too comfortable quarters, and
carried a crew of 20 men,' Michell recalled. 'My cabin – six feet
long by three feet wide – contained a bunk on top of a dresser, a
crude wash-basin, a tiny setee, an oil lamp ... our ship lacked
heating facilities except for a little coal stove (very seldom used)
in her wardroom and warmth to be found in the engine room.'[4]
After being fêted at several stops in England, the *Nimrod* finally
embarked for New Zealand on 7 August. Shackleton remained
behind to raise more cash and spend a few extra days with his
family. He would take commercial steamers and meet the ship
in New Zealand.

After a short coaling stop at St Vincent, the crew stayed four
days at Cape Town. The run eastward across the Indian Ocean
was beset with gales, and in eight weeks the *Nimrod* encountered only one other ship. Michell recorded two occasions
when England ordered a small boat put out in mid-ocean to
collect biological samples. On the second such sortie the boat
capsized, almost killing its occupants, who happened to be the
first and second officers. A jittery Captain England immediately
put an end to these scientific forays, and the crew began to
appreciate just how much one man's frayed nerves could limit
the expedition.[5]

The *Nimrod* finally docked at the New Zealand port of Lyttelton on 23 November. While the ship was refurbished and
loaded, Michell joined two scientists with the expedition for a
tour of the interior of New Zealand.[6] Shackleton, in the meantime, frantically drummed up donations in Australia and New
Zealand. His greatest coup was to persuade Professor Edgeworth David to join the expedition. David, a forty-nine-year-
old geologist at Sydney University, was a highly respected public figure in Australia, someone whose presence could give
Shackleton's expedition scientific credibility. David's support
also meant money, a great deal of it. The Professor, as he was

known on the *Nimrod*, persuaded the Australian government to donate £5,000.

The arrival of David meant finding him suitable accommodation on the *Nimrod*. Shackleton was already wedged in with England in the captain's quarters. So it fell to Michell to vacate his tiny coffin of a cabin. Michell's new quarters were 'Oyster Alley,' the name given a bunkhouse built specially for the shore party. Fifteen men were crammed into the unventilated space, the floor of which was three feet deep with scientific instruments. To make matters worse, in the frequent storms the sea leaked through, making everything damp, cold, and stinking. David was not much more comfortable in the private cabin Michell had vacated: he shared the space with a quarter-ton of his scientific equipment.[7]

One of the last things loaded onto the groaning deck before departure was nine sledge dogs. These were bought from a breeder on New Zealand's Stewart Island, where their ancestors had been dropped off seven years earlier by Borchgrevink's Cape Adare expedition. Although Shackleton placed all his transport hopes on his ponies, he had ordered forty dogs from Stewart Island as an experimental backup. Only nine could be had, but this number eventually increased to twenty-two because of litters over the course of the expedition.

The *Nimrod* officially departed for the south on 1 January 1908, the docks jammed with cheering well-wishers. The ship was so over-burdened with supplies it could not carry enough coal to steam to Antarctica. Shackleton commissioned the iron steamship *Koonya* to tow the *Nimrod* to the Antarctic Circle to conserve fuel. The ships were barely two days out when a gale struck which did not subside for more than ten days. Mountainous waves broke over the decks and the two ships often could not see one another for the fury. 'We seemed a tiny speck upon a waste of waters that resembled snow-capped peaks one moment only to find ourselves, the next instant, rushing down an immense wall of water,' Michell wrote. 'The Nimrod rolled with sickening motion over fifty degrees each way, and many of our scientists were seasick for days.'[8]

The storm turned into a hurricane between 6 and 7 January, and the *Nimrod* began taking on water at the rate of three feet an hour. Michell along with everyone else took two-hour shifts at the hand pumps. Almost as quickly as it began the gale died out, giving everyone a chance to wring sea water out of sodden clothes and bedding. 'We had become practically pickled during the past week,' Shackleton observed. The *Koonya* turned back on 15 January, just inside the Antarctic Circle. The air temperature dropped and an enormous number of icebergs were sighted, but to the surprise of all no pack ice barred the way. Although the *Nimrod* dodged bergs constantly, the captain found a relatively unimpeded route to the continent. It marked the first time a ship had crossed these waters without battling the pack.

Shackleton had promised Scott in writing before departure that he would set up his base east of longitude 170° east. Scott was planning another large scientific expedition and claimed priority over the McMurdo Sound region, where he had established his *Discovery* team in 1902. Shackleton, in a gesture of conciliation to his former leader, accepted Scott's dubious claim. He intended to erect his hut either in King Edward vii Land or on the Ross Ice Shelf, well clear of Scott's imaginary domain. Accordingly he ordered England to bring the *Nimrod* close by the ice shelf, then to steam east until a harbour could be found.

The face of the ice shelf, though, had suffered a massive rupture since it was charted by the *Discovery*. An enormous calving of icebergs had created a wide bay, which Shackleton christened the Bay of Whales. This discovery immediately scuttled plans for a hut on the ice shelf, since Shackleton feared that any shore party might also be calved unexpectedly into the sea. The *Nimrod* pushed farther east, but here pack ice and a formidable ice-locked coast prevented an entry to King Edward vii Land. Captain England grew visibly anxious about his dwindling coal supply and the threat the pack posed to the hull. Shackleton, under pressure from both the captain and the impending Antarctic winter, was forced to break his promise to Scott. On 25 January he ordered England to steam west for McMurdo Sound.

Four days later their destination came into view, but hearts sank at the sight of a vast sheet of sea ice that filled the southern reaches of the sound. Shackleton desperately hoped to build his hut at Cape Armitage, where the Ross Ice Shelf – the highway to the pole – was just in the backyard. All other points in McMurdo Sound required a traverse across unreliable sea ice to get onto the ice shelf. Cape Armitage, though, was imprisoned in sea ice twenty miles broad. Shackleton waited two days in the vain hope the ice would break up. He then had the ship ram the ice-edge, with little effect. He ordered a gasoline-powered car, the first such vehicle in the Antarctic, unloaded onto the ice in the hope it could drag loads to Cape Armitage. The wheels spun uselessly, digging it deeper into the ice. The machine was hoisted on board again, a failed first experiment with motorized vehicles in the Antarctic.

Aeneas Mackintosh, the *Nimrod*'s navigating officer, was hit in the right eye with a hook on 31 January as a barrel of beer was hoisted out of the hold. He dropped to the deck in pain and was taken to England's cabin for examination. The eye clearly could not be saved. Mackintosh was given chloroform and, with Michell assisting, Dr Eric Marshall removed the damaged tissue by the light of a single oil lamp. Mackintosh was to have remained with the shore party, but the doctors warned he could lose the other eye without careful medical attention. Michell took charge of the recovery and would see Mackintosh fitted with a glass eye in Australia.

On 3 February Shackleton acknowledged defeat in his efforts to make Cape Armitage. He ordered England to anchor at Cape Royds, the nearest the sea ice would permit the vessel. A small group, including Michell, went ashore and found a site for the hut in a small rocky valley. 'Now began an extremely uncomfortable two weeks, full of worries and delays,' wrote Michell of the frantic unloading that followed.[9] It was a gamble with the weather. The ship ran the risk of being frozen in for the winter, a risk that increased with each dying autumn day. England also had to contend with uncharted waters whose hidden rocks might rip open the hull; with violent gales that could dash the *Nimrod* on the jagged shoreline; and with deadly icebergs brushing past. He struggled to bring the ship close to shore to hasten the unloading but often had to worm out to sea when he felt the *Nimrod* was threatened. The strain on his weak nerves was almost unbearable.

The shore party quickly grew incensed with England's extreme caution. Members felt he was dangerously delaying the landing of stores and that his insistence on leaving with most of the coal was a direct threat to their comfort through the winter. England was fearful he would need the coal to navigate the pack for his return to New Zealand. And as he was captain, the safety of the ship was his foremost concern. The crew supported England as their own safety was bound to the fate of the ship. In the middle was Shackleton, responsible for the welfare of both.

Rebellion began to well up among the men of the land party. Frank Wild spoke for the group when he said England was 'off his rocker.' Shackleton was just as impatient to get supplies to shore and was annoyed by England's constant fretting. But he could not undermine the authority of a ship's captain. After several heated arguments in the captain's cabin, Shackleton persuaded England to hold the ship near to shore despite the ice and wind and to reduce his claim on the dwindling supply of coal. It was clear, though, that stronger action was needed to command any respect among the shore party in the coming winter. Shackleton silently struggled with the problem for the next few days.

In the meantime, the lip of ice that hugged the shore was wrenched out to sea by the wind and waves. The ice had been a convenient quay, but now the men were forced to land the remaining stores in a small boat. Michell was put on a coal-hauling detail, a back-breaking and miserable chore. Because the sea was a maze of large ice floes, the boat had to be poled rather than rowed. 'The crew of our small boat labouring in cold, slushy coal dust and salt spray looked like grimy stevedores. Then work continued all night, and I cannot describe the utter weariness we felt,' Michell wrote. 'Our hands got badly frozen.'[10] A series of storms lashed the *Nimrod* from 18 to 21 February, once driving it dozens of miles to the north. The same storms tore up the sea ice guarding Cape Armitage, but it was far too late to change bases.

A few more bags of coal were ferried to shore, a last packet of letters brought aboard, and on 22 February the *Nimrod* steamed north for civilization. Among the letters was sealed correspondence from Shackleton to be opened only after the ship's arrival in New Zealand. England, the letters ordered, was to be relieved of his post and given pay for a year as an 'invalid.' (The unwitting captain guarded some of the damning correspondence in his quarters during the twelve-day voyage back to Lyttelton.) Shackleton's solution assured England's undisputed authority for the return voyage, but also cooled the emotions of his shore party and affirmed the line of authority.

Shackleton had confided in the *Nimrod*'s chief engineer, Harry Dunlop, about the imminent change in command and Dunlop felt obliged to prepare the captain for the shock. On 8 March, shortly before the ship bore into Lyttelton harbor, Dunlop told England about the orders. The captain was crushed and angrily denied Shackleton's claim that illness was the cause of the dismissal. We can only surmise that Michell sympathized deeply with England, who, after all, had been a close friend for almost a year and had helped Michell obtain a paid berth in Shackleton's great enterprise. Shortly before England officially stepped down, he wrote a farewell note to Michell. It was one of the few mementoes from the *Nimrod* expedition that Michell safeguarded until his death:

Before I leave I wish to write you a few lines to express my deep appreciation and thanks for the valuable assistance you gave me and for the work you did for the whole expedition. Your personal influence for good made itself felt throughout the whole ship's company, and your unselfish devotion at all times to the success of the Expedition was very deeply appreciated by many. The professional care and attention [and] your unfailing watchfulness, for all on board, helped materially and I wished you to know before I finally separated myself from you how much I valued it. Kindest regards and good wishes for successful voyage next time.[11]

The *Nimrod* was put into dry dock for cleaning and repairs. In the meantime, Michell stayed a month at the Sydney home of fellow expedition member Leo Cotton, and while there ensured Mackintosh found a competent specialist to fit him with a glass eye. Michell, with fellow crew member Arthur Harbord, later embarked on a four-hundred-mile walking tour of New Zealand's South Island.[12]

In November 1908, the *Nimrod* prepared to sail again to pick up Shackleton's winter party. Enough coal, food and equipment to last a year was taken aboard in the event the polar party had perished and a search party had to remain for another year. Shackleton had recommended Mackintosh be placed in charge of the ship for the return journey but for reasons that remain unclear, command was given to Frederick Pryce Evans, captain of the *Koonya*. The one-eyed Mackintosh would return, but as a ship's officer.

The *Nimrod* left Lyttelton on 1 December and had fair sailing weather for most of the voyage south. Michell suffered a bout of seasickness the second day out and a rash days later. A stretch of pack ice was encountered on 20 December but two days later the little ship was through, picking up wind for a crossing of the Ross Sea. Land was sighted 1 January. Over the next two days the *Nimrod* made little progress because of the ice, which separated them from the expedition base at Cape Royds by more than thirty miles. Captain Evans finally ordered the ship anchored to the pack and sent Mackintosh and three other men with the mail across the ice to the base. Mackintosh sent two of the men back to the ship after one of them became ill and carried on with one companion.

In the meantime, the ice barring the way south broke up and the *Nimrod* steamed to the Cape Royds hut only to find that Mackintosh had not yet appeared. Expedition members grew doubly anxious that their friends and precious letters from home were lost forever. The *Nimrod* sailed north again on 7 January to search for the missing men, only to become pinned in the pack for the next eight days. Finally free on the 16th, the crew spotted a tattered tent on shore. A boat was put out and found a note from Mackintosh detailing how the sea and shore ice had conspired against their journey. He was making for the hut yet again with a lightened load. The mail, left behind in the tent, was retrieved. The *Nimrod* returned to Cape Royds by midnight and was greeted by Mackintosh, who, with his companion, had desperately struggled to the hut four days earlier having gone forty hours without food or sleep.

Captain Evans now had to pick up three field parties whose locations he could only surmise because of imprecise instructions left by Shackleton at the hut. Two of the parties were in Victoria Land to the west, one a geological party, the other a team that set out to plant a flag at the South Magnetic Pole. Evans set a course on 24 January for Butter Point, the most likely pick-up spot. There he found the geological party, which, the day of the ship's arrival, had been stranded on an ice floe rocked by killer whales. The party included Raymond Priestley, who would winter at Cape Adare three years later. 'We never saw men so glad to get back – even to such meagre comforts as our little ship could afford – as the three bearded individuals whom we welcomed on board,' Michell wrote.[13]

Finding the Magnetic Pole party meant an unnerving cruise up and down the treacherous east coast, dodging ice, rocks, and bergs. Evans had almost given up when his first officer suggested a return to the Drygalski Ice Tongue. Some icebergs may have obscured an inlet where the three missing men could have camped. Sure enough, the team, which included Edgeworth David, had arrived at the point not long earlier. They were exhausted, frostbitten, and emaciated – but triumphant, having found the Magnetic Pole on 16 January in a journey of 1,260 miles.

The final challenge was to find Shackleton and the three men he took south in his quest for the geographic pole. The rendezvous was to be Hut Point, the base for Scott's *Discovery* expedition. No one knew the fate of the polar party, which had been expected at the beginning of February. The *Nimrod* arrived back at Cape Royds on 11 February and for two tense weeks cruised between the expedition hut and Hut Point, looking for any sign of Shackleton's return. Captain Evans finally named a seven-man party, including Michell, that would overwinter if Shackleton failed to show soon. On 3 March Mackintosh told the crew he had a feeling Shackleton had arrived at the hut. He scrambled up to the crow's nest and spotted a makeshift flare sent up by Shackleton. Soon the great leader and Frank Wild were on board, and Shackleton within three hours was back on the trail to pick up his two remaining companions.

The four had trudged to within 112 miles of the pole but had to turn back because of blizzards and dwindling food supplies. The 850-mile return trek nearly killed them: they were plagued by dysentery, frostbite, enormous bursting blisters and a deadening weakness. Michell tended to the health of the polar party, including Dr Eric Marshall, who had gone limp from the journey. McMurdo Sound was already freezing over and the *Nimrod* headed north for the final run to New Zealand. The expedition pulled into Lyttelton harbour three weeks later, on 25 March. The world hailed Shackleton a hero.

Michell was discharged as surgeon of the *Nimrod* on 31 March 1909, six days after the ship docked in Lyttelton. He took a commercial steamship back to England, then another to Montreal. He had arrived in Toronto by early 1910, where he attempted to establish a private practice, apparently without success. That summer he applied to join the new Canadian navy being planned by Prime Minister Wilfrid Laurier's government, but the navy and his application were scuttled by the change in government the next year. He later joined the Royal Army Medical Corps in the First World War and served in France. Through the war he maintained correspondence with his good friend Rupert England, who lived near London.[14]

On his return to Canada following the armistice, Michell returned to Perth, and in June 1922 he became staff physician at the province's northern Academy in Monteith, just south of Iroquois Falls in northern Ontario. In the fall of 1923 he moved to Toronto for a Diploma in Public Health at the University of Toronto. Michell was appointed director of the province's public health lab in Owen Sound, Ontario, in May 1925. He married Violet Beatrice Dowdell, and spent the rest of his medical career with the Ontario Health Department. In February 1933 he was transferred to Ottawa, where he remained until retirement in October 1949.[15] Michell had no children and his health remained fragile throughout his career. He traced his lifelong medical problems directly to that brief spell in the Antarctic aboard the *Nimrod*.[16]

One evening in the mid 1950s, a quiet, frail, and elderly man appeared at a monthly meeting of the Ottawa chapter of the Canadian Numismatic Association and spoke privately for a few moments with Alfred Petrie, editor of the association's journal. Would Mr Petrie like to see an interesting medal? Might it have some numismatic interest? The octagonal silver piece bore a portrait of King Edward vii on the obverse, a scene of men before a ship and sledge on the reverse. Its clasp was inscribed 'Antarctic 1907–1909.'[17]

Petrie was indeed interested in the medal and was curious about how the gentleman had acquired it. Dr Michell, then in his seventies, broke a long silence about his role in the expedition. He explained how he had been surgeon of the *Nimrod*,

v

and had been sent the medal by the king in 1910. Petrie immediately recognized the scientific interest and importance of
Michell's recollections. Here was an unrecognized survivor of a
now-legendary expedition, perhaps with journals, photographs or letters telling of the experience. Would Dr Michell
care to put some of his memories in writing for presentation at
a meeting of the Ottawa chapter?

Several months later Petrie read Michell's memoir to the
society. The doctor, in poor health, attended but did not have a
voice strong enough to read the piece himself. So impressed
was Petrie with the document that he had it published in the
Canadian Numismatic Journal in 1958. He also inquired after
the handwritten journals the memoir was based upon, but
Michell was evasive.

Michell died in his Ottawa apartment on 20 July 1966, and
was buried two days later at his home town of Perth. Several
weeks later Petrie visited Michell's widow to receive on behalf
of the National Archives of Canada a gift of the doctor's Antarctic memorabilia. He took away a medicine chest from the
1907–9 expedition, some letters, dozens of photographs and
the Antarctic service medal. Missing were the elusive handwritten Antarctic journals. Michell had told Petrie of their existence
ten years earlier but had never allowed him to see them.

Some time later, Violet Michell confessed that the journals
did exist but she would not allow them to be made public. She
told Petrie she was bitter about her husband's experiences
aboard the *Nimrod*, which left him a semi-invalid for most of
his life. The journals detailed the doctor's terrible privations
during the expedition, she said, and she would not allow anyone to see them, even if the archives undertook to restrict
access. She said she had given the journals to an unidentified
nephew in New England, who was never to make them public.
To date they have not surfaced.[18]

THREE

The Man Who
Found the Bodies

T HE ICE in Toronto's Grenadier Pond was melting that late winter day in 1908 when Charles Wright set up his experiment. A layer of water about two inches deep had formed on the surface. Wright, wearing thin shoes, sloshed about carrying a large wooden table to the centre of the pond. Next he relayed about one hundred small lead cells to the table from shore. A tangle of scientific instruments was ferried next. Finally, he carried over a chair for himself, his feet now thoroughly soaked and numb from cold. Professor John McLennan of the University of Toronto paced the shore shouting encouragement and advice. Wright patiently wired everything together and for a few chilling hours made observations of 'penetrating radiation.'[1]

The experiment was Wright's ticket to the Antarctic, though he did not know it at the time. A twenty-one-year-old physics student, Wright was shooting for an 1851 Exhibition scholarship, worth £300 over two years. The scholarships had been created after the Great Exhibition of 1851 in London to encourage research into the natural sciences. The honour was restricted to students from the British Isles and the Dominions but the research supported could be carried out anywhere. Budding physicists, though, all went to the mecca of their profession – Professor J.J. Thomson's famous Cavendish laboratory at Cambridge University. McLennan and other professors at the University of Toronto encouraged Wright to apply for the scholarship and ensured he had access to university labs to do the requisite original research.

The Grenadier Pond experiment was Wright's final work for his science degree as well as his bid for a place at Cambridge. The 'penetrating radiation' he sought to investigate is now called cosmic rays, radiation produced in the sun and other stars. Earlier experiments with radium and uranium showed that some substances produced quantities of radiation in a natural process. It was also clear by 1908 that the earth itself radiated slightly and that some radioactive material in the atmosphere was precipitated to the ground during rainfall. Wright knew that radiation levels decreased when measured over water. But owing to the sensitivity of the recording instruments, ships could not be used for such measurements because they were unstable. The only way to do it was on the ice.

Wright's chilly experiment did record weaker radiation over Grenadier Pond. With McLennan's help, his report was hastily written up and sent in the post to London. Wright went on a canoe trip that summer to northern Ontario with his brother Adrian, up the Montreal River to Lake Temagami. He arranged to have his mail sent to a railway stop near the lake, and in the middle of the trip the pair excitedly checked with the postmaster for letters. There was indeed a letter, from the 1851 Exhibition committee. Wright had won the scholarship.

They canoed back across Lake Temagami and camped to absorb this wonderful news. Wright had to get word to his family, so he wrote a quick letter and they returned to the post office the next day to mail it. Awaiting him was yet another letter, postmarked Cambridge, England. Gonville and Caius College, to which Wright applied, had also awarded him a scholarship worth £100. Not only was Wright to study under an eminent physicist in a world-famous lab, he would be awash in money as well. He felt on top of the world.

A scant eighteen months later would find him at the bottom of the world.

Charles Seymour Wright was born in Toronto in April 1887 to Alfred Wright and Katharine Kennedy. His grandfather was a doctor who had immigrated to Canada from England and settled near Woodstock, Ontario. Alfred, educated at Upper Canada College in Toronto, had a lifelong career with the Canadian branch of the London and Lancashire Insurance Company. Katharine died giving birth to Adrian, the last of their three children, and Charles was left with no memory of her. One of his earliest recollections was connected with the University of Toronto, where he eventually was to study. On the night of 14 February 1890 University College was set ablaze when a servant stumbled carrying some lamps. Wright vividly recalled being wheeled in a pram to watch the flames. 'It was a striking display and I did enjoy it,' he wrote many years later.[2]

Wright's family doubled in size after his father remarried in the late 1890s. The new mother, Emily Nicol from Cookstown, Ontario, would bear three more Wright children. In 1899 Charles and his eldest brother, Alfred, were enrolled in Upper Canada College as day students. Charles had poor eyesight and wore glasses. This turned him away from team sports such as hockey, and towards field sports. From an early age, he felt it necessary to toughen himself physically, wearing the same kind of clothing winter and summer to show he was oblivious to the weather. He was also drawn to the sciences, already certain he wanted to be a research physicist.

From the age of about ten, just when his father remarried, Wright would spend entire summers with one or both of his brothers canoeing through the bush of the Muskokas and northern Ontario. His father and stepmother, whom Charles disliked intensely, simply did not hear from the boys between May and September each year. These forays included much fishing and moose hunting, and extended well beyond the farthest reach of the northern railways. Sometimes they would prospect, braving the clouds of blackflies and mosquitoes for a chance to stumble across gold or silver. But it was pure adventure that really attracted Wright. 'In advance we chose to examine areas of blank spaces on the provincial maps, and I now believe our interest was rather in exploring new areas than in looking for claims to stake,' he wrote in a memoir. 'Winter always found us making plans, poring over such maps as were available and discussing how best to reach the places where no maps had yet been drawn or even surveyed.'[3]

Wright finished sixth form at the college in 1903, when still fifteen, but repeated the year because he was thought too young to apply to university. He only barely passed the university entrance exam for physics in 1904, but he had accumulated enough marks in his other exams to earn admission with a small bursary. He was also awarded the Governor General's medal on graduation from Upper Canada College. In the fall he enrolled in a four-year mathematics and physics course, where most of his fellow students were schoolmasters intent on assuring their continued employment by acquiring a degree.

Wright continued to spend summers in the northern Ontario bush but, needing money, he now worked as a surveyor out of a New Liskeard, Ontario, office. He joined the Queen's Own Rifles of Canada, a militia unit then, and spent some weekends in drills. With McLennan's encouragement he submitted two research papers to the Royal Society of Canada, which published them in its bulletin in 1908.[4] Another physics paper co-authored with McLennan was published by the university library.[5] Wright also earned a little as a demonstrator in a class of young women taking a new course called Domestic Science.

Wright's memoirs refer to 1908 as an 'annus mirabilis,' the year the 1851 Exhibition prize set a new course for his life. After a late-summer crossing from New York to Liverpool, Wright took the train to London to report to the 1851 commissioner's office, then another train to Cambridge. After a few days, he met the great J.J. Thomson and was assigned a room in the lab. To Wright's great dismay, the place was as badly equipped as the University of Toronto labs. Much of his Caius College scholarship was eaten up purchasing instruments to continue his research into penetrating radiation.

The following summer, 1909, Wright took advantage of an inexpensive boat ticket and returned to Canada to see his family. He also seized the chance to determine whether he could take measurements of penetrating radiation over the ocean with newer equipment. No such luck; even a slight rolling of the ship confounded the instruments. After seeing his father in Toronto and visiting his brother Alfred in British Columbia, Wright returned to Cambridge bent upon producing a device that could be used at sea to measure radiation; over the following year he did develop a primitive form of what is now called a Geiger counter. He submitted his results to Thomson for publication, but the professor neglected to see this was carried out. Hans Geiger at Manchester University produced his own version at about the same time and the device bearing his name soon came into wide use.

Among Wright's Cambridge circle of about twenty fellow researchers was Griffith Taylor, a young geophysicist from Australia who had also won an 1851 scholarship. In December 1909 the two idly discussed joining Captain Robert Scott's second expedition to the Antarctic, which was then gathering men and money for a fresh assault on the pole. Taylor formally applied the following month after prodding by several professors. Following an interview with Scott, he was accepted as a geologist. In early February 1910, Taylor persuaded a fellow Australian, the geologist Douglas Mawson, to speak to the Research Students' Club about his work with Shackleton's *Nimrod* expedition. Mawson had been a member of Professor Edgeworth David's Magnetic Pole party and the talk rekindled Wright's interest. With Taylor's encouragement, Wright applied for a post with Scott, partly because the ocean voyage to the south would give him an opportunity to test his new radiation detection device. He soon received a rejection by mail. 'I was rather shocked about this, I didn't expect it,' he recalled.[6] His charmed life seemed suddenly jinxed.

Taylor proposed a more direct approach. Why not walk down to London to prove your fitness, knock on the door and make a pitch to Scott personally? Wright was game. They left at 5:45 in the morning and covered the fifty or so miles in about twelve hours, non-stop. Wright, who had forged a reputation as the best hiker in the university's Peripatetic Club, marched sprightly into the expedition office to request an interview. Taylor lagged behind, barely able to stand up for the blisters on his feet.[7]

Precisely what was discussed among Scott, Dr Edward Wilson, head of science, and Wright remains unknown, but he came away with the job. Wright later indicated that Scott and Wilson were eager to know about his surveying and prospecting in northern Ontario. Wright also suggested that 'somebody with pretty high qualifications had probably been appointed and then had been turned down by the doctors,' leaving an opening at the right moment.[8] Scott later recorded that he found Wright a 'charmingly simple, straightforward young man with intelligence of a high order' but who at the same time was 'decidedly anaemic.'[9] In fact, Wright, at 5 feet 11 and 165 pounds, was glowingly healthy and fit. The young man's only physical frailty was betrayed by his glasses.

Scott and Wilson had been looking for a chemist, well beyond Wright's ken, but let it be known the title meant little. Wright was to take regular readings of earth magnetism and gravity in the south, and would assist the meteorologist. He would also be permitted to carry out his penetrating radiation experiments. Wright later grew concerned that his scientific duties would keep him hut-bound and therefore disqualify him for the epic march to the pole. He proposed to Wilson that he also be appointed expedition glaciologist. Field trips, after all, were a *sine qua non* of glaciology. Wilson and Scott readily approved and so a rather large gap in the scientific program was closed, thanks to a young Canadian's taste for adventure. No matter that Wright knew nothing about glaciology. A decade later, after having immersed himself in the study of Antarctica's ice sheets, he would co-author what became the first English-language textbook in the field.[10]

As for remuneration, Wright would be fed and clothed at expedition expense but would not be paid. That suited him fine, for here was a rare opportunity to see the mysterious white continent and to conduct some key radiation experiments during the ocean voyage down. Wright had only awe for the famous Captain Scott, with whom one so junior did not argue. Later, as he grew to know this aloof and reserved leader, Wright came to respect Scott's cultivation of the scientific side of exploration but he harboured grave doubts about his judgment.

Wright asked for and received permission from the 1851 commissioners to abandon his Cavendish research early in 1910 to prepare for the expedition. He was shown how to use weather equipment by the expedition meteorologist, George Simpson. Wright also spent a week at the Kew Gardens Observatory, where he was shown the intricacies of magnetic recording instruments. He then travelled to Germany to borrow gravity-measuring instruments from the Potsdam Geodetic Institute. Wright finally arrived in Cardiff, Wales, on 14 June for the departure the next day of the *Terra Nova*.

The ship had been built as a whaler in Dundee in 1884 and the same year became part of a St John's, Newfoundland, whaling and sealing fleet. (Scott had hoped to buy back his first ship, the *Discovery*, but her new owner, the Hudson's Bay Company, turned down his offer.) The *Terra Nova* was rigged as a barque and had auxiliary engines that devoured coal at an alarming rate, restricting Scott's options in the south. The vessel had been owned briefly by the British Admiralty in 1903–4 to assist the relief of Scott's *Discovery* expedition. After being sold to the expedition for £12,500, the *Terra Nova* was stripped of her blubber tanks, and an ice house and cramped laboratory built. One of the ship's four-man cabins would house the expedition's six young scientists, including Wright, as well as a pianola. Dubbed 'The Nursery,' the cabin was situated next to the boiler and engine rooms, making it, in Wright's words, a 'perfect little hell.'[11]

Scott was poised for victory. His march on the pole in 1902–3 had been forestalled by bad weather and inadequate food supplies. The prize had also eluded Shackleton, barely, in 1908–9. Now the field was Scott's alone, or so he thought. He had the best-equipped, best-financed expedition yet to go south, and had a shore party of hardy young men, many with polar experience. This would be the crowning achievement of his naval career, his entrée into the inner circle, and a guarantee of his financial well-being. At forty-two, he was the oldest member of the expedition and already fearful of leaving no permanent mark in the world.

The ship pulled away from the Welsh quay on 15 June. The docks were filled with relatives, friends, and the curious, and a flotilla of small craft escorted the *Terra Nova* for the first few miles of its journey. Scott was not on board. He would meet the vessel at the South African port of Simonstown after tending to details. Wright began his penetrating radiation observations almost immediately, with Simpson assisting. 'We are getting some quite interesting results (Physical) already,' he wrote his father on 10 July. 'We have been getting the amount of radium in the sea and air and measuring their effects.'[12] (Simpson and Wright wrote a paper on the results, published the following year by the Royal Society.)[13] Wright was also expected to help with the masts and rigging and to lend a hand at the pumps. The *Terra Nova*, it turned out, had a rather nasty leak that would plague the crew all the way to New Zealand.

The ship made a brief stop at South Trinidad Island, ninety miles east of Rio de Janeiro, whose only inhabitants were thousands of land crabs. This was to be a scientific foray, and

Wright was assigned to collect bugs for the biologists. Next stop was Simonstown, on 17 August, where Wright packed up his radiation-measuring gear and took a train inland to the hamlet of Matjiesfontein. Here the penetrating radiation was far stronger than he had measured anywhere. The *Terra Nova*, meanwhile, underwent repairs while her crew was feted in Simonstown and Cape Town. Scott had now joined the ship and Wilson, the scientific director, was sent on by steamship to Australia, where two more geologists were to be recruited – Raymond Priestley and Frank Debenham.

The voyage to New Zealand was a time for expedition members to build a camaraderie. Once on the ice there would be no relief from one another for at least a year, so it was essential to forge these personal links. Many nicknames were dreamed up during this voyage. Scott became 'The Owner,' a name used in the British navy to refer to the commander of a warship. Dr Wilson, loved and admired by all the men, was 'Uncle Bill.' Lieutenant Henry Bowers was 'Birdie' because of his beak-like nose.

Wright became 'Silas.' The navy men on board thought it a typically Yankee name, in part because the expedition's small library included a volume by the American novelist Silas K. Hocking. Bowers, though, claimed all the credit: ' "Silas" struck me one day on the ship as a typical Yankee name and in a happy moment I called him Mr. Silas P. Wright of the Philadelphia Educational Seminary. Since then he has never been called anything but Cousin Silas or Silas.'[14] The men also knew Wright was sensitive about being mistaken for an American, so 'Silas' was a poke at his patriotism. The name stuck fast, and colleague Priestley ensured it was used by Wright's friends and family long after the expedition.[15]

The ship reached Melbourne on 12 October, where a devastating nine-word telegram awaited Scott: 'Beg leave to inform you *Fram* proceeding Antarctic. Amundsen.' Roald Amundsen, the Norwegian explorer, had struggled to equip an expedition for an assault on the North Pole. But the prize had apparently been taken in the meantime by either Robert Peary or Dr Frederick Cook, whose claims were still being sorted out in 1910. Amundsen decided privately he would go for the South Pole, and would keep silent until after departure lest his backers pull out. He broke his silence to his crew at the island of Madeira, where he left instructions to send the fateful cable. 'I think we all felt at first that this change of plan was a bit offside,' Wright recalled, 'especially because it was not sent before he had reached Madeira. For my part my chief regret was that ... [he] should send such a curt message apparently not followed by a letter or any explanation ... Not in the best of taste!'[16] Scott, whose capture of the pole had seemed assured, suddenly was in a race with a skilled polar explorer. Amundsen's intrusion into the field left expedition members confused at first, then irritated that gentlemanly rules of conduct had been violated.

The ship next stopped at Lyttelton, where an inspection in dry dock finally located the annoying leak. Wright, Taylor, and Debenham were sent to inspect the Tasman Glacier and Mount Cook, more than 12,000 feet high, for a taste of the coming ice-work in the south. The excursion marked the trio's first experience with skis: 'The question then arose who should use the ski down [the glacier],' Wright recorded in his diary. 'I had one pair on the strength of my announcement that there could be no difference in operation of skis to a man used to skates and to Canadian snow shoes.'[17] He made the descent with Taylor standing behind him on the skis hitching a ride. They arrived at the bottom with limbs and confidence intact.

While Wright and Simpson calibrated instruments, the crew attended to the final loading of the ship. Finally, on 29 November, the sluggish, overloaded vessel left Port Chalmers, New Zealand, for the most dangerous waters in the world. The crowded deck held nineteen ponies, thirty-three dogs, hundreds of sacks of coal, three motor-sledges, petrol cases, mutton carcasses and dozens of other items for which there was no room in the bulging holds.

'We met our first gale on December 1st. It was a corker and nearly the end of the expedition,' Wright recalled.[18] The storm worked up its fury during the evening and by midnight was at full force. Some of the deck cargo was loosened by the swell, and once free the crates would smash into everything in their path. Waves hammered the ship, knocking off deck timbers. The steam pumps were ineffective, the hand pumps clogged and the *Terra Nova* rapidly filled with sea water. A bucket brigade was formed, with men strung along a ladder. 'We were always cheerful,' Wright remembered, 'and passed the buckets up and down to sea shanties and any scraps of doggerel known to more than a single member of the team.'[19] The pumps eventually were cleared, the water level lowered, and the ship was saved. On 3 December a grim accounting showed that two ponies and a dog had died, ten tons of coal and sixty-five gallons of petrol had been lost.

The first icebergs were sighted on 8 December and a day later the ship entered the pack ice. The appearance of the frozen mass meant Wright had to remain on deck night and day keeping a detailed record of ice formations, according to a list of ten observation instructions Scott had provided. This included taking photographs and making sorties on skis over the pack to inspect proximate specimens of icebergs. It also meant little sleep until landfall and painful flirtations with snow blindness.

Christmas was spent with the ship still wedged in the pack. Roast penguin, plum pudding, and grog were followed by songs and bantering. Late on 29 December the *Terra Nova* finally escaped the ice after a twenty-one-day imprisonment. A quick crossing of the Ross Sea and the ship entered McMurdo Sound. A rocky cape on the east side that had been known as the Skuary during the *Discovery* expedition was eventually chosen as the site for the hut and renamed Cape Evans, after Scott's second-in-command, Lieutenant Edward (Teddy) Evans. The spot was roughly halfway between Scott's old *Discovery* hut farther south and Shackleton's 1908 hut to the

north. Unloading began on 4 January. Two weeks later the outpost was reasonably complete – a large, heat-tight hut, pony
stables, meteorological screen, and hundreds of stacked crates.

Wright pitched in for the initial unloading, then turned to his
immediate scientific task, the creation of an ice cave for the
magnetism-measuring instruments. The constant temperature
of the L-shaped grotto would ensure accurate readings from
the device, which recorded information on photographic
paper. The three-foot-high entrance opened horizontally into a
larger chamber twenty-five feet deep. Wright lined the interior
with dark felt to make it light-tight, and strung wire to the main
hut so that automatic time signals, one every two minutes,
could be transmitted to the recording device in the cave.
Wright and Simpson together needed four days to hack out the
cave, and another day to build a wooden framework to hold the
felt sheets.

Finally, Wright had to observe the stars by telescope for a
time check on the hut clock. This was a procedure 'complicated by a temperature of –40 degrees [F] with a slight wind,
quite sufficient to keep one nursing his nose, and to be very
careful not to put one's eye to the telescope lest it freeze and
remain there,' he wrote.[20] This agony had to be endured every
fortnight. Wright 'seemed to be impervious to the elements,'
Herbert Ponting, the expedition photographer recalled, 'and
used to kneel for hours beside his transit telescope, observing
the occultation of stars – with a telephone receiver at his ear
and the transmitter at his lips by which means he communicated the exact moment of contact to his confederate, Simpson, at the sidereal clock inside the Hut.'[21] Frequently, Wright
would let loose a string of 'Canadian' profanities over the telephone when something went wrong, Ponting noted. This happened once as a Sunday service was being held inside the hut,
much to the embarrassment of Simpson.[22]

Soon after the ice cave was complete, Scott ordered Wright
and Taylor to break off duties for a round of 'ponting.' This verb
the men coined to describe posing perfectly still in the bitter

cold for a photograph by Ponting. (Wright's diary describes him as an 'abominable nuisance.')[23] The first series of still shots was of an extraordinary 150-foot-long ice cave from whose interior one could see the *Terra Nova* in the distance. Wright and Taylor posed in several of the photos to provide human scale, and the series proved to be Ponting's most famous from the expedition. 'I doubt if any mass of ice has ever been photographed so thoroughly,' Taylor wrote.[24] That same afternoon, the pair were asked to climb the sixty-foot summit of the stranded iceberg containing the cave while Ponting operated a cinematograph. The sequence, staged only after the pair had carefully cut ice-steps into the berg, was later incorporated into Ponting's popular forty-minute film of the expedition.

On 15 January Taylor and Wright took another day trip, this time across the nearby Barne Glacier to inspect Shackleton's hut at Cape Royds, which had been abandoned in 1909. 'It seemed extraordinary that so many empty boxes and such piles of debris could have been the result of fourteen months' stay,' Taylor wrote of the mess they encountered.[25] At the door of the hut they found a note by Professor David giving a brief account of the expedition. Inside, not a grain of snow had penetrated. In the galley were scones and a loaf of bread that had been pulled from the oven just before the hut was hurriedly abandoned. And on the table, a meal of condensed milk, biscuits, jam, and gingerbread. Wright and Taylor enjoyed the lunch set out almost two years earlier.

On 24 January, with some order established at the expedition base, Scott led a twelve-man depot-laying party to the south with supplies for the spring assault on the pole. Three days later Wright, with the geologists Taylor and Debenham, and seaman Edgar Evans, were taken by the *Terra Nova* to Butter Point, on the west side of McMurdo Sound, to begin a six-week field trip. Some of the territory – including a mysterious ice-free valley – had already been discovered by a four-man team Scott led in 1903, which included Evans. But then Scott's group had been unprepared for snow- and ice-free terrain and returned to base by another route without exploring the formation. The new team under Taylor would descend into the so-called dry valley and chart the adjacent glaciers and mountain ranges to carry out a full scientific and geographical survey.[26]

The trip was the only occasion on which Wright supplemented his scientific work with geographical discoveries. The team carried out the first exploration of a dry valley in Antarctica, a hitherto uncatalogued topographical oddity. The three-thousand-foot deep gouge, carved by a tremendous glacier, apparently became ice-free as the mountain range rose cutting off the source of glacial flow. Extremely dry winds from the polar plateau sweep through picking up stray moisture. No precipitation has fallen there for at least two million years and seals that sometimes wander into the area are mummified soon after death. (The area is so unique that NASA scientists carried out investigations there to determine what the surface of Mars might be like.) The valley had been viewed from its eastern and western ends by 1911, but Taylor's team was the first to cross it.

The four were burdened with a full complement of scientific instruments, including a twenty-two-pound array of photographic equipment, a five-pound polariscope or 'barrel organ' for viewing ice crystals and an 11.5-pound theodolite to measure position. A few days after being deposited by the *Terra Nova*, the team cached most of the food to begin the descent into the valley. With some difficulty, they crossed the small, slippery glacier that poked into the valley from the landward end. 'We rolled about all over the place, and someone remarked that we had all the appearance of being drunk and none of the pleasure of it,' Taylor wrote.[27] They set up their tent at the edge of the ice, then began exploration of the four-mile-wide, twenty-five-mile-long curiosity.

Although the valley has had no precipitation in eons, the adjective 'dry' is perhaps misleading because glacial meltwater creates small streams that feed frozen lakes. The first night in the tent, Wright woke up to complain that he was perspiring badly, only to learn he had slept in a three-inch puddle of melt-water. The water of one of the lakes was found to contain dissolved minerals that when ingested acted as a laxative. The lake was duly christened Lake Chad after the name of the firm that manufactured the expedition's toilet paper. Unable to use a sledge, each of the group devised his own method of carrying equipment. Wright's choice was the pack strap or tumpline, the North American Indian method of carrying a pack using a strap around the forehead, leaving the hands free. Skis and crampons (ice-cleats) were useless in the valley, and the men's boots took a beating on the gravel surface.

During the week spent in the dry valley, Wright made several geographical discoveries: a new glacier was named the Canada Glacier, and the peaks adjoining it were called Mount McLennan, after his mentor at the University of Toronto, and Mount Falconer, after the university president. A peak just east was named Mount Coleman, for Arthur Philemon Coleman, head of geology at the university. Farther west, another peak became Mount J.J. Thomson after his Cambridge professor and a nearby ice formation was called the Cavendish Icefalls, for the world-famous laboratory. (Scott formally agreed to the names on 15 July and they retain them to this day.) On a later trip to an area immediately north, Taylor named a new ice sheet the Wright Glacier (now the Wright Lower Glacier) after his colleague and friend. In the 1950s it was discovered that the Wright Glacier led to another ice-free area and this was charted as the Wright Valley.

The team emerged from the valley on 8 February and spent the next five weeks wending south, examining the Koettlitz Glacier and several small dry valleys adjacent to it. During this period Wright began to have doubts about the adequacy of Scott's sledging rations. His diary is filled with references to food, and the four sledgers regularly made bets with one another in which the stakes were full meals back in civilization. When it was his turn to cook, Wright, ever the scientist, established precise tests to determine whether the 'hoosh,' or pemmican stew, was ready. One was the drop-test to determine viscosity, another was an estimate of its meniscus or curved surface. Indeed, so dedicated a scientist was he that while the others chose Browning and Tennyson to fill their one-pound quota of books, Wright brought two mathematics texts, both in German.

The team met the returned depot-laying party on 15 March at the old *Discovery* hut, where all sixteen men were forced to wait more than a month before the sea ice was safe enough to cross back to the Cape Evans base. With the help of ponies, the depot party had hauled a ton of supplies to a point just north of 80° south, dubbed One Ton Depot. Seven of the eight ponies died on the journey, two of them after they fell into the sea from an ice floe. Atop this disaster, Scott learned that Amundsen had set up his base at the Bay of Whales. This was only about four hundred miles to the east, in the region Scott had determined to establish a second base. Twice now, the brash Norwegian had upset the code of gentlemanly conduct.

The day after Taylor's party arrived at the *Discovery* hut, Scott asked for eight men for yet another depot-laying sledge trip. Wright volunteered, partly to get some experience of sledging on the Ross Ice Shelf preparatory to the spring attack on the pole. 'It was very sporting of Wright to join in after only a day's rest,' Scott wrote. 'He is evidently a splendid puller.'[28] Wright, however, grew to regret his offer. His gear was still full of ice and water from the western journey, and the barrier conditions were colder and less predictable. The lowest temperature encountered during their week away was –42.5 F, and Wright found it took him three hours to get warm inside the sleeping bag at night. The party had dangerously short sledging rations and inadequate oil supplies. And Teddy Evans got so muddled in navigating that the party initially missed the target depot by several miles.

They returned to the *Discovery* hut on 23 March and waited another nineteen days before setting out over newly formed sea ice towards the base at Cape Evans. By 13 April, Wright was back at the main hut to begin the long winter routine of meteorological and magnetic readings, and to continue his glaciological studies. This last he was inclined to neglect in favour of his radiation experiments, a situation that drew mild rebukes from both Wilson and Scott. 'This morning I gave Wright some notes containing speculations on the amount of ice on the Antarctic continent and on the effects of winter movements in the sea ice,' Scott wrote on 14 May. 'I want to get into his head the larger bearing of the problems which our physical investigations involve.'[29]

Scott's criticism grew more pointed five days later when it was Wright's turn to deliver one of a series of evening lectures. The topic was 'Ice Problems,' and the talk was illustrated with fifteen slides, some from his journey to the western mountains. Wright called it a 'fearful business' because he could not say all he wanted in the two and a half hours allotted to him. Scott was more biting: 'He had a difficult subject and was nervous. He is young and has never done original work; is only beginning to see the importance of his task ... Passing to the freezing of salt water, he was not very clear ... There was a good deal of disconnected information.'[30] The group decided another lecture on the Ross Ice Shelf and the interior ice sheet was needed. 'I think I will write the paper to be discussed on this occasion,' Scott sniffed.[31]

Despite his occasional badgering of Wright, Scott appears to have developed a genuine affection for his young Canadian glaciologist. The two had little contact before the enforced confinement of the Antarctic night, but during the winter at Cape Evans they came to know one another better. In October, after seven months of almost daily contact, Scott wrote: 'One of the greatest successes is Wright. He is very thorough and absolutely ready for anything. Like Bowers he has taken to sledging like a duck to water, and although he hasn't had such a severe testing, I believe he would stand it pretty nearly as well. Nothing ever seems to worry him, and I can't imagine he ever complained of anything in his life.'[32]

Complain he did, but usually it was restricted to cursing a troublesome telescope or to a short journal comment. Wright was not a regular or prolific diarist and of Scott he said little. He found 'The Owner's' naval reserve inappropriate and noted, for example, that Scott always insisted his tent mates urinate outside regardless of how bitter the conditions became.[33] But Wright was eager to be picked for the four-man party that would sledge to the pole and so kept his tongue. On 1 June, Scott told Wright he was, in effect, on the short list – he would join the parties hauling supplies south in the spring. The final assault party would be chosen from among these men. It also meant Wright would stay at least another year in the Antarctic. He welcomed the challenge and was determined to show he had the right stuff for the pole journey. He had to maintain cordial relations with his leader.

As for the rest of the shore party that winter, Wright was repeatedly ribbed about his Canadian background. On midwinter day, 22 June, small gifts were handed round by Birdie Bowers. Wright's was an envelope marked 'In memory of my native land' which contained an American flag. 'This, as a loyal Canadian, he threw away with contumely,' Taylor noted.[34] Taylor was a conspirator himself. Two weeks later, on July the Fourth, he wrote: 'Have just been ragging "Silas" Wright as an American ... on this auspicious day. Whereupon he fell upon me and succeeded in tearing my pocket.'[35] Part of the reason for the friendly ribbing was Wright's insistence on proclaiming his roots in the face of an overwhelmingly British expedition. His two silk sledging flags, for instance, contained the emblems of a beaver and a maple leaf and were displayed in the hut on festive occasions.[36]

Scott's attack on the pole was to be led by two motor sledges hauling supplies, followed by a caravan of ponies, each dragging a sledge and led by one man each. On 1 September Wright learned he was assigned to Chinaman, dubbed the 'Terror of the South.' The smallest and oldest of the ponies, Chinaman was ornery and pathetically slow. In preparation for departure the next month, Wright fought with his charge for ninety minutes each morning to condition him for the polar journey. On 13 September Scott outlined in a lecture his final plans for the march south, detailing weights of sledges, approximate travelling times, depot locations, and contingency plans. Wright was alarmed that the calculations failed to take into account pony meat as a source of food, since the animals were to be shot at the end of their hauling. Wright mentioned this apparent oversight to Wilson, but heard no more about it.[37]

The motor sledges finally sputtered south on 24 October (they broke down soon after and were abandoned). And on 1 November Wright and two other pony-leaders assembled into a party at Hut Point. Chinaman slept inside the hut but kept everyone awake through the night with his snoring and pawing. The journey proper began the next day, as did problems that were to plague the party for the next month. The ponies' hooves sank deeply into the surface of the Ross Ice Shelf. The animals also tended to tire easily, requiring frequent rests. And because ponies sweat through their hides, unlike dogs, they became caked with ice. At each camp, Wright and the others had to build windbreaks out of snow blocks to protect the forlorn creatures. He also had to rise earlier than the main group of seven pony leaders because Chinaman and two other ponies needed extra time to keep pace with the party. Wright called the trio of weakling ponies the 'Agony Column.'[38]

Finally, on 28 November, Wright recorded in his diary: 'Chinaman died tonight of senile decay complicated by the presence of a bullet in the brain.'[39] The two dog teams on the march south were short of food and needed a meal. The killing took place almost at the farthest-south point reached by Scott, Wilson and Shackleton in 1903. The death of Chinaman brought an end to one set of frustrations for Wright but marked the beginning of a far more gruelling exercise: manhauling. Wright found the rations for the journey wholly inadequate for the climate, especially with the added burden of dragging a sledge across the ice shelf. Snow blindness was a recurring and painful hazard. And to compound the strain, he was part of a four-man team whose leader, Teddy Evans, he disliked. 'Hope I do not stay long in Teddy's tent,' he wrote, 'am sure to have a row sooner or later.'[40] He later referred to Evans, Scott's second-in-command, as clumsy, a quitter, and a hypocrite.[41]

At the foot of the Beardmore Glacier, on 9 December, the remaining ponies were shot and manhauling began in earnest up the glacier slopes to the polar plateau. Wright's team dragged 170 pounds per man. Two of the team – Evans and seaman William Lashly – had been pulling a sledge almost from the start of the polar journey, so the group was the weakest and most dispirited of the three manhauling parties. The sticky, four-foot drifts at the base of the glacier turned the sledge into a snow-plough. The dog teams headed back to base on 11 December, leaving three four-man sledge parties pushing on towards the south. On 18 December, from glacial moraines near the peak called Cloudmaker, Wright picked up a handful of marble pebbles, one of which, on examination at the base months later, was found to contain the first large Archaeocyathid, or sponge fossil, discovered in Antarctica.[42]

Two days later Scott announced that Wright and three others would head back to base the next night. The gamble had been lost – Wright would not be going to the pole. Scott had become convinced that older men stand the cold and drudgery of manhauling better than the young, and felt that the thirty-to-forty-year range was ideal. Wright was just twenty-four. And to confirm Scott's suspicions, Dr Edward Atkinson, who was in Wright's manhauling party, reported on 10 December that Silas was showing clear signs of being 'played out.'[43] The assessment may have been prompted by a bout of insomnia Wright experienced at the higher altitudes. After breaking the news to the four men who were to return north, Scott noted in his diary: 'All are disappointed – poor Wright rather bitterly, I fear.'[44] At the same time in another tent, Wright recorded in his journal: 'Scott a fool ... Too wild to write more tonight.'[45]

Wright felt certain he was in better condition than at least one of the eight picked to go on. He did not complain to his leader, but his expression betrayed him. As compensation, Scott made Wright navigator for the returning party. There had been no sign of Amundsen as they crept along the Beardmore Glacier, the only proven route to the pole. So despite the rigours of manhauling, optimism prevailed; the goal was almost within Scott's grasp. On 21 December Dr Wilson pressed a sundial into Wright's hand as a memento, and farewells were exchanged all round. Eight bone-weary men trudged forward 'and the last we saw of them as we swung the sledge north was a black dot just disappearing over the next ridge,' wrote Apsley Cherry-Garrard, one of the returning party.[46]

Wright's group had a miserable return trip. They got tangled in a jumble of crevasses soon after turning north; Wright inadvertently led the team in a wide circle during one horizonless day; two of them (Patrick Keohane and Atkinson) suffered dysentery; eyes were dangerously strained trying to follow a faint trail; and the food was inadequate. 'I get hungry again one hour after lunch,' Wright jotted on New Year's Day, 1912. 'Am certain could do more and better work on a bigger ration.'[47]

Aware that there was almost no margin of error in the rations, Wright constantly urged the party to make long marches to build a food surplus in the event some disaster overtook them. Towards the end of the trip, as they neared base, food depots were better stocked and the four pulled in to Cape Evans on 28 January exhausted but with full bellies. Ponting, the photographer, insisted that no one take a bath until he could get some pictures, including a cinematograph of the party manhauling back to base. As usual, the sequence was staged. The next day Wright's legs swelled up badly in reaction to the strain of manhauling on the ice shelf. His brief diary entry: 'Overate. Unhappy.'[48]

The final supporting party, three men, had an even more difficult return from the polar plateau. Teddy Evans got a life-threatening case of scurvy and had to be dragged back on a sledge. The *Terra Nova*, meanwhile, had landed fresh supplies at Cape Evans, along with eight Indian mules and fourteen dogs. Evans was invalided home, and was joined for the return to civilization by Simpson, Taylor, Ponting, and others. Atkinson, now the only naval officer, took charge of the dozen men left at the base.

Scott's pole party, meanwhile, was long overdue and obviously in trouble. On 27 March Atkinson and Keohane made a desperate rescue bid. They travelled only a few dozen miles before turning back in face of the bitter temperatures. Atkinson led one last rescue attempt, this one aimed at Lieutenant Victor Campbell's stranded northern party. On 8 January the *Terra Nova* had dropped off a six-man team under Campbell's command more than two hundred miles to the north of Cape Evans. (This was the group, including Raymond Priestley, that had spent the first winter at Cape Adare and were picked up by the ship for transfer south.) The group was to geologize in the western mountains for about six weeks but the sea ice prevented the ship from returning as scheduled. The six had only summer clothing and sleeping bags and, at most, 10 weeks' food. Could they survive the winter? With Wright and two seamen, Atkinson planned to travel across the new sea ice to Evans Coves, the spot the *Terra Nova* had dropped off Campbell's men. If the sea ice was too weak, the rescue party would travel up to the polar plateau along a glacier, go north along the plateau until they could find the glacier that led down again to Evans Coves. 'On the face of it, this was insane,' Wright recorded in a memoir. 'If the Northern Party was in trouble we would only add more mouths to feed there during the winter. And all this by moonlight since the sun would have disappeared.'[49]

Wright, however, kept his opinion to himself and the teams set out on 17 April. Crippling temperatures, unstable sea ice and a blizzard drove them back less than a week later. The mercury had dipped so low that no body perspiration could escape their clothing and sleeping bags – it simply froze in the fabric and fur. Wright's sweater, for example, weighed thirteen pounds more after the journey than before. 'Wright, from the very first, had been entirely against this journey,' Atkinson recorded in his diary later. 'He had some knowledge of a previous sledge trip on the western coast. Not until after I had told him that we should have to turn back, did he tell me how thankful he was at the decision.'[50]

Winter at the Cape Evans hut in 1912 was sombre as the attenuated party buried itself in routine. They knew Scott's five-man party had perished and Campbell's group would have a desperate time surviving. A grisly task awaited them in the spring: to find and count the dead. The stout hopes of a year ago had withered to foreboding and resignation. With the easy-going Atkinson in charge, and with a common plight to unite them, the stiff division between seamen and officers-scientists faded. It was in this spirit that Atkinson put it to the men to decide what course should first be taken in the spring – head north to help Campbell's team or south to find Scott's party and diaries that might tell how disaster overtook them. Atkinson and eleven men voted to go south, one abstained. Part of the reason for the near-unanimity was a fear the British Admiralty would send rescue ships as they did unnecessarily in 1903 when Scott's ship the *Discovery* was unexpectedly locked for a second winter in the Antarctic ice.

On 29 October they set out, seven mules led by seven men, a dog-team party following, and Wright leading as navigator. He had carefully constructed a map showing every depot, lunch, and night camp made on the trail south in their two sledging seasons. Suspicious snow cairns would thus be easily identified. They had only enough provisions to get to the Beardmore Glacier and back, so that if the party had perished on the polar plateau the bodies likely would never be found. Despite the grim task, Wright was eager for a second chance to examine the great glacier.

On 12 November, barely fifteen days out, Wright squinted

against the snow-glare at a dark speck about half a mile to the west of the trail. At first he was only mildly curious, certain that the polar party had not made it this far north. There had been two false alarms in the last five days, and this was likely another. He looked at the dark patch again through the field glasses and skied on until he was nearly abreast of it. He then motioned to the rest of the search party to continue, and with a shove on his ski poles, glided over to investigate. As he approached, the speck resolved itself into a the tip of a tent, once a shelter, now a canvas tomb.[51] 'It ... was a great shock as I had been so certain that the Beardmore crevasses had been their downfall,' he wrote later. 'I considered it would be a sort of sacrilege to make a noise. I felt much as if I were in a cathedral and found myself with my hat on.' Wright motioned with his arms to attract the search party. The rest of the men finally noticed the frantic signals and turned off the trail. Wright bade them make camp about a hundred yards from the tent because 'it was wrong to trample the snow round and about what was obviously their last camp.'[52]

After an hour or so, party leader Dr Atkinson arrived. The snow was cleared from the outside of the tent and the tie-string at the entrance loosened. Atkinson entered. After a few minutes he emerged with several journals and silently read the chronicle of doom. The party had arrived at the pole on 17 January, only to find Amundsen had been there first, more than a month earlier and by a new route. Dispirited, the five men had trudged home in deathly cold temperatures with inadequate rations and fuel. Evans died on the Beardmore Glacier. Titus Oates, ailing terribly with a frostbitten foot, walked to his death in a blizzard a few miles south. Another storm pinned the three survivors at this spot for four days, just a few miles south of a huge food depot. Scott's last diary entry was dated 29 March.

Atkinson insisted all those in the search party look at the bodies inside. All three men were in their sleeping bags. Wilson, arms crossed, was on the left, Bowers on the right, both huddled securely in their bags. In the centre, Scott was half out of his bag, his coat flung open, and one arm stretched towards Wilson. To Wright, the end appeared to have come peacefully. Others weren't so certain. 'It was clear he [Scott] had had a very hard last minutes,' Tryggve Gran wrote. 'His skin was yellow, frostbites all over.'[53] Another witness, Thomas Williamson, wrote: 'I saw a most ghastly sight ... [Scott's] face was very pinched and his hands, I should say, had been terribly frostbitten ... the other two bodies I did not see, nor did I care to see them poor fellows.'[54] Headgear was removed and Atkinson read the lesson from the Anglican burial service. After a few prayers, the men sang 'Onward Christian Soldiers,' then some gear and documents were taken from the tent. Wright in particular suggested they retrieve the men's chronometers, which had been borrowed from the Greenwich Observatory. Atkinson agreed and Wright removed the one carried by Bowers.

The bamboo poles were tugged away and the canvas fell to become a funeral shroud. The men erected a large snow cairn and placed a cross made out of skis at its peak. And just in case there was a need to find the spot again, perhaps because of an inquiry by the Admiralty, they built two other cairns nearby, each surmounted by vertical sledges. They never even considered hauling the bodies back to base. The men would rest where they died, in accordance with British military tradition, although the Ross Ice Shelf, creeping slowly northward, would someday dump the bodies into the sea.

Two of the weakest mules were shot, most of the supplies depoted, and the men marched south about twenty miles. Oates's sleeping bag was spotted lying in the drift, along with his theodolite, socks and fur boots. One of the boots had been split down the middle to contain Oates's grotesquely swollen foot. They continued south the next day but there was still no sign of the body. Here they erected another cross.

On return to the Scott cairn, they retrieved about thirty-five pounds of geological specimens that the polar party had dragged from the Beardmore Glacier. Among them was the first Antarctic example of a Glossopteris fossil, which later became part of the continental drift theory. Among the gear they also noticed a letter from Amundsen to Norway's King Haakon that Scott had retrieved from Amundsen's tent at the pole. Wright tucked it in a pocket.

The main party pulled in to Hut Point on 27 November, where they discovered that Campbell's party had miraculously survived the winter in a snow-cave, living off seal and penguin meat, and had sledged back to base. (In 1922 Campbell moved to Newfoundland, where he spent the rest of his life.) The men now awaited the return of the *Terra Nova* while continuing to take observations and short sledge trips in the vicinity. They also developed the films that had been found with the bodies of the polar party. The photos were a chilling illustration of the tale told by Scott's diaries: dispirited men gazing at Amundsen's tent at the pole; an official portrait suggesting fatigue, hunger, and frostbite; five men clasping sledging flags with a look of resignation rather than victory. One negative, slightly blurred, spoke of another unexpected emotion. Four of them are laughing heartily as some mishap befalls Bowers, the photographer.

By mid-January, with the ship long overdue, it looked as though the nineteen survivors might have to spend yet another winter in the south. On 18 January, the day they began to dig an ice cave to store seal meat for another year, the ship finally hove into view. The sad news was shouted from the shore, and the shocked crew hastily removed the setting for a banquet planned to celebrate the conquest of the pole. A few days later the ship's carpenter built a nine-foot cross of heavy Australian jarra wood with the names of the dead and the inscription 'To strive, to seek, to find and not to yield.' The line, from Alfred Tennyson's *Ulysses*, had been inscribed on the flyleaf of a book of Browning's poems that had been taken to the pole by Scott and had been retrieved by the search party. Wright and seven other men dragged the cross to the top of Observation Hill, where it was erected facing south.

The *Terra Nova* anchored off Oamaru, on the east coast of

New Zealand, on 10 February, where the first press bulletin inflated the disaster: 'it is believed that 66 scientists and sailors lost their lives.' Toronto papers receiving the bulletin immediately contacted Wright's father, who, already suffering from a cold, was reported to be 'prostrated with grief' at the apparent loss of his son.[55] The following day a welcome cable arrived from Christchurch: 'Will be home in June. Am coming via Vancouver. Charlie.'[56] As details of the Antarctic disaster hummed along the telegraph wires, Charles Wright became an instant celebrity in his home town.

The *Terra Nova* docked on 12 February in Lyttelton, flags at half-mast. Repairs were carried out over the next few weeks before expedition members could start the long voyage home to England. Wright would not join them. He had to check the swing of his gravity-measuring pendulums at Christchurch, Wellington, and the Melbourne Observatory. With two of the dogs and his sledge-mate Frank Debenham, the geologist who would become first director of the Scott Polar Research Institute in Cambridge, Wright took a commercial ship to San Francisco.[57]

One of the dogs was given as a gift to Wright's older brother, Alfred, in Prince Rupert, British Columbia, the other to his younger brother, Adrian, in Vancouver. All four men spent two weeks in the British Columbia bush with a surveying party from Alfred's office, then Debenham and Wright went to Winnipeg. There, on 7 June, Wright delivered a short afternoon speech about the expedition before the members of the city's Canadian Club. 'One of the most remarkable things about this expedition of ours is the way it seems to have appealed to everyone,' he began. 'It is certainly not because people like a deal of adventure and dash; for nobody can say that a Polar expedition even approaches dash.' Instead, it 'has struck people suddenly as a surprise, that men can go into the wild places of the earth merely to seek knowledge. It has, I say, struck people as a surprise that there are men willing to give up their lives in the search for knowledge.'[58] The rest of the address was a plodding narrative of the expedition, with Wright's own role and personal impressions notably absent. Indeed, throughout his life he played down his role and did not mine his experiences for publication, as did so many of his colleagues, including Taylor, Priestley, Cherry-Garrard, Ponting, and Evans. The *Winnipeg Free Press* reported that 'with words simple and unadorned, he moved the Canadian Club more deeply than probably any orator has ever moved it.'[59]

The next day Wright, with Debenham in tow, took a train to Toronto. He had been warned about his new celebrity and about plans by the city to present him with a gold watch. To avoid reporters and politicians at Union Station, Wright sent a cable from Minneapolis saying he had missed his train connection. Another cable went to his family saying he would arrive as scheduled on 10 June. The ruse failed. A throng awaited him at the station and he was front-page news the next day. Wright was shy and untalkative – 'a very disappointing subject to the would be hero worshipper' one frustrated reporter wrote.[60] Only once did emotion overcome his natural reticence. He was asked why the search party did not bring back the bodies of the dead. 'The thought never entered our heads,' he replied sharply. 'It seemed perfectly obvious to us that his last resting place should be in the tractless ice fields which were the scene of his life work.'[61] Wright's father had hoped to board the train at Lambton, outside the city, and travel the last few miles beside his son. But the engineer did not make the usual stop and Wright was greeted by the stepmother he never got along with. Together they went to the family home in the exclusive Rosedale district, then to the university to see colleagues and former professors. A week later he was formally welcomed to the city in a ceremony at city hall and presented with a gold watch.[62]

Wright and Debenham soon embarked for England. Wright went to the Potsdam Geodetic Institute to return the pendulums, one of which was declared defective. He had to pay out of his own pocket for the manufacture of a new one, although the

blow was softened by a £150 honorarium given all the expedition scientists out of the flush of donations that Scott's death
had triggered. Wright then joined Debenham, Taylor and
Priestley in Tewkesbury, England, where Priestley's father was
headmaster of a local school. Since there were no classes in the
summer, the four used a schoolroom attached to the Priestley
household to write up their scientific reports and personal
accounts. Wright soon fell in love with one of Priestley's sisters,
Edith Mary, and they married in June 1914. The first of their
three children, a son, soon followed. Taylor married another
Priestley sister, Doris. In the fall of 1913 the four young scientists together went to Cambridge, where Wright became a lecturer in cartography and surveying.[63]

Wright joined the Signals Section of the Cambridge University Officers' Training Corps, specializing in the new technology of wireless transmission. It marked the beginning of a
lifelong career in military research. With the declaration of war
in August 1914, Wright became a second-lieutenant in command of the 2nd Army Wireless Company, Royal Engineers,
and was posted for a time to the Scottish Army Troops Signal
Company based in Glasgow. He was sent to France, where he
developed wireless techniques and equipment for use in the
trenches. Wright was eventually promoted to captain in the
Intelligence Division of the General Staff and was awarded an
MC and OBE.

At the end of 1918, with the armistice, Wright joined his old
professor from the University of Toronto, John McLennan, to
help establish a new military research arm for the Admiralty.
His employment as a scientist with the Admiralty would continue for almost three decades and had a touch of irony, since
Wright had found Scott's naval reserve and authoritarianism
ill-suited to the broader needs of scientists. In these early years
Wright managed to steal enough time to prepare short reports
on the aurora and gravity as well as a full-length glaciology
report, all based on his observations during the Scott expedition. The war, his growing family, and the administrative bur-

den of creating a new naval section had forced a delay in these studies. Raymond Priestley and he decided to combine efforts for the glaciology report. Their *Glaciology*, published in 1922, was the first in-depth study of glaciers other than those in the European Alps.

In 1934, Wright was made director of scientific research at the Admiralty and oversaw the early development of radar and methods to detect magnetic mines and torpedoes. He received a knighthood in 1946 for this work and retired to Canada the following year, eventually settling near Victoria. Wright continued to accept offers of short-term employment during his retirement, including stints at the British Joint Services Mission in Washington, DC; the Scripps Institute of Oceanography in La Jolla, California; the Pacific Naval Laboratory in Esquimalt, British Columbia; the University of British Columbia in Vancouver; and the Royal Roads Military College in Victoria. He died on 1 November 1975, and twelve days later his body slid into the sea following a ceremony aboard HMCS *Restigouche* off Esquimalt.

'Hope I have set foot on Barrier [the Ross Ice Shelf] for the last time,' Wright jotted in his diary on 27 November 1912.[64] The search party was then making its way back to base, all looking forward to the arrival of the ship and release from a continent that once held wonders but now seemed only bleak and menacing. Wright had no intention, much less desire, to return to Antarctica. But return he did, in 1959–60 as a guest of the United States government and again in 1965. He revisited the Cape Evans hut with journalists in train, and did not tell them his old bunk had for some reason been moved out of its original spot. He stood again beneath the Observation Hill cross, which he had dragged to the spot almost half a century before. He was taken by helicopter over the western mountains to a dry valley, the curious geophysical phenomenon he had explored in early 1911. He was also taken on a huge C-130 transport plane for a visit to the South Pole, the windswept geographical point he had so yearned to travel to with Scott.

In 1973, two years before his death, Wright was asked by an interviewer whether there was anything about the expedition that still haunted him. 'Starvation' was the instant reply.[65] Wright's first experience of short rations came during the six-week sledge trip led by Griffith Taylor to the dry valley. And to confirm his suspicions, the short depot-laying party that he joined on the Ross Ice Shelf soon after was dangerously short of food considering the lower temperatures and likelihood of blizzards. Scott's calculations always seemed to leave Wright hungry. Indeed, as he looked back six decades later, the tragic deaths of the polar party seemed the result of desperately underfed men.[66]

Wright believed Scott took a too-cavalier attitude about the pony meat. The carcasses of ponies shot at the foot of the Beardmore Glacier were carelessly abandoned rather than depoted to supplement the rations. As navigator of one of the return parties, Wright well understood that the line of retreat was too thinly stocked. His four-man party, already on inadequate rations, was forced to make long marches to build a surplus of food in the event the depots had not been re-stocked as planned. Teddy Evans, in the return party that followed Wright's, nearly died of scurvy because of vitaminless rations. Manhauling turned the body into a furnace burning calories at a wild clip. With the addition of extremely low temperatures, food became a critical factor.

Food, Wright believed, was at the heart of the polar party's slow decline. Scott at the last moment decided to take a fifth man with him to the pole, upsetting the food calculations in all the depots since they contained four-man ration packages. Evans's three-man returning party simply had to guess how much pemmican and biscuit to leave in a package for the returning party. Before his death, Scott said he could not have predicted the low temperatures his party experienced on the return trip. But Wright noted later that the temperatures conformed with those experienced by the only other man to travel the route, Shackleton. The low temperature, itself a drain on the body, also changed the character of snow crystals on the surface. Hauling a sledge over them was compared to dragging a weight across a sand surface, a deadly undertaking for hungry, cold men.

'You know, one would dream things like ... apples, apples,' Wright recalled. 'Heavens, what one wouldn't have given for one. Apples.'[67]

FOUR

A Geologist
Adrift

ADIPLOMATIC TIME BOMB was set ticking in 1909 when a group of Danish explorers, led by Knud Rasmussen, drew up an ambitious arctic program. At meetings in Copenhagen, Rasmussen proposed a permanent base on the west coast of northern Greenland, opposite Ellesmere Island. From this spot, small groups would make forays into the surrounding regions to study geology, physiography, and the ethnology of the Inuit. One of these proposed field trips would take a party across Baffin Bay to establish a post on Ellesmere Island. The Danes, who long had possession of Greenland, regarded the remainder of the northern Arctic as a no man's land and therefore fair game for explorers who need not consult any national government.[1] The Canadian government, however, had been diligently making repeated claims to Ellesmere Island. Britain transferred sovereignty over most of the Arctic archipelago to Canada in 1880. And on three voyages of exploration, Canadian government representatives took official possession of Ellesmere, the most recent expedition headed by Captain Joseph

Bernier. On 12 August 1907, Bernier raised the Canadian flag at King Edward VII Point and had a cairn erected over a metal box containing a statement of Ottawa's claim.[2]

The Danes made no effort to secure Canada's permission for Rasmussen's proposed expedition. The plans were published in an obscure Danish journal in 1910, and the permanent base, christened 'Thule,' was established in the same year. The Great War, meanwhile, interrupted most polar exploration and it was not until 1919 that Rasmussen again turned his attention to the Ellesmere Island expedition.

The following year, press reports about the proposed Danish incursion into Canadian territory triggered alarms at the tiny Department of External Affairs, which had been established only eleven years before. On 28 October 1920 the department's legal adviser, Loring Christie, alerted Prime Minister Arthur Meighen that the 'necessity for taking concrete steps to confirm the Canadian assertion of sovereignty over the northern arctic islands has now become more urgent.'[3] Indeed, so concerned was the government that a group in the Department of the Interior drew up a bizarre emergency plan to assert sovereignty. Canada would borrow a dirigible from the British government, load it with Mounties and supplies, launch it from Scotland, and fly it across the North Pole. As it drifted over Ellesmere Island, the Mounties would parachute down to cut off the raiding Danes.[4]

Christie had a less dramatic solution. He proposed enlisting the aid of Vilhjalmur Stefansson, the colourful and outspoken Canadian explorer who had commanded the government's 1913–18 Arctic expedition. Another extended assault on the region under Stefansson would forestall any Danish territorial claims and emphasize Canada's sovereignty. Besides, Christie advised, Stefansson could probably do the job cheaply since he was an expert at living off the land.[5]

Stefansson was quick to exploit the government's political quandary to promote his personal agenda. For several years he had contemplated a voyage to unexplored areas of the Beaufort

Sea – the so-called Zone of Inaccessibility – where new lands were supposedly awaiting discovery. The government, on the other hand, was more concerned about the Eastern Arctic, the scene not only of Danish field-work but of proposed Norwegian and American expeditions as well. Indeed, the MacMillan Expedition, led by a college teacher from Maine, had spent 1913–17 exploring Ellesmere, Axel Heiberg, and other high Arctic islands without seeking Canada's permission and ignoring Canadian wildlife laws. The ever-ambitious Stefansson exploited Ottawa's insecurity by pressing for an epic Arctic voyage that would encompass the entire region, the bill to be picked up by the Canadian taxpayer. His letter to the prime minister on 30 October 1920 dashed any hope that an assertion of sovereignty might be had at bargain-basement prices. Stefansson proposed a five-year, fifteen-man expedition that would cost half a million dollars. The voyage would include stops at Ellesmere Island and other islands fronting Baffin Bay to 'more or less fence off any other country from islands lying further west.'[6] The Department of the Interior proposed a more focused approach. In a report delivered late in the summer of 1920, a department board recommended establishing four permanent RCMP posts in the Eastern Arctic to be manned each summer. The cost? Perhaps $130,000, although the project could easily be scaled down by reducing the number of posts.[7]

The earliest an expedition could leave was the following summer, and the first reports of a Danish Ellesmere expedition turned out to be premature, so the government dithered searching for short cuts and less expensive solutions. Fortuitously, Ottawa had received a surprise offer that was made without reference to the sovereignty question and could save the government a lot of money. At the urging of the Royal Geographical Society, Sir Ernest Shackleton wrote from Britain in the summer of 1920 that he planned to explore the Canadian Arctic in what he claimed would be his last expedition. Would the government put up some cash?[8]

Shackleton's intended field of action was also the so-called

Zone of Inaccessibility. Stefansson later insisted that Shackleton had stolen his own proposal and misrepresented him to the Canadian government by claiming that Stefansson had abandoned plans to go north again. Stefansson reiterated to the prime minister that he was eager to lead an expedition to the Eastern Arctic, with just one condition. Stefansson had signed a lucrative contract to lecture for thirty-five weeks throughout North America, beginning in the summer of 1921. He told Meighen the latest he could extricate himself from the contract was 1 February, and he had to have a commitment from Ottawa before that date if he were to lead an expedition in the summer.[9]

Stefansson was himself a potential source of trouble for Canada's sovereignty claims. He repeatedly pressed the government to annex Wrangel Island, an uninhabited and desolate patch of land north of Siberia. Most of the crew and expedition members of the *Karluk* were stranded on Wrangel Island after their ship became frozen in the pack ice and sank at the outset of Stefansson's 1913–18 Canadian Arctic Expedition. (Stefansson was off on a hunting trip at the time the *Karluk* was beset.) When rescue came months later, there were just fourteen survivors of the original twenty-five aboard. Stefansson had continued his expedition unaware of the fate of the *Karluk*, but he now urged the Canadian government to claim the island on the basis of this grim and unplanned occupancy. The Department of External Affairs dismissed his pleas by noting that because the island was so far outside the region of Canada's Arctic, any such claim would undermine Ottawa's argument that the Arctic archipelago was a mere extension of Canada's southerly land mass.[10] Stefansson was undaunted. He made repeated and unauthorized claims of Canadian sovereignty for the island and later sent a four-member expedition to Wrangel, all of whom died. He was fast becoming *persona non grata* in Ottawa. Meighen was not about to place such a strong-headed and unpredictable character in charge of the delicate task of establishing sovereignty in the Eastern Arctic. Stefansson's

1 February deadline was allowed to pass with no commitment given, leaving Shackleton's rival bid the only outside offer on the table.

Shackleton met Meighen on 4 February in Montreal to sound him out personally on the possibility of Canadian funding. Meighen listened politely and sent the explorer on to Ottawa, where Shackleton met the minister of the interior, Sir James Lougheed. Shackleton again received no commitment but was now fully briefed about Canada's sovereignty problem. He was told of the still-secret plan to establish the four RCMP posts in the Eastern Arctic, one of them on Ellesmere Island.[11] Shackleton's original proposal placed him only in the Beaufort Sea, where he hoped to discover new land and perhaps make a dash to the pole. The expedition would nicely round out his career as a polar explorer by adding Arctic successes to his string of Antarctic accomplishments. But, tantalized by the scent of money, Shackleton was ready to tinker with his plans. On 5 April, during a return trip to Canada, Shackleton put his best offer in writing. He asked Meighen for $100,000 of the $250,000 needed for the expedition. Another $25,000 had been promised by a wealthy businessman in England, he said. And Sir John Eaton of Toronto – third son of Timothy Eaton, and president of the department-store chain – was committed to a $100,000 grant, no strings attached. 'The whole character of the expedition and status will be Canadian,' Shackleton wrote to the prime minister from Ottawa's Chateau Laurier Hotel.

I discussed this matter with my personal friends who have given me the ship and the $25,000.00 and they have no objection to my having the expedition entirely Canadian in action and publicity.

Scientific and navigating staff of the expedition will consist of fifteen (15) officers, nine (9) of whom have been with me on previous expeditions, the remaining six (6) will be drawn from Canada. I am, at the present moment, in touch with university authorities in this country for the selection of suitable young scientific men. These officers will be supplemented by a few French-Canadian and North-West dog drivers.[12]

International political currents, rivalry among ambitious explorers, the penny-pinching of a Canadian government – these forces converged one evening at Montreal's McGill University to pluck an obscure young man from a legion of adventure seekers and send him exploring with the great Shackleton. George Vibert Douglas, twenty-nine, was finishing a master of science degree in metallurgy at McGill in the spring of 1921 when Shackleton delivered a lecture at the university. Douglas showed up, his ambition ignited when he heard Shackleton announce he was looking for young men to go north with him. 'As I left the lecture hall, Professor [of Mining Engineering] J.B. Porter said "Do you know of any men who would like to go north with Shackleton." I said, "I know one." Prof. Porter said "Well then come and I'll introduce you to Sir Ernest." Shackleton came into the room, looked me over from head to foot and said – "Are you fit." I answered – "Yes Sir I am." "Well then go and see my secretary, Mr. Cook."'[13] Shackleton had unceremoniously bagged a Canadian scientist as part of his calculated bid for a $100,000 government grant.

Shackleton returned to England on 20 April to inspect repairs to the expedition ship, which had been purchased in January from a Norwegian whaling fleet. Built in 1917 as an Arctic sealer, the wooden *Foca I* was soon renamed the *Quest*. She was 111 feet long, 125 tons, and had 125-horsepower auxiliary steam engines. Shackleton immediately realized that with his own supplies, officers and crew, there was little additional room for a Canadian RCMP contingent and their prefabricated huts. He immediately cabled his Canadian lobbyist, John Bassett, publisher of the Montreal *Gazette*, to negotiate alternative schemes that would give Shackleton his money and Canada its outposts.[14] The government was now under renewed pressure to act. A Copenhagen newspaper report, dated 9 April 1921, confirmed the Danes were planning an expedition to Ellesmere

Island that summer under Rasmussen.[15] Something had to be done. Balance sheets were drawn up comparing an all-Canadian voyage to the Eastern Arctic with a hybrid that would include the British explorer. Viewed this way, Shackleton no longer seemed such a bargain. A veteran Canadian polar ship, the *Arctic*, had already undergone $55,000 worth of repairs and could relieve the RCMP posts year after year. Shackleton's offer was a one-shot deal. Still, the government decided to postpone a decision as long as possible.

A frustrated Shackleton finally dictated a telegram sent to Meighen on 6 May: 'Please cable government's definite support and amount ... urgently awaiting your action.' Meighen, annoyed with Shackleton's insistence, let the axe fall. 'Our arrangements now do not admit of assistance your expedition this year.' A final plea in a 12 May telegram was to no avail.[16] A few weeks later, a short diplomatic message vented the international steam and allowed Canada to postpone the voyage yet again until the next year. In a memorandum to the Colonial Office in London, through which Canada then dealt with non-Commonwealth countries, the Danish embassy conveyed its government's guarantee 'that the expedition has no political or mercantile aims but is of entirely scientific character and that no acquisition of territory whatsoever is contemplated in the regions in question.' Then the *pièce de résistance*: 'it would be much appreciated if the consent of the Government of Canada to the landing and further progress of the expedition might be obtained as soon as possible and communicated to this Legation.'[17]

The memorandum marked a victory for Canada and a significant saving for the federal Treasury that year. Shackleton, on the other hand, had waited so long for an answer from Ottawa that his plans for a summer voyage to the Arctic had to be abandoned. Never one to accept defeat, he simply turned his plans upside down à la Amundsen. There was still time to catch the Antarctic summer. He had a ship, a trusted and loyal crew, and a new offer of funding from Irish businessman John Quiller

Rowett. Hell, he'd even take his token Canadian scientist along for the ride.

George Vibert Douglas was relatively old to be taking a master of science degree. But he had decided to interrupt his studies in 1915 after two McGill professors urged him to sign up for the war. Born in Montreal on 2 July 1892, Douglas lost his mother to 'breast fever' shortly after the birth of his sister, Allie, in 1895. Brother and sister were raised by their maternal grandparents, the Reverend George Douglas and his wife, Maria, and their two unmarried daughters. George and Allie inverted their last names accordingly, even though their father, John Vibert, lived until 1908, when he died of complications from tuberculosis.[18]

George's paternal grandfather, J.A. Vibert, had been a captain from Jersey who sailed the North Atlantic and Caribbean, eventually becoming port warden of Montreal. Reverend Douglas was founder and first principal of the city's Wesleyan Theological College, then affiliated with McGill. After graduating from the Westmount Academy, Douglas entered McGill in the fall of 1911 for a B SC in mining engineering and economic geology. After the war broke out in August 1914, he joined the university's officer training corps and went to England in the autumn of 1915 as a second lieutenant with the Northumberland Fusiliers. He soon rose to the rank of captain and was later awarded the Military Cross for service in France and Flanders.

Demobilized in 1919, Douglas took a seven-month course at Britain's Royal School of Mines, then returned to McGill to complete his BS C the following year. He registered in the autumn of 1920 for an MS C in metallurgy, and had his fateful meeting with Shackleton early the following year, a few weeks before completing his course work. By 16 May it was clear Shackleton's plans for an official Canadian expedition had come unravelled. Douglas, assuming he was no longer needed, went to Alberta that summer for some paid geological fieldwork and left Shackleton no forwarding address.[19]

Shackleton, meanwhile, was dangling a new proposal before his backers and friends. During a two-year voyage, the *Quest* would explore and chart dozens of sub-Antarctic islands and map two thousand miles of the Enderby Land coast in Antarctica. The expedition would also seek mineral deposits and beds of guano – a fertilizer – for commercial exploitation, and carry out oceanographic, biological, and meteorological studies. This rambling, over-ambitious program grew like a weed when Shackleton stumbled on the ultimate backer, every explorer's dream-come-true: Rowett, an old school chum, had agreed to pick up every bill.

Shackleton acted quickly to corral his scientific crew. Douglas clearly had made an impression, for Shackleton made special efforts to find him. He contacted humorist Stephen Leacock, an arctiphile and McGill professor, who eventually tracked Douglas down in Edmonton.[20] Late that summer, Douglas finally received Shackleton's cabled offer to go to the Antarctic as geologist on the *Quest.* He accepted at once, took a train to Quebec City, a steamer to Liverpool in August, and another train to London. At Shackleton's office he was told to order whatever geological equipment was needed and to interview anyone who might be interested in buying guano. They also discussed how to exploit copper deposits that had been reported on the Antarctic Peninsula. Douglas would be paid £41. 8s. per month in a year-long contract.[21]

Work on the *Quest* continued in fits and starts. Shackleton had planned to install a diesel motor to replace the worn and antiquated steam engine, whose boiler had been built in 1890. Strikes in the city, however, prevented the work from being carried out. The useful range of the vessel was thus severely restricted. Shackleton was more successful in festooning the ship with the latest gadgetry. There was electric lighting throughout, the crow's nest was electrically heated, two wireless sets were installed, and an electrically powered Odograph would automatically record the ship's speed and movement. Jammed in the port alleyway was the fuselage of a small seaplane, a so-called Baby Avro. Shackleton planned to be the first to use an airplane in the Antarctic. Because of space constraints, the Avro's wings and floats had been sent ahead to Cape Town; they would be picked up before the ship headed into the pack ice. Douglas's bunk was one of several along the walls of the mess, a heavy green curtain its only defence against the commotion of the common room. Like all of the scientific staff, he was expected to tend the ship, and stand watch.

Also taken on was George (later Sir Hubert) Wilkins, an Australian naturalist who had served on Stefansson's Arctic expedition of 1913–18 and on a failed British expedition to Antarctica's Graham Land in 1920–1. Wilkins had been in New York planning an expedition that would be the first to use airplanes in the Antarctic. The German Junkers company agreed to lend him two aircraft for the venture. In late May Shackleton cabled a warning to Wilkins that this association with a German manufacturer so soon after the armistice would ruin his reputation in the British Empire. Why not come south on the *Quest* and fly in the British-made two-seater monoplane? Wilkins had no illusions about motives. 'The simple truth was that Shackleton didn't want anyone else working in the Antarctic while he was in the field,' he wrote later.[22] But he succumbed to Shackleton's entreaties by regarding the *Quest* expedition as a rare apprenticeship under a great leader. Wilkins still intended to take the Junkers airplanes into the Antarctic the following year. With New Zealand pilot Roderick Carr, he helped to custom design the expedition's Baby Avro. Wilkins and Douglas became fast friends and together would carry out the only professional scientific work of the *Quest* voyage.

On Saturday, 17 September, Douglas pencilled his first expedition journal entry: 'Amid scenes of unparalleled enthusiasm the Quest sailed at 1 p.m. proceeded upstream to London Bridge ... I hope that we may accomplish something which may justify all this enthusiasm.'[23] At sea, Douglas was sporting about doing routine jobs and even volunteered to make breakfast one morning after the cook wounded his hand. A boy scout that Shackleton had taken along, James Marr, observed with relief that the cook was back in action the next morning 'and so a possible mutiny was averted.'[24]

There were brief stops at the islands of Madeira, St Vincent, and St Paul's Rocks, where Douglas did some quick geological surveys. The Atlantic voyage soon exposed the gross inadequacies of the *Quest*. The ship's top speed under steam was far slower than its reputed seven to eight knots, and there were frequent problems with the engines. Worse still, the vessel was so small it lurched with the slightest wave. The crew was constantly tossed about, across the mess table, out of bunks, over the decks. Food frequently became airborne and even seasoned sailors struggled against seasickness. Wilkins ventured that the agent who had bought the temperamental little vessel for Shackleton must have been 'drunk and seeing double.'[25]

Shackleton – the 'Boss' to his admiring crew – quickly realized the *Quest* would need at least four weeks of overhaul at Rio de Janeiro. A stop at Cape Town to pick up the airplane wings, floats and other supplies was thus out of the question. The austral summer would then be too advanced to do any work in the Antarctic. On 1 November he advised Douglas and Wilkins they would be sent ahead to the sub-Antarctic island of South Georgia while the *Quest* was being repaired. If arrangements could be made with whalers in the area, they might even be placed on the Antarctic Peninsula itself to do some prospecting. The *Quest* would fetch them later.

The South American coast was sighted on 21 November, and the ship hove into Rio harbour soon after, its keel warped and propeller shaft out of alignment. Douglas and Wilkins made their way by mail steamer to Montevideo and sailed on 28 November for South Georgia to carry out field-work on the island until the *Quest* arrived. Their ship, the *Woodville*, arrived at the whaling station of Grytviken on 8 December and two days later the pair took a short rainy hike inland to survey the territory. A few weeks later, they each went to opposite ends of the island for extended field trips.

South Georgia is a mountainous, heavily glaciated crescent whose complicated geology was not well understood in 1921. The island was discovered in 1675 by a British merchant, but the first landing was made exactly a century later by Captain James Cook, who claimed it for Britain. Seal colonies attracted commercial hunters, who had nearly wiped out the population by 1810 and who returned twice in the nineteenth century when the numbers recovered. In 1904 the first whaling station, Grytviken, was built by a Norwegian group and for the next half-century South Georgia was the world's whaling centre. The island also became the last way station for several expeditions heading for the Antarctic, but is perhaps best known for a forced seventeen-mile march across it by Shackleton in 1916. The hike was the climax of his efforts to rescue the men of the *Endurance*, the vessel that was to have landed an expedition for the first crossing of Antarctica. The ship was crushed in the pack ice at the outset, and Shackleton led his crew through the ice floes in rowboats to the uninhabited and desolate Elephant Island. With five men, he sailed a small open boat across eight hundred miles of treacherous ocean until reaching South Georgia. Bone-tired, hungry, and cold, Shackleton and two companions crossed the mountainous interior and stumbled into the whaling station of Stromness. He eventually rescued the survivors on Elephant Island, not a life lost. Shackleton in 1921 was eager to see South Georgia again to rekindle memories of what had been his most heroic journey.

While ashore at Rio, Shackleton suffered a heart attack but would not let the ship's surgeon, Alexander Macklin, examine him. He insisted it was a mere fainting spell, and ignored Macklin's advice to rest. He also began drinking, entirely out of character and a cause for concern to the men. The *Quest* finally steamed out of Rio harbour on 18 December for a stormy crossing to South Georgia during which further problems with the ship became apparent. A water tank leaked dry, the boiler furnace cracked, and the engines sputtered. South Georgia was sighted on 4 January. Shackleton and his mates from the

Endurance peered excitedly at the old landmarks through binoculars and anchor was dropped at Grytviken. That night the 'Boss' penned a last poetic entry in his diary: 'In the darkening twilight I saw a lone star hover, gem like above the bay.'[26] He died in his bunk a few hours later.

Douglas had set up his research camp on the shore of a small bay near Godthul, two hours' journey by sea from Grytviken, and was unaware of the arrival of the *Quest*. Wilkins and Marr came in a small whaling boat early on 9 January to break the sad news. 'We have lost a great leader. R.I.P.,' Douglas wrote in his journal that day. 'The expedition will carry on ...'[27] He and his equipment were immediately brought back to the whaling station. The *Quest*'s wireless failed just as the crew tried to get out word of Shackleton's death. Frank Wild, an old Antarctic hand and mate, took over the command of the expedition. Without instructions on where to bury his leader, he decided to send the body back to Rio with one of the men.

Shackleton had left no indication of his latest expedition plans, so Wild proposed to map parts of the Antarctic coast between the Ross Ice Shelf and Coats Land. Warm clothing and other supplies in Cape Town could not be retrieved because of the lateness of the season. Wild hoped to scavenge some supplies left on South Georgia by the ill-fated German *Deutschland* expedition of 1910–12. But the stores had been opened and the contents scattered. Wild's crew would have to make do with supplies at hand and whatever the whalers could spare.

The Grytviken whalers were a congenial lot, but the station itself was a scene of unparalleled butchery. 'The water of the harbor was red with blood, and everywhere was the awful, nauseous stench of rotten whale carcasses,' Marr wrote. 'We spectators found it treacherous work walking on the slip, which was several inches deep in a slimy horror of blood and blubber.'[28] Douglas and Carr, the pilot without prospect of a plane, escaped upcountry to Cooper Bay equipped with a kayak. They carried out more field investigations inland and reported evidence of a volcano in eruption. They were picked up by the *Quest* on 17 January to begin the journey south.[29]

No landing could be made at the first land encountered, the volcanic Zavadovskiy Island. Sulphuric fumes and a reddish cloud issued from caves on the south side, stinging their eyes, noses, and throats. Meanwhile, bad luck continued to plague the expedition. Douglas, beginning to chill in his inadequate clothing, badly sprained his ankle on 30 January while skipping to keep warm. The next day Frank Worsley, ship's captain, was knocked by a swinging lifeboat the crew was trying to move. 'There was a cry, the splintering of wood, the awful snapping of human bones, and Worsley's ribs gave to the impact of the weighty craft,' Marr wrote.[30] Wild 'felt sure Worsley was killed. His faced turned a deathly grey and was covered with perspiration, and he could scarcely breathe.'[31] Worsley survived but needed several weeks to recover.

Mutinous thoughts took root as they entered the pack ice on 4 February. The *Quest* was an uncomfortable, difficult ship and underpowered for the battle with the ice. They zigzagged south and north in a game of tag with the pack to avoid being frozen in. Wild noted a 'discordant element in the personnel'[32] at the same time as Douglas was writing in his diary: 'This senseless rummaging around putting in time is absurd. I think if nothing is done when we reach Cape Town I will go home. Far better prospects in Canada.'[33]

Wild decided to spin out the ship's dwindling coal by heading to Elephant Island, where elephant seals could provide blubber for the furnace. Exasperated, Douglas called it a 'futile attempt by grown up infants to reach the Antarctic Continent' and listed in his journal the many inadequacies of the *Quest* and crew. The ship was the 'wrong shape and poorly built,' and as a makeshift meteorologist, Carr was a 'joke.' Worsley was vain 'to the point of absurdity.'[34] Similar sentiments were exchanged in hushed tones by several other men. The grumbling made its way to Wild, who was 'surprised to find that the men affected were those in whom I had placed the most implicit

trust. It was a condition of things that required prompt measures. I assembled each mess in turn, and going straight to the
point told them that further continuance would be met with
the most drastic treatment ... I was glad to notice an immediate
improvement.'[35] Douglas's journal that night: 'Wild gave a general dissertation on the ethics of being afloat and not knowing
where you are going.'[36] Talk was muzzled but dark thoughts
lingered.

Elephant Island was sighted on 25 March, about a month
after Wild's stern lecture. The long days at sea only added to
Douglas's frustration – there was precious little work for a geologist among the waves. Elephant Island offered a welcome
opportunity to do some science. For Wild and Worsley, the barren rocks stirred emotions about the landing they had made
there eight years previous, after the *Endurance* was crushed in
the ice. For 105 days, Wild and twenty-one other men had eked
out a bare existence on the pebble beach.

Douglas was among the *Quest*'s seven-man shore party on 26
March. While the crew slaughtered seals for blubber, he hacked
away rock specimens and made hasty sketches of the terrain. It
was a short stay, though, a bare twenty-four hours' worth of
geologizing in two landings. A hurricane blew up and sent the
ship at a reckless clip in the direction of South Georgia. Anchor
was dropped again at Grytviken on 6 April and the blubber collected at Elephant Island – not needed because of the strong
winds – was tossed overboard to float among the whale detritus
in the harbour.

Shackleton's body, meanwhile, had been returned for burial
on South Georgia at the request of Lady Shackleton. The 5
March interment was a small affair attended only by the Grytviken whalers while the *Quest* was at sea. On their return,
Wild's crew agreed to build a cairn in honour of the 'Boss.'
Douglas picked a high site overlooking the harbor and sketched
a design for the monument. Digging and blasting began on 2
May and the work was completed three days later. Attached
was a plate inscribed in rough letters 'Sir Ernest Shackleton

Explorer. Died here January 5th 1922 Erected by his comrades.'
But even this expression of a common bond did not muffle
Douglas's dislike of the present leadership. Of the cairn-build-
ing, he noted it was 'the usual messing about with Worsley
making a nuisance of himself.'[37]

Douglas was allowed to continue his geologizing of South
Georgia for most of April, although without a field assistant.
The *Quest* and crew finally steamed away on 9 May for visits to
half a dozen South Atlantic islands. Again, Wild's attitude
miffed his Canadian scientist. As Douglas later put it, Wild 'did
not know what to do with the expedition after Shackleton's
death. His idea was to sail around from point to point, but he
had no conception whatsoever of scientific inquiry. "Gough Is.
– yes there is Gough Is. I suppose you want to go ashore? How
long do you want?" "Four days" – "You can have two days."
Here is an island rich in geology and biology and we've spent
days and days getting to the place and then a quibble about
how long we can stay there ... Shackleton fairly bubbled with
good humour and until his death it was a happy ship ... for me
it was as if the main spring had snapped ... the loyalty did not
transfer itself to Wild.'[38]

The *Quest* finally returned to London's St Katharine's Dock
on 17 September, a year to the day after setting out. Douglas
gave his geological specimens to the Museum of Natural History in South Kensington, and wrote his reports in Cambridge
at the Scott Polar Research Institute, then a one-room affair at
the Sedgewick Museum of Geology. He also worked at Emman-
uel College, where he became an honorary fellow. His initial
report, part of the official account of the expedition in 1923,
apologized for the incomplete data: 'It was found to be seldom
possible to do accurate and close geological mapping, owing to
the limited time that was available for work ashore.'[39] A fuller
account of his work was published by the Museum of Natural
History.[40]

Douglas met his future wife, Olga Margaret Crichton, when
he visited a friend in County Sligo, Ireland, whose property

adjoined the Crichton farm.[41] They married after a brief court-
ship in 1924 and eventually had four children. His association
with the great Shackleton soon began to open doors. 'There is
no question about it,' Douglas wrote years later, 'if one goes on
an expedition with a public figure like Shackleton you are a
marked person.'[42] He was invited to teach at Harvard University for three years, studied at the Massachusetts Institute of
Technology, and spent several summers geologizing in British
Columbia and northern Ontario. Douglas abandoned work on
his PH D to become chief geologist at the Rio Tinto copper mines
in Spain. He returned to head office in London for a year, then
was sent to what is now Zambia to head a team of thirty geologists.

Copper prices plummetted in the Depression and Douglas
was given word in 1931 that he would be laid off. He successfully applied for the newly created Carnegie Chair of Geology at
Dalhousie University in Halifax and remained in the post for
the next twenty-five years, until retirement. Although Douglas
was forty when he began teaching, students remarked on his
skill, energy and enthusiasm. In 1933–4, he gave a few lectures
and radio addresses about the *Quest* expedition, but beyond
this did not capitalize on the experience.[43] During the Second
World War he served without pay as provincial geologist,
examining old mines for minerals made scarce by the war.
Each summer he would lead students into the bush in Newfoundland, Labrador, Quebec, and Nova Scotia. Retired in
1957, he moved with his wife to Toronto and became a consultant, sometimes lecturing at the University of Toronto. A heart
attack felled him on 8 October 1958. Douglas Crag, a 5,500-foot
peak in the Salvesen Range of South Georgia, was named in the
1950s to commemorate his geological work on the island.

Shackleton's Baby Avro airplane, stripped of its wings and
floats, was the harbinger of an age to come. The *Quest* expedition was the last of the so-called heroic age in Antarctic exploration, when men, dogs and ponies supplied all the motive

power and primitive machines gave more trouble than they were worth. As it turned out, a member of Shackleton's crew would inaugurate the new age. Naturalist George Wilkins (as Sir Hubert Wilkins) made the first airplane flight in the Antarctic, on 16 November 1928. One of his first discoveries by air, a strait along the Antarctic Peninsula, was named after a Canadian, Vilhjalmur Stefansson. He also took along a young Canadian pilot fresh from the northern bush.

Hugh Evans, taxidermist and zoology and photography assistant with the first expedition to winter on the Antarctic continent. The ten-man party, under Carsten Borchgrevink, spent the winter of 1899–1900 at Cape Adare, where one man died.

Dr W.A. Rupert Michell (right) was ship's surgeon with the *Nimrod*, which served Ernest Shackleton's 1907–9 Antarctic expedition. Michell is shown here aboard the *Nimrod* with Aeneas Mackintosh (left), the ship's navigating officer, who lost his eye in an accident. Geologist Leo Cotton is centre.

Charles Wright, a Toronto-born physicist, shown here in 1911 in full sledging gear on Captain Robert Scott's second Antarctic expedition

George Douglas taking measurements of the sun at Leith Harbour, South Georgia, December 1921

Members of Hubert Wilkins's second expedition to the Antarctic Peninsula, 1929–30. Al Cheesman (second from right) was the main pilot of the expedition's Lockheed Vegas, one of which is pictured here. Second pilot Parker Cramer is at left, Wilkins is standing, and Orval Parker is right.

Wilkins's two Lockheed Vegas undergoing checks in late 1929 at Deception Island. Cheesman is seated at the right.

Frank Davies, physicist with Richard Byrd's first expedition, 1928–30. Davies's scientific duties at the main base at the Bay of Whales prevented him from joining field parties.

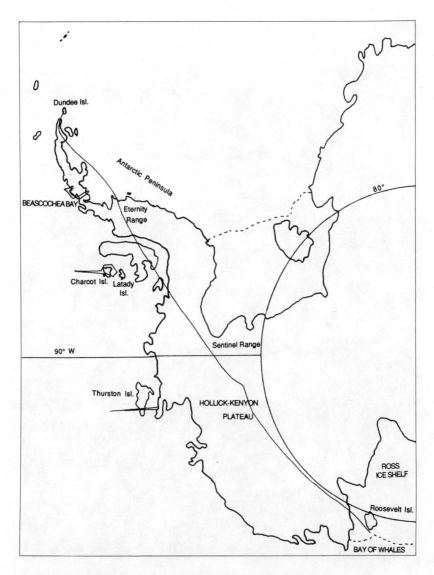

Map of three 1929–30 flights of exploration by Al Cheesman, to
Beascochea Bay, Charcot Island, and Thurston Island; and the 1935
trans-Antarctic flight of Herbert Hollick-Kenyon from Dundee Island
to the Bay of Whales

Herbert Hollick-Kenyon (left) and Lincoln Ellsworth aboard the *Wyatt Earp* in January 1936 after their flight across Antarctica. Hollick-Kenyon was a skilled pilot and navigator, but his silent disposition unnerved Ellsworth.

A May 1936 homecoming celebration for Hollick-Kenyon, Red Lymburner, and Patrick Howard in Winnipeg, which included live radio speeches. Hollick-Kenyon is at the microphone, Lymburner is over his shoulder (centre of photo). Howard is next to Lymburner.

Ellsworth and Lymburner (right) load their Northrup Delta on 11 January 1939 for their major exploratory flight near the Amery Ice Shelf.

Ellsworth's Aeronca scout plane ready for a reconnaissance flight by
Lymburner on 1 January 1939

Four Canadian Antarctic aviators, *c.* 1940: left to right, Burt Trerice, Herbert Hollick-Kenyon, Red Lymburner, and Pat Howard

Captain Andrew Taylor, surrounded by his surveying gear, relaxes inside the expedition hut at Port Lockroy in July 1944.

Andrew Taylor taking survey photos at Wiencke Island, off the Antarctic Peninsula, in October 1944

Four-man field party led by geologist Fred Roots in the Barkley
Mountains of Queen Maud Land, in February 1951, about six
hundred kilometres from base

Field party, *c.* 1951, led by geologist Fred Roots in the mountain mass later named Rootshorga, the highest summit in Queen Maud Land

FIVE

A Wayward
Bush Pilot

T HE *Polar Record*, an authoritative journal in matters of polar history and science, made a belated announcement in the obituary section of a 1945 issue: 'Flying-officer Al Cheesman, Royal Canadian Air Force, was reported missing in January 1943. In 1929 he was a member of Sir Hubert Wilkins's expedition to [Antarctica's] Graham Land. He also piloted a plane in 1937 in Sir Hubert Wilkins's air expedition in search of the six missing Soviet trans-polar aviators.'[1]

This brief notice was hardly a fitting tribute to Cheesman's flying career, which began in the northern Ontario bush. He was more than merely a member of Wilkins's expedition – he was the primary pilot, responsible for some of the earliest air exploration of the continent. His flights uncovered hundreds of square miles of new territory, with no loss of life or aircraft. Just getting a plane into the air over Antarctica was a challenge. There were no runways, no parts or fuel depots, no repair facilities. Aircraft technology was primitive, often improvised. Antarctica's storms were the world's worst and there were no weather forecasts. A blizzard could envelop a fragile airframe in minutes without warning. Cheesman had beaten some pretty long odds.

The obituary was inadequate in another respect; Cheesman, in fact, had not died. His plane was forced down by a January 1943 snow squall in northern Labrador, as the notice indicated, but he walked away from the wreck unhurt. Using survival skills, he and two companions rested comfortably and welcomed their rescuers eight days later by offering them cups of hot coffee.[2] That was pure Cheesman. He was a survivor and not even the venerable *Polar Record* could finish him off.

Cheesman came late to the cockpit and only after years of tinkering with internal combustion engines. He was born in Saint John, New Brunswick, on 14 May 1900, to Thomas Walter and Jenny Edythe Cheesman and claimed to have carried out his first flights when he was ten.[3] These were on a sled rigged with a sail with his brother Charles as test pilot. The pair found that with enough downhill speed the wooden runners actually left the ground for brief periods. By his early teens Cheesman had become hooked on engines. He became so adept that the Saint John Power Boat Company let him perform small repairs on their machines, and motorists with breakdowns were frequently directed to Cheesman for help.

Cheesman's mother pulled her son from school when he was fourteen and got him an office job. He struggled as a clerk for four years while training and working after-hours at a local machine shop. At the age of eighteen, Cheesman quit office work to become a partner with a sixty-three-year-old businessman in the Peerless Motor and Machine company. He worked in the firm on and off for another four years, beginning as a foreman machinist and eventually becoming a marine engineer.

For a brief period in 1920 Cheesman was a mechanic with the Frelinghusen motor-boat racing team in Florida. In July that year he joined the Canadian armed forces as a private, based in Calgary, but lasted just 169 days. Twice punished for unrecorded offences, Cheesman was discharged in January 1921, an officer noting on the exit papers that the young man was unpunctual and showed lack of keenness.[4] In the summer of 1922, he met Canadian pilot 'Duke' Schiller while on a trip to New York. Schiller gave him work as an air mechanic for several months before Cheesman enrolled at Boston's Franklin University to study engineering and electricity.

Cheesman returned to Peerless the following summer but, still aimless and unsettled, headed for California in the fall of 1923. While awaiting a train connection in Detroit, he visited the local airfield and struck up a conversation with an employee of a passenger air service that flew between Michigan and Florida. Cheesman was soon offered training as an airplane mechanic. He eagerly accepted but was out on the street the next year when the firm folded, forcing his return to Saint John.

For the next year Cheesman helped run the Saint John machine shop, but he was now determined to get back into aviation. With Schiller's endorsement, he applied to Ottawa in April 1925 for certification as an air engineer and within two weeks got his licence. Cheesman then landed a job that summer servicing a fleet of thirteen flying boats in the Ontario government's new air service, based in Sault Ste Marie. In November 1926 the province sent Cheesman to an RCAF training course at Ontario's Camp Borden to become licensed as a commercial pilot. His instructors were impressed. After only two weeks, and based on a fifteen-minute solo flight, Cheesman was found to have 'a natural aptitude for flying ... should make a sound and reliable pilot.'[5]

Meanwhile, Harold 'Doc' Oaks, a pilot with whom Cheesman worked at Sault Ste Marie, quit his job with the Ontario government to help set up Western Canadian Airways. The company, incorporated at Winnipeg on 10 December, was kick-started with $200,000 from grain baron James Richardson. Even before the firm's incorporation, Oaks offered the post of mechanic to

Cheesman, who promptly quit the Camp Borden course and headed north again. Western Canadian Airways, with operations based in Hudson, Ontario, was to serve Manitoba and northern Ontario primarily as a transport airline. Cheesman joined Oaks in flying the company's first aircraft, a Fokker Universal monoplane dubbed the *City of Winnipeg*, from New York to Hudson. They left on 16 December but did not complete the trip until Christmas Day after nineteen hours and fourteen hundred miles of stop-start flying through repeated flurries. Even though he still had no pilot's licence, Cheesman flew the aircraft on the third leg of the trip from Hamilton to Camp Borden.

Cheesman got an unexpected second chance to fly the plane on 8 February 1927, during a rescue mission. Oaks had taken off from Hudson six days earlier with eight hundred pounds of supplies but never arrived at his destination, Narrow and Clearwater lakes. Cheesman set out by dog sled to find his friend and located the aircraft at Woman Lake, about 120 miles north of Hudson. Oaks had been forced down by bad weather. The aircraft's undercarriage was smashed but Oaks was uninjured. Pilot Dale Atkinson of rival Patricia Airways flew Oaks out, leaving Cheesman to begin repairs to the Fokker. He lashed birch saplings together for an improvised undercarriage, climbed aboard, and piloted the aircraft to Hudson for a complete overhaul.[6]

On the strength of this limited cockpit time, Cheesman applied for a flight test finally to win his licence. He got his chance on 23 February at Hamilton. He and a federal inspector took off in a wheel-equipped plane from an ice-strip in Lake Ontario. 'He should be a good pilot if he does not become careless,' the inspector noted afterward.[7] Cheesman was finally granted his licence that May after completing a last requirement, a solo two-hundred-mile flight over the bush.

In March and April, Western Canadian Airways carried out a contract to ferry fourteen federal engineers and almost nine tons of equipment from the head of steel at Cache Lake, Mani-

toba, to Fort Churchill (then being examined as a possible sea-
port), a distance of 280 miles. During one of these flights the
City of Winnipeg was forced down by a burst oil line, and the
pilot abandoned the aircraft for an overland trek to Cache Lake.
A rescue aircraft dropped off Cheesman at the disabled plane,
then continued to search for the missing pilot. Cheesman
spent a night alone, fighting the chill by sleeping on his knees
and elbows while howling wolves circled his encampment.
After frantic repairs, he took off at first light to return to Cache
Lake.

Norwegian pilot Bernt Balchen, sent north by the Fokker
company to break in the new planes, described Cheesman's
unexpected return:

We are heating our oil the following morning to take off for the
downed plane, when we hear the drone of a motor in the distance.
There is no other airplane within a thousand miles, and we stare at
the sky incredulously as the second Fokker staggers into view. It is
seesawing and wobbling like a wing-shot goose, lurching and yawing
as it drops toward the lake, and thumps onto the ice. Al Cheeseman
[*sic*] crawls out and reels like a wooden man into the mess hall.[8]

Cheesman married Eva Meryl Greer (Schiller's sister-in-law) at
Sault Ste Marie in June 1927 and the newlyweds spent their
honeymoon at Hudson in a tent. In March the following year
Oaks left Western Canadian Airways to form a mineral exploration company, also backed by Richardson, called Northern
Aerial Minerals Exploration Limited. Again Cheesman followed
his friend, this time as a fellow pilot helping to establish fuel
caches along the northwest shores of Hudson Bay to support
the transport of prospectors hired by the company.

That same autumn of 1928, on the other side of the planet, Sir
Hubert Wilkins was making history by completing the first
flights in Antarctica.[9] Wilkins had been contemplating air
exploration of the south polar regions as early as 1921, when he

abandoned his plans in favour of a berth on the *Quest* and a chance to fly the Baby Avro. The British Natural History Museum sent him on an expedition to central Australia from 1923 to 1925, but Wilkins was back in the polar regions in the late 1920s to carry out Arctic flights from Alaska. The most daring of these was the world's first trans-Arctic flight, on 15 April 1928. Wilkins and American pilot Ben Eielson flew across the high Arctic from Barrow to Spitzbergen. Their twenty-two-hour flight turned up six undiscovered islands.

This success acted as a magnet for financial backing of Wilkins's next venture, an air survey of Antarctica's Graham Land, part of the long peninsula that stretches like a horn towards South America. As a youth, Wilkins had experienced first-hand the devastation of drought in his native Australia and believed a world-wide network of weather stations could at least give warning of impending disaster. He declared it a personal mission to help establish a ring of such stations in the Antarctic. Besides, there was much still to be discovered on the continent, whose interior remained a blank apart from the thin trails to the pole cut by Amundsen and Scott.

Wilkins had used a Lockheed Vega, the *Los Angeles*, in his Arctic flights, and the firm sold him a second at cost in appreciation of the publicity. Cash flowed from the Detroit Aviation Society, the Vacuum Oil Company of Australia, and the Hearst newspaper chain, which was guaranteed exclusive news rights in return for its $25,000 cheque. The American Geographical Society bestowed a scientific seal of approval, and Eielson and another Alaskan pilot, Joe Crosson, ensured Wilkins would have polar expertise in the cockpit.

The American explorer Richard Byrd, then planning his first Antarctic expedition, visited Wilkins in New York asking that he sign a document guaranteeing Byrd the first flight to the South Pole. (Byrd had learned that the Hearst chain was offering Wilkins a $50,000 bonus to beat him to the pole.) Wilkins refused to sign the document, but assured Byrd that his base of operation was confined to Graham Land and that no dash to the pole was contemplated. This was so in part because Wilkins had no expedition ship to act as a base. He had to rely for transport on whaling ships operating out of Deception Island, near the northernmost tip of Graham Land.

Deception Island looks like a ring with a narrow breach for an entrance, and in fact is the cone of a still-active volcano. The water of the inner lagoon sometimes steams and burbles with sulphur fumes as minor eruptions churn the depths. Wilkins planned to use the protected inner harbour as a ski- or sea-runway, depending on conditions. He hoped to establish an advance base some six hundred miles south using aircraft transport and then make the first trans-Antarctic hop, ending at the Bay of Whales, which was to become Byrd's base. As it turned out, conditions were appalling. The ice at Deception Island harbour was weak and honeycombed. An improvised land runway on the beach proved unsatisfactory for taking off with full loads, and after failed efforts to find another suitable runway in the area Wilkins had to abandon plans for his transcontinental flight. But he did beat Byrd into the air. On 16 November, five days after arrival, one of the Vegas went up for a short reconnaissance flight, thus inaugurating a new era in Antarctica. And on 20 December, Eielson and Wilkins made their longest flight, almost thirteen hundred miles, from Deception Island along Graham Land. From this flight, Wilkins mistakenly concluded that Graham Land was not a peninsula but rather an archipelago, and gave the name Stefansson Strait to an inlet at the most southerly point of the flight to honour his Canadian mentor.

In mid-1929, Cheesman, now the father of a year-old son and based in Sioux Lookout, Ontario, received a request from Wilkins that he recommend a backup pilot for a second Antarctic expedition. Parker Cramer, an American pilot with flying experience in Labrador and Greenland, had already been picked to replace Eielson, who was on contract with Alaskan Airways. Wilkins's other Antarctic pilot, Joe Crosson, was also at Alaskan Airways and suggested to Wilkins that Cheesman would know some skilled pilots who might be available for work in the south. Cheesman took one look at Wilkins' request and promptly came up with two candidates: himself and another flying buddy. According to Wilkins's account, he looked up the records of both and rejected Cheesman because he was headed for bigger things in Northern Aerial Minerals Exploration Limited. A stint in the Antarctic could derail a promising career. Wilkins sent a wire offering the post to the other man. 'Cheesman pocketed the telegram, got a six-month's leave of absence from his company, and came down to meet me in New York,' Wilkins wrote later. 'He turned out to be as fine a pilot and companion as one could wish for.'[10]

The goal remained a transcontinental flight from Graham Land to the Ross Sea. The expedition members departed New York on 22 September aboard a commercial vessel for Montevideo and from there on a whaling vessel to Deception Island. The weather was even milder than the year previous, dashing any hope for long flights from the harbour ice. The Lockheed Vegas had been left on the beach at the end of Wilkins's previous expedition, the wings detached and covered but the fuselages exposed. Within hours of arrival at Deception, Cheesman and Cramer cleaned out the snow, attached the wings, and installed larger-diameter tires. The engines growled to life with no hesitation.[11]

Wilkins had brought down a tractor and small car to help rebuild the pebble-and-stone runway (the previous year's work was carried out using only picks and shovels) but the ground remained too soggy for safe takeoffs with full loads. After a few short flights in the vicinity, Wilkins decided to trans-ship one plane, the *Los Angeles*, farther south to find a suitable ice runway. The British Colonial Office had put their research vessel *William Scoresby* at Wilkins's disposal on the strength of his accomplishments during the 1928–9 expedition. The loaded ship sailed from Deception Island on 12 December and for the next week wandered south in search of firm pack ice or calm ocean. Finding neither, the expedition headed north again for the uninhabited harbour of Port Lockroy, where on 19 December tranquil seas invited a short flight.

Cramer was by far the more experienced pilot, but ironically that was a handicap. Wilkins preferred to use Cheesman as main pilot to ensure Cramer would be available for any rescue flight. Accordingly, Cheesman took the controls of the *Los Angeles* for the first takeoff on floats, with Wilkins as navigator. The goal was to cut eastward across Graham Land to the Weddell Sea, less than one hundred miles away, to re-examine territory crossed during Wilkins's 1928 flight along the spine of the peninsula.

After takeoff, Cheesman climbed sharply to more than nine thousand feet to clear the mountain tops and was immediately faced with headwinds of more than sixty miles an hour. The engine began to sputter. The pair decided to head south along the west coast to escape the gale and give the pistons a chance to recover. Fifty miles farther south, with the engine sounding healthier, they cut into the east wind again and across the spine. They had barely reached the other side when the fuel gauge indicated half a tank and Cheesman brought the aircraft around for the return. They soon reached the circular head of Beascochea Bay, which makes a long cut into the west coast, and with a furious tailwind they ran into trouble. Wilkins wrote: 'The great cirque at the head of the bay is the most awesome thing I have seen from the air. I had directed Cheesman to fly over it, and with ready obedience and skill he did so. But he opened the engine throttle wide. It was no place over which to linger. Whirling currents caught the machine. We looked down into what seemed to be a cylinder leading down to hell.'[12] Cheesman recovered control and brought the craft down safely near the *William Scoresby*. 'Today Cheesman made his first flight in the Lockheed fitted as a seaplane,' Wilkins wrote in his log that night. 'He proved his skill and ability. I am well satisfied with his performances.'[13]

Wilkins now ordered the ship to head for Beascochea Bay to determine whether sea ice in the area could support a takeoff on skis. They soon moored to the ice at the entrance to the bay and lifted the *Los Angeles* and the Austin motor car over the side. The eight-wheel Austin was intended to haul gasoline farther west to the takeoff point but almost as soon as it roared off, the sea ice gave way beneath. Another submerged layer of ice caught the machine's wheels. The air temperature had by now reached an extraordinary 54° F and the thin ice was growing thinner. The legs of crew members regularly broke through, and the ice beneath the plane's skis stretched like rubber. The two machines were hastily hauled aboard. The expedition again headed south in desperate search of a solidly frozen airfield.

Christmas Day was overcast, with high winds and a deep swell. The men cobbled together a little cheer with penguin eggs and hoosh, and by wireless from San Francisco received greetings from friends and family. The lee of a big iceberg they encountered on 27 December offered a calm patch of sea, and Wilkins and Cheesman decided to try to take off on floats. Wilkins wrote:

It was from the start almost hopeless. The plane rocked and rolled in the water and with the engine running bucked about on the seas like a thing run wild. Cheesman at the controls did his best to keep the machine on course and, when in the most favorable position, he gave her the gun.

She sprang from wave to wave with leaps like a hunted kangaroo. In the cabin the pounding of the pontoons on the water sounded like the rattle of artillery fire. As soon as our speed began to increase, the shocks, as we struck the high waves, were terrific; and the wooden sides of the machine, where the pontoon bracings are fastened, heaved and buckled. In a few seconds the pontoon gear was so strained that it would have been madness to continue the effort, and, as I was about to give the order, Cheesman cut the gun with difficulty and taxied to the small lee afforded by the iceberg.[14]

A second attempt that day failed as well. But after the ship steamed to a calmer stretch, the pair did manage to get airborne and headed towards Charcot Island, 150 miles due south. This first extended flight over the pack ice was nerve-wracking because there was no possibility of landing on floats anywhere along the route. For the first fifty miles the sea was too littered with ice fragments that would tear the pontoons to pieces. Farther towards the mainland, the pack ice was solid, smooth and featureless. Without landmarks, navigation was strictly by dead-reckoning. To add to these difficulties, cloud cover and snow squalls forced Cheesman to fly lower than five hundred feet. The cliffs of Charcot were at least two thousand feet and tension built as they neared the rock with visibility straight ahead almost nil. Guessing, Wilkins finally ordered Cheesman to turn back – and seconds later caught a glimpse of a dark cliff wall that might have been their end.

Clear weather the next day beckoned a return to Charcot Island. During this four-hour flight, which extended to the limits their fuel supply, Cheesman and Wilkins flew around the coast of Charcot, proving what had only been surmised before, that it is detached from the mainland. At two points over the island, they dropped cannisters containing the British flag and documents claiming the territory on behalf of King George V. They also discovered three small islands and what they believed to be about 250 miles of coast farther south. (In fact, the land sighted in the distance was Latady and Alexander islands, the mainland being a further 250 miles.) Wilkins took movies and photographs of all that they saw.

With the Vega strapped on deck once more, the ship steamed north for refuelling at Deception Island. When they arrived at Port Lockroy, Parker Cramer, desperately eager to get at the controls of an aircraft, flew Wilkins ahead to Deception, where the beaches were steaming furiously in the wake of a minor eruption beneath the harbour two days before. The ship arrived several hours later, on 5 January, then headed to the Falkland Islands for three weeks of reprovisioning while Wilkins and company waited impatiently at Deception for one last foray south.

The vessel re-entered the harbour on 25 January, and the expedition cruised southwest for more than one thousand miles before pulling into a bight in the pack ice for the last flights of the season. Attempts on 30 January were aborted twice. First the engine would not start because of an ice-clogged fuel system which had to be laboriously taken apart, thawed, and re-assembled. The second time, Cheesman got the craft airborne but a bitter snowstorm to the south proved too risky to penetrate. The *Scoresby* steamed farther southwest and on 1 February, the weather clearing, Wilkins ordered the last flight.

The day was overcast and although the cloud cover held to fifteen hundred feet, winds were so strong at that altitude that Cheesman kept the aircraft at about five hundred feet for the first two hundred miles. Even at that level the air was rough. Navigation was extremely difficult; the light conditions were poor and there were relatively few features in the pack ice below. They soon ran into dark cloud and the temperature rose rapidly. 'The warmer, damper air filled the cabin and cockpit of the plane as if with the smoke of many cigarettes,' Wilkins wrote. 'The engine also felt the change, and I worried somewhat as the revolutions died slowly down. Cheesman replied to my inquiry that he had not changed the throttle, and even when he tried it in several different positions the engine failed to recover. We sank low in the misty air.'[15] At this critical juncture the aircraft emerged from the storm cloud and the engine, gulping dry air, picked up speed again.

After about fifty minutes in the air, Cheesman spotted dark patches in the mist that suggested land to the southwest. Wilkins saw two other patches to the east, but in the poor visibility they could be certain of nothing. The variation from white was nevertheless a relief to their eyes after flirting with snow blindness.

About that time I looked below and was much startled by what I saw, [Wilkins wrote]. There, it seemed, were two men running for their lives.

The shock was instantaneous and was over almost as quickly. They were great emperor penguins of course ... We could not help but laugh loudly at the comic figure they cut and craned our necks to watch them as they were speedily left behind. Never once did they hesitate or stop to look around. With their broad backs toward us, their bodies swaying like pendulums, they hurried from the thundering noise of the engine.[16]

Again, a dark strip ahead appeared to indicate land, but as they approached, it resolved itself into a patch of water at the edge of an iceberg. The patches sighted earlier also turned out to be weak shadows cast by bergs. The aircraft again entered a thick haze, forcing Cheesman to bring it down to 150 feet for the next ten minutes. Finally they were completely engulfed by a snowstorm, and Wilkins ordered Cheesman to head north. At their farthest south – latitude 73° south, longitude 101° – Wilkins dropped a cannister containing the British flag and a document claiming the area in the name of the king. The run home to the ship was uneventful, and the aircraft was soon lashed on deck.

Cheesman and Wilkins were sorely disappointed that their 450-mile flight did not turn up any undiscovered land, but in fact they did cross the western end of Thurston Island. This low land mass is normally smothered in ice and almost impossible to detect from the air, especially in poor light. And at the most southerly point of the flight, the cannister fell at the edge of the mainland now known as Eights Coast. (The region was more fully explored by air in 1940 during a United States' expedition led by Byrd.) Britain has never made a formal claim to the territory.

The ship arrived at Deception harbour on 14 February, and expedition members caught a return voyage to Montevideo on a whaling supply ship within two hours. Both aircraft were loaded aboard, later to be sold to the Argentine government. Wilkins booked his men on the commercial steamer *Eastern Prince*, which arrived in New York on 19 March amid public acclaim. Cheesman was greeted by his wife at the wharf in New

York and they travelled by train to visit his parents in Saint John.

Cheesman was flippant with a reporter who travelled the last few miles in the Pullman coach with him. 'He spoke laughingly of a terrible ordeal the explorers underwent in returning to navigation routes on the little British tender-ship 'Horsby' [*Scoresby*] which rolled and surged in the tempestuous icy seas to the accompaniment of whale-meat and other such foods as could be secured – an experience Cheesman himself hopes never to duplicate.'[17]

After a brief stay in Saint John, Cheesman returned to Sioux Lookout to resume his five-year contract with Northern Aerial Minerals Exploration.[18] That July he had one of his many brushes with death, when his airplane caught fire during a flight in northwestern Ontario. Cheesman was forced to ditch the plane in a lake but managed to swim away uninjured. A Depression-forced layoff in December 1930 prompted his return to Western Canadian Airways two months later. His second son, Thomas, was born June 1931, and by the autumn Cheesman was based in Vancouver, flying the company's fisheries patrol. In 1933 the young family settled back in Ontario in Port Arthur, after Cheesman landed a job as pilot for the Pigeon River Company. He eventually purchased the firm's lone aircraft, a Super Universal Fokker, and launched Explorers Airways, a one-man, one-plane transport operation serving prospectors.

Sir Hubert Wilkins sought out his former pilot again in the summer of 1937 for what would become an eight-month, fifty-thousand-mile search for six Russians believed to have crashed during a trans-Arctic flight from Moscow to Fairbanks, Alaska. Soviet air pioneer Sigismund Levanevsky radioed on 12 August that one of his four engines had conked out north of Alaska and that he was taking the aircraft lower. Nothing was ever heard again from Levanevsky or his five-man crew and the Kremlin hired Wilkins to conduct the search. Cheesman joined as co-pilot and the first flight took off from Alaska on 19 August. No wreckage or bodies were ever located.

In February 1940 Cheesman joined the RCAF to train new pilots at Trenton, Ontario. On 24 May he narrowly survived death when, during a night training flight, the aircraft's right wing hit an airport wind-sock. Cheesman, in the rear cockpit, was only slightly injured. His student pilot from Saskatoon was killed.

Cheesman was later transferred to Scoudouc, New Brunswick, in late 1941 to conduct air patrols on the lookout for German U-boats. On 17 January 1943, his single-engine Norseman with two others aboard was reported missing after being long overdue from its eight-hour flight. Eight days later the wreckage was spotted near Sandwich Bay, Labrador. Cheesman had been caught in a sudden snow squall and forced to pancake the aircraft onto a small frozen lake. The radio was smashed but no one was injured and Cheesman's survival skills got the trio through the week in comfort.

Cheesman was given a medical discharge in April 1945 because of a progressive hearing loss. The Department of Transport then denied him renewal of his commercial pilot's licence on account of a newly discovered heart condition in January 1946, and he bitterly fought the ruling for a decade. He never flew solo again. In 1950 one of the three small islands Cheesman and Wilkins had discovered off the coast of Charcot Island two decades earlier was officially christened Cheesman Island by British authorities to honour his pioneering flights.

Cheesman had returned to Fort William by 1953. He suffered a heart attack in 1956, another shortly before Christmas 1957, and died of complications on 2 April.

SIX

Byrd's Men

ON 14 JULY 1929 Frank Davies felt the call of nature and shuffled his chubby frame to the latrine in the Administration Building of Little America. The toilet facilities were unheated and primitive, just a trench in the ice surmounted by a wooden bench with a hole and seat lid attached. In temperatures hovering at –30° F, a great column of frozen body waste would climb to the height of the bench hole within a week. The Crystal Palace, they called it. The men of Richard Byrd's first Antarctic expedition played intense games of poker each week in which the losers got the job of knocking down the tower of excrement.

Davies closed the door behind him, dropped his pants and flipped down the toilet seat. At that moment, a flash shot out from the hole as an explosion rocked the building. Outside the door, a huddle of pranksters led by an Irishman named Jack O'Brien doubled over in laughter. O'Brien had wired the latrine to set off a charge of flash powder when the seat was lowered. The device had been armed to get Davies, the expedition's Canadian physicist, as O'Brien saw him head for the john.

But as the laughter petered out, there was no sound from inside the latrine. The men banged on the door, calling out Davies's nickname, 'Taffy,' but to no response. Finally, they broke the door off its hinges to find their victim peering through thick lenses and asking in mock curiosity: 'What's the matter, gentlemen?' Davies, a camp clown himself, tried his best to turn the gag around on its perpetrators by his seeming unconcern. But the men would not let it drop. A notice later posted on the bulletin board announced:

Coronas, streamers, arches and many other phenomena were brought home vividly to Professor Frank as he sat on the crapper this morning planning his day's magnetic work and disposing of Great Britain's food problem. A FLASH, A FLAME, AND SMOKE GALORE, SCORCHED HIS BOTTOM FOREVERMORE![1]

Richard Byrd's first expedition to the Antarctic, in 1928–30, was the formal debut of the United States in a region that had been dominated by the British, Norwegians, and Australians.[2] And in the American way, it was launched on an unprecedented scale. It was the first million-dollar Antarctic expedition, for example, more than twice as expensive as those of Scott or Shackleton. The forty-two-man party was the largest ever to winter over. Byrd had secured three modern aircraft to begin the first systematic aerial mapping of the continent. The latest radio equipment would keep field parties and aircraft in touch with the base and the United States. It was also to be typically American, hence the name Little America, an expedition that would showcase Yankee technology and talent to the world.

Yet behind the scenes, Byrd's team sometimes behaved more like a college fraternity house than skilled explorers proudly waving the Stars and Stripes. The incident that left Davies's buttocks scorched was but one practical joke among dozens, often the byproducts of boisterous drinking sessions. The pranksters frequently fastened on the good-humoured Davies partly because he was so obviously un-American. Born in Wales before emigrating to Canada, he had a thick Welsh accent and a quite unfamiliar way of looking at the world.

'The large percentage of foreigners in the personnel of the expedition has quite frequently been the subject of comment,' wrote Harry Adams, an expedition member. 'Many persons have wondered why an exclusively American crew was not selected.'[3] Part of the answer may have been that Byrd welcomed whatever talent showed up on his doorstep. There were five Norwegians, for instance, including Martin Ronne, a sailmaker who had been on Amundsen's South Pole expedition, and Bernt Balchen, the Arctic pilot who had flown with Byrd before.

But the addition of Davies to the expedition likely had more to do with necessity than with broad-mindedness. Byrd's ambitious plans called for a full scientific program. He had received more than fifty thousand applications from seamen, pilots, and others, but only a handful from genuine scientists willing to work for no pay. Among the sacks of mail was a letter from Frank Davies, then a graduate student at McGill University in Montreal. On learning of Byrd's plans, Davies had written to Charles Wright, the Canadian physicist who had been with Scott eighteen years earlier. He asked Wright, then working for the Admiralty in London, what geophysical observations were still needed in the Antarctic. Wright offered some ideas, and Davies sent his application to New York.

'I thought that at the age of 24 ... I'd be assistant to some much older fellow who was a physicist,' Davies recalled years later. 'And on that basis, I applied and he [Byrd] invited me to come down to see him in New York. And I had a long chat with him and he took me on. I asked him later on, on the expedition, how it was that he took me on. He didn't know anything about me. And he said, "Well, I had lots of applicants calling themselves physicists. But," he said, "I'm not a physicist, I'm a sailor. I don't know what the dickens to do with a physicist in the Antarctic. And your letter was the only one that explained what a physicist was going to do".'[4]

Davies's childhood gave little hint of a polar future. The son of a schoolmaster, he was born on 12 August 1904, in Merthyr Tydfil, Wales.[5] While still a boy, he was taken to a slide lecture on Scott's last expedition that sparked his imagination. Davies's high school mathematics teacher in 1917 turned out to be Alexander H. Macklin, formerly ship's surgeon with Shackleton's abortive trans-Antarctic expedition of 1914–16. The mathematics job in Wales had become available because recruitment for the Great War sent most male teachers to France. The boys knew of Macklin's Antarctic connection but he never talked about his experiences.

Drawn to the sciences, Davies enrolled at the University College of Aberystwyth, in Wales, and graduated in June 1925 with a B SC, specializing in physics. Then shortly before his twenty-first birthday he emigrated to Canada, working as a farm hand in northern Saskatchewan before becoming a demonstrator in physics and a lecturer in mathematics that fall at the University of Saskatchewan in Saskatoon. The following year he enrolled in McGill University as a graduate student. By the spring of 1928 he had earned an M SC in physics, supporting himself all the while as a demonstrator in physics. Davies intended to press on with a PH D at McGill when Byrd's offer sidetracked him. Byrd sent Davies to Chevy Chase, Maryland, in May 1928, where he was given a crash course at the terrestrial magnetism department of the Carnegie Institution and was loaded down with specialized equipment.

Science had steered Davies south, but for Newfoundlander Jack Bursey, the only other British Commonwealth member at the outset of the expedition, it was pure polar passion that brought him to Byrd's doorstep. 'I first fell under the spell of Antarctica when I was a boy of ten in the north of Newfoundland where I was born and where I read by candlelight all I could lay my hands on about the mysterious southern continent,' Bursey later wrote.[6] He was born Jacob Bursey on 20 September 1903 at St Lunaire, a community of fewer than sixty people at the northeastern tip of Newfoundland. The village was so isolated, Bursey grew up without ever seeing a car, train, tractor, horse or telephone. In the summers he would help his father catch cod on the family schooner. In the winters he would hitch nine dogs fan-style to a sled and hunt seals out on the ice. Dogs were the only transportation available when the boats were frozen in. 'I didn't know what the future held, but my dream – of following in the footsteps of the polar explorers whose adventures I lived over and over again – continually beckoned,' Bursey wrote.[7]

Among the occasional visitors to the Bursey household was Wilfred Grenfell, the British medical missionary knighted for his work in Newfoundland and Labrador with the Royal National Mission to Deep Sea Fishermen. In 1900 Grenfell had established a headquarters at St Anthony, about twelve miles south of St Lunaire, and sometimes preached in surrounding outports. Longing to escape the tiny community, Bursey took a dog team through a blizzard one day to St Anthony to announce to a startled Grenfell: 'I want an education.' With financial help from Grenfell's mission, he was soon studying to be a machinist in Boston, working summers on a private yacht. He later moved to Nyack, New York, where he studied for a year at the Missionary Institute. There he was jolted one day by a newspaper story announcing Byrd's plans for an expedition.

Bursey immediately posted his letter of application and soon received a notice that selection would begin in the spring. He quit school and found a job in New York City to be nearby if called. And if Byrd would not have him, he'd simply sail as a stowaway. Weeks stretched into months and still no word from the expedition office at the Biltmore Hotel. Burning to go south, Bursey finally turned up at the third-floor suite in person, first making a friend of Charlie Lofgren, Byrd's assistant, to get an interview with the commander himself. 'Then suddenly all the tension and anxiety left me,' Bursey, short and wiry, recalled of his meeting days later with Byrd. 'I was unprepared to find a man who was so quiet, efficient, unassuming, and easy to meet.'[8] Byrd made no immediate promise, but was approving of Bursey's background in Newfoundland (then still a British colony), and of his skills as a dog-driver and seal-hunter. More than a week later, on his way to work, Bursey learned that his fifteen-year-old dream had finally taken form: Byrd gave him a job as dog-driver.

Dreams also welled up in Byrd, but unlike most dreamers he had the skills to transform them into ships, planes, supplies and volunteers. Born 1888 at Winchester, Virginia, by the age of fifteen Byrd was determined to follow a naval career.[9] But his slight frame and weak muscles brought his plans to a halt soon after he joined the US navy in 1908: he broke the bones in his right foot on three occasions, and was retired as an ensign. Aviation, he soon reasoned, required no great strength and so he re-joined the navy during the First World War as a pilot, specializing in navigation. The navy refused Byrd's repeated requests in the 1920s to conduct daring flights that would prove the capabilities of aircraft across the Atlantic or over the Arctic. So he left the service and mounted a private expedition to become the first to fly over the North Pole.

With Floyd Bennett, an old navy buddy, Byrd secured a ship, a plane, and fifty men to sail to Spitsbergen, the Norwegian islands that lie just 750 miles from the pole. On 9 May 1926 Bennett completed the flight with a crew that included Byrd as navigator. (Doubts have since been raised about whether they did make the pole.)[10] Byrd returned to acclaim in the United States, winning the rank of commander through a special act of Congress. He followed with a New York–to-Paris flight on 29 June 1927. A second ticker-tape parade through Manhattan confirmed his hero status. For both flights, Byrd had charmed support out of well-heeled sponsors, such as John D. Rockefeller, Jr and Edsel Ford, and persuaded volunteers to put their lives on hold for a chance at glory.

Flush with acclaim, his entrepreneurial instincts awakened, Byrd now hatched a far more daring stunt: a flight from the edge of Antarctica to a landing at the South Pole, then a takeoff to continue to the opposite coast. This, on a continent where no aircraft had ever flown before. The expedition would be phenomenally expensive, requiring ships, planes, radios, dogs, equipment, and supplies to last a year or more. It would be a private expedition, and Byrd planned to enrich himself on his return with a lucrative lecture tour and book sales.

The commander's flair for publicity soon coaxed a steady flow of donations from commercial producers each eager to use their official sponsorship for advertising. In the end, Byrd had to scale back his plans to a simple return flight to the pole without a landing. He soon bought and equipped two ships. The *Samson*, an oak-hulled Norwegian sealing vessel built in 1882, was recommended by Roald Amundsen as the strongest ice ship in Europe. The three-masted vessel was 170 feet long, with sides 34 inches thick to withstand the crushing pack ice. It was rechristened the *City of New York*. The second was a steel-hulled former British minesweeper that had been confiscated by the US government for rum-running; it became the *Eleanor Bolling*, for his mother. The vessel bobbed about so badly even in the calmest seas that to the crew she was the 'Evermore Rolling.'

Frantic weeks of packing and loading preceded the departure of the *City of New York* on 25 August 1928 with a complement of thirty-three men, including Davies and Bursey. Davies had come aboard at Hoboken, New Jersey, and immediately wondered where the crew was. 'I found I was it,' he said, quickly accepting that the division of labour would remain fuzzy for the next eighteen months.[11] Russell Owen, a *New York Times* reporter, was watching the chaos of loading when Davies appeared:

A tubby little scientist, cap over one ear, unshaven and red-eyed, came tumbling down a plank to the deck with a box clutched in his arms. 'Hey, where'll I chuck this damn thing?' he barked at nobody in particular, looking helplessly at the clutter around him. 'Aw, throw it anywhere,' yelled a man nervously taut, running back breathlessly for another box. So the scientist dumped it, mopped his forehead, and went back up the plank to the wharf for more.[12]

Relative good weather for the first few weeks gave the crew a tolerable breaking-in period while they learned seamanship. (The *Eleanor Bolling*, a faster vessel, would leave later with other expedition members; Byrd would travel on the whaler *Larsen* to rendezvous in New Zealand.) The men detested their captain, Fred Melville, who was related to Herman Melville, author of *Moby Dick*. Melville insisted on creating an officer class aboard that would take meals apart from the crew. Davies, as scientist, was regarded as an officer but he took all his meals with the men in defiance of the captain.[13] Between Panama on 16 September and the ship's arrival in Tahiti on 1 November, Davies volunteered for three weeks of coal-stoking on the fire deck when two other men collapsed on the job. Without ventilation in the ship's belly, temperatures soared over 100° F and Davies lost about fifteen pounds.

Following the stopover at Tahiti, Davies began the expedition's first scientific work by counting dust particles in the atmosphere. Earlier observations had demonstrated the obvious: in industrial areas, pollution increased the dust counts, which in turn altered the electrical conductivity of the air. But until Davies's experiments for the Carnegie Institution, no one had tested the air over the open Pacific. Compared with data obtained later at Little America, Davies found that the pristine Antarctic environment was about half as dusty as the Pacific Ocean, itself a relatively dust-free environment.[14]

The ship arrived at Port Chalmers, New Zealand, on 26 November 1928 and was immediately put into dry dock. With Paul Siple, a boy scout chosen from among the thousands to apply for a place in the expedition, Davies took a walking tour of the countryside. 'Frank complained that I took up the whole path as I walked,' Siple noted, 'and I, likewise, disapproved of his walking with his legs so wide apart that it looked as though he were straddling a barrel – victims we were of the famous disease, sea-legs.'[15]

The expedition finally set out for the Antarctic on 1 December, the two main ships, badly overloaded, led by a factory whaler. During the battle with the pack ice, word came by radio that Hubert Wilkins's tiny expedition had beaten Byrd into the air with a short flight on 16 November. Christmas was celebrated at sea. The role of Santa fell to the rotund physicist with a cheery disposition and infectious laugh. Davies raided the ship's pharmacy for cotton, which was stuck to his cheeks for a beard. A pillow was stuffed into his red parka, and between ho-ho-hos he passed out small gifts provided by Byrd's wife for each of the men.[16] The celebration was rounded out with ice-cream, strawberries, candy, nuts and a gallon of champagne.

The voyage, meanwhile, sounded some sour notes for Bursey. Three school chums from Harvard University led by Norman Vaughan were elbowing Bursey to the margins of the expedition's dog operations. Vaughan had driven dogs in Labrador for Grenfell in the winter of 1925, and began to consider himself an expert.[17] Once accepted in the expedition, Vaughan joined dog breeder Arthur Walden at his kennels in Wonalancet, New Hampshire. Seventy-nine huskies had been donated by Frank Clark, a Canadian whose Clark Trading Company operated outposts along the Labrador coast. Another sixteen were bred at Wonalancet for a total of ninety-five animals. Walden, at the age of fifty-seven, soon regarded Vaughan as an upstart rival and the elder man's growing mental instability forced Byrd to hand Vaughan responsibility for all dog operations in Antarctica. Bursey, with more sledging experience than all except Walden, was shunted aside during this clash of egos. Assigned to the *City of New York*, he was excluded from caring for the dogs during their voyage south to New Zealand on a whaling ship. And when it came time to divide the surviving eighty-four dogs into teams assigned to each man, Bursey was handed the dregs.

'I took one look at my pack of bedraggled huskies and turned away, heartsick with disappointment,' he later wrote. 'What a scrubby, sorry-looking lot! They were so inferior to the dogs I had known in Newfoundland and Labrador, and to the other dogs already claimed, that I was thoroughly ashamed of them. I felt cheated and abused, and thought I had not been treated fairly.'[18] Nevertheless, one animal later proved himself an excellent lead dog. Named Luny – short for St Lunaire – he remained a lifelong companion for Bursey after the return to civilization. But on the bleak Ross Sea, before the nine-dog team could prove itself, Bursey's hopes seem dashed.

On 28 December the ships finally pulled into the Bay of Whales along the Ross Ice Shelf, the same inlet that had sheltered Amundsen's vessel eighteen years before. Soon began the soul-destroying task of hauling 665 tons of supplies by dog-team nine miles to the site chosen for Little America. Weeks of numbing routine were occasionally enlivened with near disasters. On 24 January Bursey's team was hauling a sledge heavy with coal towards Little America when the dogs' feet began to break through a snow bridge concealing a deep crevasse. Bursey shouted them on but the sledge was too heavy and sagged into the crack. He immediately grabbed the gang line to save the load, waved his knife and shouted for help to Quin Blackburn, who was driving another team fifty yards ahead. Blackburn glanced back at him but pressed on, apparently oblivious to the danger. As the sledge continued sinking, Bursey was about to cut the load loose when a team that had seen his plight rushed up from the ship. 'When rescued, he was in the early stages of hypothermia and could not have held on much longer,' Vaughan recalled.[19]

A more dramatic rescue came six days later when a massive chunk of the ice shelf gave way under the legs of two men who were helping to haul up a rope loaded with supplies from the ships. As tons of ice thudded onto the deck of the *Eleanor Bolling*, nearly tipping her over, one of the men was tossed into the sea. The other, assistant meteorologist Henry Harrison, managed to cling to the rope with Davies at the summit anchoring him. 'I held on to the rope where I was and dug my feet in,' Davies said later. 'I couldn't see what happened but there was a load on it down below.'[20] Davies kept his position for half an hour, his hands bleeding from the strain, until a second rescue line could be lowered. Much as the men liked to kid him about his stockiness, Davies proved himself physically powerful and tenacious. He was also droll. Surveying the mess left by the thunderous calving of the ice shelf, he remarked dryly: 'That would discourage immigration down here.'[21]

Byrd grew concerned about the strain placed on the dogs by the relentless unloading. He radioed his New York business manager, Hilton Railey, to send twenty more dogs and a handler to catch the *Eleanor Bolling* on a second trip from New Zealand. Railey called Edward Farn, manager of the Pacific & Arctic Railway and Navigation Company, based in Vancouver, to ask for help. By luck, a candidate was visiting Farn that very moment – Alan Innes-Taylor, a former RCMP officer with years of northern experience. Innes-Taylor was game, and Byrd's all-American expedition acquired another Canadian.[22]

Alan Innes-Taylor was born in England at Little Berkhampstead, about twenty miles north of London, on 12 February 1900 to a New Zealand father and British mother.[23] His only sibling, Ian, was born a year later and the family soon emigrated to New York, then to Toronto in 1906, where his father sought work as a printer. Three years later, Innes-Taylor was sent to boarding school at Bobcaygeon, Ontario, graduating in 1917 to enter the aeronautics school at the University of Toronto. After earning his wings at Camp Mohawk, Ontario, he became a pilot with the Royal Flying Corps – too late to see action in continental Europe, where his father had died of wounds. In 1919 he helped survey the Trent Valley Canal and became a farm hand near Bobcaygeon before joining the Royal Canadian Mounted Police. After training at Regina, Innes-Taylor was posted to Vancouver, Esquimalt, British Columbia, and Whitehorse in the Yukon. It was there he learned to drive dogs.

On leaving the Mounties in 1926, Innes-Taylor became a Yukon miner at Keno Hill, a purser on a Yukon riverboat that hauled freight between Whitehorse and Dawson, and a treasurer for the Yukon Airways and Exploration Company. Not yet thirty, he had deep-set eyes, a heavy brow, and a small mustache, and was prematurely bald.

Innes-Taylor obtained fresh dogs from a breeder at Grouse Mountain, near Vancouver, and sailed on a passenger liner for New Zealand on 9 January. He transferred to the *Eleanor Bolling* but pack ice late in the season barred the way south, forcing the ship's return to New Zealand. Innes-Taylor spent the winter keeping his fifteen dogs and nine pups fit by hauling seventy thousand pounds of supplies and building materials up the Tasman Glacier for a resort on Mount Cook. The work helped earn his keep while he awaited the austral summer for another attempt south.[24]

The start of Davies's scientific program on the ice was badly delayed by the achingly slow process of unloading the ships. An estimated twelve thousand miles was covered in the shuttling operation from the ships to Little America and back again. On days when foul weather halted all labour, the men drank liberally from the supplies of liquor they had purchased in New Zealand. Although the United States was bound by prohibition, Byrd raised few objections to drinking on his expedition and he himself often imbibed. Among the supplies were fifty-gallon barrels of 'medicinal' or 'photographic' alcohol that would fuel many soirées during the long Antarctic winter. Bursey was not a drinker, but party-hound Davies enjoyed these sessions immensely. During one drunken bash that filled a lull in the unloading, he entertained the men with a mock strip-tease on a messroom table.[25]

Even sober, Davies provided quirky comic relief to the strain of hauling. His technique for crawling into a sleeping bag, for example, was clearly intended to draw laughs and made its way into several of the men's diaries. 'He took off all his clothes

except a suit of dirty gray underwear, much too large for him,'
wrote Russell Owen, the *New York Times* reporter who stayed
the winter. 'Then he put his feet in his fur sleeping bag and
jumped up and down while he hauled it up until it was around
his shoulders. He looked behind him, selected a place on the
floor and fell backward, and had a book in his hand almost
before he stopped bouncing. He said he was too fat to get into
bed any other way.'[26]

The *City of New York* left the Bay of Whales on 21 February
to winter in New Zealand. The *Eleanor Bolling* had left on 2
February and its failure to return later posed an immediate
dilemma for Davies, for the ship had been carrying materials
to build an iron-free hut for his magnetic experiments. The
expedition carpenter hammered together a frame using non-
magnetic nails (copper and brass), and sailmaker Martin
Ronne sewed a canvas shell for it. The makeshift hut was then
fitted into a square hole dug into the ice, seventy yards south
of an underground tunnel that connected the main administration building to the mess hall. A foot of snow covered the
roof, making it flush with the surface of the ice shelf and creating a light-proof, temperature-stable environment. A crew
then turned out to dig an underground tributary from the
main snow tunnel so the hut could be safely visited in bad
weather.

Davies then drove wooden piers two feet into the ice, where
they were frozen fast. A table was fastened over them and the
instruments from the Carnegie Institution for measuring magnetism were placed on top. The devices – to record magnetic
declination, and the horizontal and vertical intensity of the
earth's magnetic field – used light beams bounced off mirrors
onto photographic recording paper, which was wrapped on a
drum driven by a clockwork mechanism. The mirrors were
connected to magnetized needles so that they would alter position slightly as the earth's magnetic field fluctuated. The reflected light beam would exaggerate these tiny movements to
form continuous lines or 'wiggles' on the recording paper. The
results could then be compared with Carnegie magnetic sta-

tions in places such as Australia and Chile, and aboard the institution's research ship, to provide a daily snapshot of world magnetism.

A storage battery located fifteen yards away in a cave in the tunnel wall powered the lights and had to be changed twice a week. Each day Davies and his assistant, Arnold Clarke, had to retrieve the recording paper for developing in the photo lab. They then attached fresh, unexposed paper to the drum, and rewound the clockwork mechanism. The instruments, especially the mirrors, had to be kept frost free. Davies experimented with an oil stove to keep the hut warm but it simply aggravated the frosting problems. All the work, therefore, had to be done in temperatures that dropped as low as –35° F. The first of 240 observations was made in May 1929 and they were concluded on 18 February the following year.[27]

A second magnetic observatory was built on the surface nearby out of ice blocks covered by a canvas roof. At intervals of about a week to ten days, the expedition geologist, Larry Gould, would help Davies with the four to five hours of celestial observations necessary to establish absolute magnetic values used to calibrate the underground instrument readings. This was bone-chilling work with fingers exposed in temperatures that could drop to –70° F. An added nuisance was the puppies that wandered over in search of entertainment and had to be chased away. 'The last time Commander Byrd paid us a visit he almost received a whack on the nose before we discovered that he was not another of Josephine's numerous progeny,' Davies wrote at the time. 'We had to shoo him away, however, for fear he had some iron on him that would affect the instruments.'[28]

Detailed magnetic observations had been carried out in Antarctica previously, by Erich von Drygalski's *Gauss* expedition of 1901–3, Scott's 1901–4 and 1910–13 expeditions and Douglas Mawson's expedition of 1911–14. But Davies's work had a special importance because it coincided with the eleven-year peak in the cycle of sunspots, which affect the earth's magnetism and auroras. Previous efforts had coincided with troughs in the cycle. The advent of radio had also made the study of the earth's magnetism more urgent as fluctuations in the field affected transmissions in still-mysterious ways.

Davies demonstrated a quiet determination that verged on the heroic in this often painful work. He would have to pull on many layers of clothing before heading out. O'Brien, his nemesis, called him 'Sister Veronica' for the parka hoods that made him look like a fat woman with a cowl.[29] Referring to Davies and his assistant, Siple wrote: 'Many days when they were taking absolute readings with their delicate instruments they would come in so cold that the tears would fill their eyes as the warmth slowly came back to their icy hands.'[30] Owen bumped into Gould returning from one of the sessions in the aboveground magnetic observatory. 'Ice was hanging [on] to his mustache and whiskers, and he looked wild. "Get out of my way," he yelled. "I was never so cold in my life."'[31]

Davies also took charge of a series of visual observations of the aurora australis, or southern lights, which can range from darting sprays to rustling curtains. Little America was located in an aurora-rich belt and the long Antarctic night allowed near-continuous observation. The first such display was recorded on 16 March. With the help of six volunteers, the multi-hued spectacle was observed every thirty minutes and described in a log using standardized terms. Regular watches from 3 April to 26 September (after which the summer sun shone continuously) produced 7,412 observations.[32]

Byrd had arranged special Saturday night broadcasts to Little America from station KDKA in Pittsburgh, and on 11 May time was devoted to a series of messages for Davies from the faculty at McGill University. Among them was one from physicist Howard Barnes, who urged Davies to take information on the structure and density of old glacier ice; and from physicist A.S. Eve, who asked Davies to report by radio any conspicuously strong southern lights, quoting Greenwich time, for comparison with observations of northern lights.[33] Added to his load were the counts of Antarctic dust particles; temperature and conductivity readings of ice in the Ross Ice Shelf (using equipment supplied by McGill); measuring and photographing ice crystals in crevasses; and helping the doctor in medical experiments to determine how quickly human flesh cooled. Byrd also called on Davies to use his magnetic equipment to try to locate Amundsen's 1910–11 camp, Framheim, under the ice (they failed).

Even chief meteorologist Bill Haines co-opted the physicist, as Davies liked to say. Like Tom Sawyer, Haines was a master at finding others to suffer the cold and perform outdoor meteorological tasks so he could remain inside near the stove. Owen's diary entry for 27 June noted: 'The Physicist was helping the Meteorologist place some thermometers which register electrically indoors. They had to be placed deep in the snow. The Physicist came in after a time, red faced and puffing, after being out in the cold wind, and said: "I've been cooperating with him again. Somehow, he always manages to get on the inside."'[34] Davies tried the same trick by persuading some men to take his magnetic readings. Byrd wrote: 'To his horror he found them, when he went out to supervise the job, working heartily under Haines, who had recognized their possibilities and over-night proselyted them to meteorology.'[35]

Davies's most bizarre activity was the exploration of crevasses, which often opened into grand crystalline chambers and sapphire corridors that stretched for miles. Enormous ice crystals clung precariously to the walls of these 'fairy palaces,' as they were called, giving the sensation of being inside a giant's chandelier. Davies and Gould would measure and photograph individual crystals, sometimes observing their growth over several weeks. 'No Aladdin with his wonder lamp ever dreamed a crystal palace one half so lovely as this ice palace of ours,' Gould wrote. 'The walls were completely studded with an unthinkable maze of paper thin ice crystals of unbelievable fragility, and in places they hung in great masses from the roof like huge candelabra, and the thin snow cover let enough light filter through to give the whole atmosphere just the right touch of unreality.'[36]

The broad scientific program, added to his camp duties, kept Davies off the trail during the whole of his sojourn in Antarctica and stole any time he might have had for a diary. 'Our Welsh magnetician therefore was one of the busiest men in Little America,' Byrd wrote. 'With a carefree impunity we had to admire, he scrambled in and out of some of the worst crevasses about the camp, during the winter, risking life and limb for the sake of getting a few temperature readings at varying depths, a cluster of ice crystals or a specimen of ice.'[37]

Davies worked hard and liked to play hard as well. On Saturday nights he would have violent wrestling matches with O'Brien, the mad latrine bomber. Sunday mornings were often spent repairing the furniture broken up by these fights.[38] Davies bunked with Haines and two others in a corner of the administration building that O'Brien dubbed the Rat's Nest. 'Here, with Taffy and Bill as ring leaders, was concocted much of the deviltry that delighted and enraged the camp, and the subdued chuckling that was frequently overheard from that corner soon came to mean that some new outrage was afoot,' Byrd wrote.[39]

Asked by Byrd that winter what he missed most in the Antarctic, Davies replied: 'Temptation.'[40] That was likely a reference to sex, because he certainly succumbed to the temptation of alcohol. Davies particularly enjoyed a glass or two of Blowtorch, a mixture of pure alcohol and lemon powder, or an improvised cocktail with marmalade as flavouring. 'One can do wonders with a little alcohol, some fruit juice and snow,' Owen noted.[41] The men began these winter parties in earnest on 9 May 1929 to celebrate the anniversary of Byrd's North Pole flight. Davies declared to Gould, the geologist, that no Yankee could outdrink a Welshman – and promptly proved himself wrong by winding up drunk on the floor.[42]

Badly hung over the next night, Davies dutifully took the evening watch in the photographic lab as scheduled. After the 10 p.m. lights out, Bursey decided to visit Taffy. Bursey wrote in his diary: 'When I opened the door I noticed a rather stuffy smell, but thought nothing of it until I walked over to the box where Captain Mac [Ashley McKinley] kept his pup, Ski, trying to break him in as a house dog. The pup was almost dead. I could not think what was wrong, because I had been playing with him a little while before. Then I saw that Taffy was acting strangely. Dr. [Francis] Coman came in and said, 'There is something wrong with Taffy. Better get him out of here.' We found the trouble was carbon monoxide gas coming from the gas stove.'[43] The ventilator had become clogged with snow during a recent storm.

'Davies was as limp as a rag, completely out,' Byrd reported, 'and while Dr. Coman worked over him on the mess table, I never saw the men so grave – for everyone in Little America loved Taffy ... We hustled him out into the open and walked him up and down. The cold air brought him to all right, but in our anxiety to get him out we overlooked the fact that we had stripped off most of his clothes, and he very nearly froze to death before we got him back.'[44] Davies's head exploded with a violent headache the next day, but he otherwise recovered. Were it not for Bursey's fortuitous visit, he might well have died.

While Davies chummed with his bunkmates in the Rat's Nest, things were not so jolly for Bursey. He had been shut out of caring for the dogs on the trip to New Zealand, given the worst animals once down south, and now the Harvard trio forced him out of his bunk. Bursey had been living with all the other dog-drivers in a crowded prefabricated hut, known as the Biltmore, next to the mess hall. When two bunks became vacant in the mess hall, Byrd picked two men to be transferred out of the Biltmore to create more room. But the Harvard boys objected to Byrd's choices and demanded that Bursey and another man clear out instead, for reasons that remain unclear. Byrd acceded and the outcast Newfoundlander packed his kit.[45]

Bursey's musical tastes also won him no friends. The expedition library had a Victrola and a variety of records but Bursey

seized on only one, 'The Bells of St Mary,' and played it over
and over, night after night. It was 'one of the things that drove
us nuts,' Davies recalled forty-three years later.[46] '"The Bells of
St Mary" is a tune I am not likely to forget,' said Byrd. 'I was
working on my polar reports nearby, and had all the feelings of
a distracted fugitive fleeing from a mad minstrel.'[47]

Bursey seemed to find a private joy in his dogs, especially
Luny, his leader. And it was his intense, nurturing relationship
with these animals that finally won him a measure of respect at
Little America, for his team proved indomitable on the trail. On
a depot-laying trip from 7 to 13 March, Bursey's dogs joined a
six-man party that travelled fifty miles south and back through
blizzards and extreme cold. 'Bursey's leader, St Lunaire, a
brown Labrador husky, [was] one of the hardest workers I ever
saw, and possess[ed] an uncanny sense of direction,' Byrd
wrote.[48] For that reason, Bursey's team led six others east
toward the newly discovered Rockefeller Mountains on 19
March, just days after the depot-laying trip. They were to
relieve a party that had landed by aircraft but had seen their
machine wrecked on the ground by gusts of up to 120 miles per
hour. It was a dangerous sortie for dogs and men: Amundsen
had warned Byrd that no field trip should be undertaken after
15 March because of the killing winds and chill of the Antarctic
winter. A second aircraft managed to carry out the actual rescue of the stranded Rockefeller Mountain party while the
sledge teams were sixty-three miles out from Little America.
With Luny again in the lead, the party rushed back to base in
thirteen straight hours, breaking by one mile Amundsen's
record of sixty-two miles in a non-stop march.

At base, Davies was constantly ragged about his Welsh
accent and British origin. His companions heard 'Michigan'
come out as "Mitchigan," for instance, and he was harrassed
for sounding an 'f' in lieutenant. Every night, the men would
listen to a radio program from Wellington, New Zealand, that
began with 'God Save the King.' As the music began, so did
good-natured shouts for Davies to stand at attention like a loyal

subject. He refused, but did agree to a request from Byrd to raise the British flag in a ceremony marking the return of the sun on 22 August. The commander wanted to honour Amundsen and Scott and had the Norwegian and British flags flown beside the Stars and Stripes.[49]

The return of the sun heralded preparations for summer journeys. Byrd's primary goal, a flight to the pole and back, required depots laid at regular intervals all the way south to the Queen Maud Mountains in case the aircraft was forced down. A geological team led by Larry Gould would also travel overland to the mountains, and would dip into the same string of depots. Byrd badly needed more dogs on the trail and so on 28 September radioed Innes-Taylor in New Zealand to book passage for himself and the extra dogs aboard the Norwegian whaling vessel *Kosmos*. The 570-foot factory ship with a crew of three hundred was soon plying southern waters, slaughtering up to ten whales each day. As an experiment to boost efficiency, the ship carried a De Havilland Moth aircraft for spotting whales from the air.

Innes-Taylor and his dogs spent several months on the butcher ship.[50] The captain refused to make a special trip to Little America but agreed to transfer his passengers to the *City of New York* if the whaling vessel got through the pack. During this long sojourn, one of Innes-Taylor's dogs had a litter of thirteen pups – far too many to nurse. The ship's doctor suggested catching a female whale that was nursing a calf and giving her milk to half the pups, despite the fact it contravened international whaling laws. The captain agreed and, unknown to a whaling inspector on board, had a nursing whale quietly caught and slaughtered and her milk frozen for use as needed. 'Six weeks later the pups were twice the size of those left with the mother,' Innes-Taylor reported. 'We decided that whale's milk was the answer to raising giants.'[51]

Innes-Taylor made friends with the pilot of the pontoon-equipped De Havilland, Lief Lier, and often sat beside him on whale-scouting flights. Keen for adventure, the pair planned some aerial exploration over the nearby Balleny Islands, whose mountains rise to ten thousand feet, north of the coast of Victoria Land. They conducted a short test flight on 20 December, loaded down with emergency fuel and supplies. A calm day beckoned on the 26th, but as Innes-Taylor prepared for the flight the ship's doctor, Ingvold Schreiner, pleaded to take his place beside Lier. 'I didn't have the heart to refuse him,' Innes-Taylor recalled. 'It was disappointing, but then I thought there would be another time.'[52]

The aircraft took off and was never heard from again. Lier and Schreiner became Antarctica's first aviation victims. Weeks of searching failed to locate any wreckage or bodies, and the cause of the disaster remained a mystery. 'On the last day of the final search the wind died, the sea became calm, and for a few moments it was still,' Innes-Taylor wrote years later. 'I had a feeling then that has persisted since, that somewhere high on the islands' mountaintops, my two friends lie amidst the wreckage of their plane, enveloped by that peace to be found where no man has ever trod or ever will, and I have wondered many times why I was not along on this adventure in the unknown.'[53]

Byrd, meanwhile, had scored an aviation triumph sixteen hundred miles to the south. On 15 October Bursey's dog-team led the main depot-laying party more than two hundred miles south. The loads were horrendously heavy, and the group suffered through fogs, blizzards, temperatures in excess of –40° F, a surface like sand, and searing snow blindness. But the worst obstacle was a heavily crevassed area the men christened Chasm Pass. 'The area was all hollow beneath our feet,' Bursey wrote. 'Portions of the Barrier [Ross Ice Shelf] kept dropping with a cannon-like booming that made our spines creep as we skimmed over it ... We were worn out, so we camped, but sleep was impossible. The moaning, roaring, and cracking of the splitting and shifting ice on which we lay made continual thunderous noises as the Barrier settled beneath us, collapsing somewhere in its depths.'[54] Miraculously, no one was killed by the crevasses and the party depoted six hundred pounds of supplies on 1 November. St Lunaire picked out the trail home, and the men pulled into Little America on 9 November demanding a huge meal of ham and eggs.

Ten days later, Byrd and a crew flew to the base of the Axel Heiberg glacier in the Queen Maud Mountains to depot gas for refuelling on the return leg of the planned polar flight. And on 28 November, with the weather finally clear, he and three others made a sixteen-hour flight to the South Pole and back in a three-engine Ford monoplane. The only drama during the trip was the ascent up the Liv Glacier. Pilot Bernt Balchen could not gain the altitude needed to reach the polar plateau and twice ordered emergency provisions dumped overboard. The lightened aircraft gained the plateau with only feet to spare. The route had already been blazed by Amundsen, and there were no geographical discoveries, but the flight took nerve and demonstrated the enormous possibilities of aerial exploration. Writing in his diary as they cruised over the pole, Balchen remained unimpressed: 'Somehow our very purpose here seems insignificant, a symbol of man's vanity and intrusion on this eternal white world. The sound of our engines profanes the silence as we head back to Little America.'[55]

The polar flight concluded, Byrd now faced the double problem of getting the geological party back safely from the mountains and the *City of New York* through the pack ice for the return to civilization. The pack was extremely heavy that year, and even the sturdy whaling ships were reluctant to ram their way through. Innes-Taylor and his dogs transferred to the *City of New York* from the *Kosmos* during a rendezvous north of the pack. Weeks of frustration followed as the *City of New York* scouted in vain for a route through to the Ross Sea. Byrd and some of the men grew anxious at the thought of being forced to winter another year. Many began to dip deeply into the alcohol supplies again to ease the strain. Davies cheerily volunteered to spend an extra year at Little America to continue the magnetic work, but the commander turned him down. The ship finally broke through the pack and arrived at the Bay of Whales on 18 February to great jubilation. But Innes-Taylor's thirteen-month, ten thousand-mile mission to bring Byrd the extra dogs had ended with a whimper: he arrived far too late for any field-work and was able only to help load the ship. The next day, Little America was abandoned and men, dogs and equipment headed north for the long voyage home. Innes-Taylor had been on the ice less than twenty-four hours.

The South Pole flight brought Byrd enormous acclaim and many honors in the United States, including a promotion to admiral. His lecture tour was a success and his 1930 book about the expedition, *Little America*, was a runaway bestseller with one hundred thousand copies sold. Byrd's Antarctic adventures were just the psychic balm Americans needed in the aftermath of the 1929 stock market crash. For Davies, Bursey, and Innes-Taylor, all needing jobs in the thick of the Depression, the cleanup of Byrd's expedition continued to provide a meal ticket. Davies returned his equipment to the Carnegie Institution and was kept on as a scientist for the next two years to analyse the magnetic and auroral observations from Little America. Both Innes-Taylor and Bursey were among twelve expedition members who worked aboard the *City of New York*, which was sent on a fund-raising cruise to coastal cities and eventually berthed at Chicago for the 1933 World's Fair. There Bursey met Ada deGraff, a woman who came aboard for a tour and wound up marrying her Newfoundland guide the following year.

Innes-Taylor, cheated by fate from Antarctic adventure, was soon given another chance. Byrd was planning a second expedition to the continent and asked Innes-Taylor to join him as a dog driver. Norman Vaughan, ringleader of the Harvard trio, had also been asked back to head the expedition's dog unit and to serve as one of four men who would winter in an isolated hut to be situated at the foot of the Queen Maud Mountains, half-way to the pole.

Byrd later claimed that his change of plan – to occupy the advance base himself without any companions – came about only after the expedition had arrived in the south. In fact, as Vaughan later revealed, the admiral came to this decision long before embarking from Boston and confided his intentions to Vaughan. 'Two days later the truth finally struck me,' Vaughan wrote. 'Publicity. By taking three of us with him, Byrd would have to divide the publicity among four. By staying alone, he would be the only man in the world who had endured such hardship ... I saw his decision as a grab for glory.'[56] In anger and despair, Vaughan quit the expedition and turned over all responsibility for the dogs to Innes-Taylor.

Innes-Taylor gathered and trained the dogs and drivers at the same Wonalancet kennels that had served Byrd's first expedition. About fifty of the animals were a Wonalancet crossbreed of the Alaskans from the 1928–30 expedition with Siberian and wolf. Another seventy-six Labradors were obtained from Quebec's north shore and the Labrador coast. Among these were Toby and Pierrette, which at almost ninety pounds each were the expedition's biggest animals. Vaughan had bought them from a French-Canadian farmer in Quebec who was using them in place of draught horses. The remaining thirty animals were huskies bred by John Isfeld at Gimli, Manitoba.[57]

Byrd's two expedition ships were a bargain this time around because of the Depression. The steel-hulled *Jacob Ruppert*, a war-surplus freighter, was leased from the United States shipping board for one dollar a year. The oak-hulled *Bear of Oakland*, an ice ship built in 1874, was obtained for $1,050 at an auction partly rigged by the City of Oakland. Byrd had also obtained four aircraft, including an autogiro, precursor of the helicopter; six snow-tractors; three cows, to provide fresh milk daily; and a record fifty-six-man wintering party, including eighteen who had been with the first expedition.

When the *Jacob Ruppert* sailed from Boston Harbor on 11 October 1933, Innes-Taylor was in charge of more than 150 dogs. Disaster constantly threatened. Sixty of the dogs were accidentally soaked in fuel oil during a refuelling stop at Bayonne, New Jersey, and were heavily powdered with coal dust during a coaling stop at Newport News, Virginia. Innes-Taylor put the dogs on a diet of barley water to help get them through the tropics, and built wooden platforms shaded with awnings that were hosed down twice a day to keep them cool. After a six-day stopover in New Zealand, the ships headed south on 12 December.

The day before Christmas, with the vessels struggling through the pack ice, Innes-Taylor let a half-dozen dogs run unleashed on the forward well-deck for some needed exercise. One of the animals, Olaf, inexplicably took a flying leap into the sea, and was plucked from the water eight minutes later with great difficulty. 'Innes-Taylor gave the dog artificial respiration, and tonight Olaf appeared to be suffering less from exposure than from a hang-over produced by a liberal shot of excellent whiskey,' Byrd jotted in his diary. 'When Innes-Taylor revealed the cure, it was all we could do to restrain the entire ship's company from jumping overboard.'[58]

The ships finally gained the Bay of Whales on 17 January 1934, with fewer than ten dogs lost on the voyage from Boston. The first order of business was to inspect the buildings at Little America to determine how well they had stood up after four years. Thirty minutes of hard digging and the men finally broke through into the old administration building. Several beams had cracked under the weight of snow, a film of ice covered the walls, and crystals hung in dense blooms from the ceiling. Otherwise, the place looked just as unkempt as when it was abandoned, with dirty underwear draped here and there and a half-finished meal on the table. One of the men flipped an old light switch and miraculously the bulbs glowed feebly, drawing power from four-year-old storage batteries. 'While we were standing there the telephone rang,' Byrd recalled. 'I'm not joking; it actually rang.' The first expedition had boasted a hut-to-hut telephone link. 'Nobody moved for a second. "Did somebody miss the boat?" asked George Noville with raised eye-brows.'[59] In fact, the telephone system had also survived intact and one of the men in the other building was testing it.

The next day unloading began in earnest. The dogs were in poor physical condition because of their long inactivity and were puckish. 'For the first few days dog transport was a three-ringed circus,' Byrd wrote. 'The teams were forever fighting, tangling, breaking away. Two days after we landed there were few drivers with voice enough left to speak above a whisper.'[60] The dog-drivers took alternate twelve-hour shifts, back and forth along the seven-mile trail between the ship and Little America II, which consisted of eight new buildings erected near its predecessor. The route was soon dubbed Misery Trail, and several thousand gruelling trips were made over three weeks before the job was finished in mid-February. Byrd was impressed enough with Innes-Taylor's work to promote him to chief of trail operations, responsible for the logistics of all ground transport during the expedition.

Innes-Taylor and George Noville, the expedition's executive officer, erected private quarters for themselves to provide some peace as they drew up work sheets and trail instructions. Just twelve feet square with an eight-foot ceiling, it was dubbed Dog Heim and soon attracted so many visitors that its original pur-pose was entirely defeated. 'Originally built with the hope it would insure some privacy, it became (in tribute to Noville's skill as a cook) a sort of Antarctic Coffee Shoppe, always crowded, nearly always merry,' Byrd wrote.[61]

Innes-Taylor's first trail operation was a depot-laying trip south that would supply field parties the next summer – a trip that closely paralleled Bursey's four years earlier.[62] The depot group would consist of a main party of four men and twenty-seven dogs led by Innes-Taylor, and a supporting party of two men and eighteen dogs. There was a secondary goal as well: to scout a safe route for the snow tractors, which would carry sup-plies and materials to build the advance base that Byrd intended to occupy for the winter. No snow vehicle had ever performed satisfactorily in the Antarctic. On Byrd's previous expedition, the lone snowmobile had broken down about seventy-five miles south of Little America and was abandoned. However, significant technological advances had since been made, especially by the Citroen company of France, which provided three modified tractors originally designed for desert use.

The depot group, bone-weary from unloading the ships, set off on 1 March on their month-long, 360-mile journey. Innes-Taylor's team, consisting of Gimli huskies with a powerful dog named Sam in the lead, broke trail. The first night under canvas was ominous as the men shivered in badly designed sleeping bags with zippers that would not zip. The trail radio also refused to function and three containers leaked away gallons of precious cooking fuel. Four days out, a blizzard pinned them down. Then came one of those moments in which technological advances turn a familiar world upside down. Early on 6 March three men from Little America II pulled into the camp after an all-night trip on a puffing, clanking Citroen. They delivered ten gallons of kerosene, sturdier fuel containers and wool liners for the faulty sleeping bags. One of the tractor men also made a quick repair of the trail radio.

The Citroen crew was to return to base, but the machine was working so well that Byrd ordered it to continue south. The men loaded it with one-third of the six thousand pounds on the sledges of Innes-Taylor's group. On 9 March the tractor men got bored with travelling in low gear to match the speed of the dogs. They spurted ahead to drop supplies at a depot 123 miles south of Little America, then turned north again. They covered the distance back to Little America in just sixteen hours, stopping only to coax free meals out of the slower dog parties. 'It seems strange hearing a motor horn in this strange white silence,' a fatigued Innes-Taylor scribbled in his diary.[63] The next day, when his group finally caught up to the depot, there was a hint of bitterness. 'Time changes many things,' Innes-Taylor wrote. 'Tractors, airplan[e]s, autogiros, all [on] their way speeding over the unknown, while the humble sledger and his faithful dogs are forgotten. It is an era of new technique in Polar transportation that is upon us.'[64]

Byrd was a fast convert to the snow machines. He noted their journey was 'a new day's record for surface travel in Antarctica, and the first successful demonstration of mechanized transport in field operations.'[65] (The record would be broken again by a Citroen months later.) Shivering in his inadequate sleeping bag that same night, Innes-Taylor tried valiantly to produce a list of reasons why dogs were still useful in polar transport. On 14 March his group established a depot about 180 miles south, christened Camp Yukon, and continued to their farthest south a few miles on. The low that day was a killing –47° F and Innes-Taylor spent another sleepless night in agony, shivering in an iced-up sleeping bag. The dogs also suffered terribly in the low temperatures, their condition aggravated by bad pemmican. The great ice shelf growled ominously around them. 'While we were all in the cook tent this morning, suddenly there came on a tremendous roar like the oncoming of a thousand locomotives,' Innes-Taylor's 16 March diary entry reads. 'It culminated in a loud report and the whole barrier surface for miles settled 3″ to 4″.'[66]

On 21 March they pulled back to the depot at 123 miles, where tractors carrying the prefabricated advance base and its supplies were waiting. The next day Byrd arrived by aircraft and the men set to work digging a hole in the barrier for the hut and assembling it. Innes-Taylor chafed at this order as he considered the worn-out state of his dog-drivers. 'Such careless indifference to the welfare of the men I have never seen,' he confided to his diary. 'It took the spirit out of all my men.'[67] Towards the end of construction, Innes-Taylor mentioned his foot had frozen. One of the men quickly pressed the ice-hard sole into the warmth of his stomach. 'He held it there fifteen or twenty minutes, until the circulation revived it with a pounding pain that brought sweat to Innes-Taylor's forehead,' Byrd recorded.[68]

Construction was finished on 23 March and the men elected

Innes-Taylor as chef for a meal of celebration inside. Turkey, chicken and corn niblets were on the menu. 'The kerosene in the stove had frozen, and the meat was so rigid we had to thaw it out with blowtorches,' Innes-Taylor later recalled. 'We tried to make it lively, but couldn't quite pull it off.'[69] Fourteen men squeezed into the tiny hut for the feast, five of them forced to stand for lack of floor space.

Poor weather forced Innes-Taylor's party to remain in camp another two days, teeth chattering in tents while Byrd and the tractor men slept inside the hut. On the morning of 25 March just as they were about to head north again, Paul Siple dropped a bombshell. He said the admiral had selected Siple and two others to undertake a major exploratory sledging trip next summer – and neither of Siple's helpers would be from the depot-laying party. 'This is a blow,' Innes-Taylor wrote in his diary. 'I had no knowledge of such plan from the Admiral. Looks as though my title of "Charge [of] Trail Operations" was just a title. A disappointment for me.'[70] Earlier, the dog-drivers had groused to one another that they derived no pleasure from the gruelling work of hauling supplies for explorers. They wanted a piece of the action as well. 'Talked over our hopes for next year. Possibly a trip into the unknown. Taxying [sic] scientists to the Queen Maud Range [Mountains] doesn't particularly appeal to us,' Innes-Taylor wrote in his diary.[71] But Byrd's grand scheme reserved no special place for the hardy dog-drivers. They would be the expedition's hewers of wood and drawers of water.

The trip back to Little America was horrific, as temperatures plunged to a low of –61° F. On 27 March one dog died in harness and two others collapsed half frozen. They had to be shot. Even the revolver took eleven minutes to thaw before it would fire. Another failing dog was left to make its own way back, and many animals suffered from bleeding paws. Then the final indignity: on 28 March the red-and-black Citroens carrying the tractor drivers chugged merrily by on their way back from advance base, where they had left Byrd alone. 'Those bloated daredevils were lolling on cushioned seats, chewing gum and eating chocolat like so many millionaires on a tour,' Innes-Taylor said later, only half kidding. 'Stop? Hell, those fellows went by with their noses stuck up in the air as if they were passing a family of peasants having a humble dinner in their miserable hovel!'[72]

Innes-Taylor's party pulled into Little America on 31 March, their Canadian leader eleven pounds lighter from the month-long strain. Immediately, a debate was ignited between the 'dog catchers' and the 'limousine explorers' about whether the dog days of the Antarctic were numbered. The 'dog came out second best,' concluded Charlie Murphy, the expedition chronicler, in summarizing these spirited repartees. 'In the decisive matters of speed and payload the tractor ... was well out in front.'[73] Even Innes-Taylor grudgingly admitted that for hauling supplies, tractors outperformed dogs, which were best reserved for detailed survey work after being flown to the survey area.[74]

Technology had triumphed over tradition, and for proof one needed look no further than Little America itself. The main buildings all had electric lights; the kitchen, an electric coffee and meat grinder; the workshops, electric saws and drills. An electric sewing machine stitched torn parkas. An electric movie projector clattered away Monday, Wednesday, and Saturday nights. Telephones linked the huts. One man shaved daily with an electric razor. Even the cow barn came equipped with an electric milking machine. Aircraft were shown to be invaluable in 1928–30, and now tractors – long a disappointing failure in the Antarctic – had finally proved their worth.

The Citroens soon proved themselves yet again. At advance base Byrd became seriously ill from carbon monoxide poisoning when a gas-powered generator malfunctioned. Although he kept silent about his grave medical condition during his regular radio transmissions, it became clear to the men at Little America that their leader needed rescue. Dog-team transport was out of the question in the frigid Antarctic night so the job fell to the tractors. After three false starts, a Citroen crew finally reached the admiral on 10 August at the end of more than two days of travel. Byrd's lone sojourn on the Ross Ice Shelf and his brush with death provided the drama needed to match the 1930 pole flight. His book about the ordeal, *Alone*, would become a bestseller. But the larger story behind the expedition was the rescue by tractor – and the death knell of an era in polar exploration.

Innes-Taylor gave up his bunk in Dog Heim to Byrd, who needed weeks of quiet recuperation after being flown back to Little America in mid-October. Meanwhile, the fall field-work was begun in earnest. Innes-Taylor had been pegged to head another depot-laying party to the south, again leaving exploratory work to others. But perhaps despairing of a mere supporting role, and acknowledging the superiority of tractors for such transport, he had a change of heart. 'After a resurvey of the operation, Captain Innes-Taylor recommended that his own Supporting Party be cancelled and its function taken over by tractors,' Byrd wrote. Blind to Innes-Taylor's disappointment, the admiral was impressed by his apparent self-sacrifice. 'I should rather find such bigness in my associates than discover a mountain range,' he wrote.[75]

Dogs continued to play a role in the field, but normally only at the end of supply lines laid down by tractors. The only dog-driving left for Innes-Taylor was the back-breaking monotony of reloading the ships for the return to New Zealand. On 7 February the ships headed north and Little America was abandoned once again. The expedition had marked a turning point in polar exploration. Gone were the days when European explorers rediscovered centuries-old techniques of polar survival. Machines increasingly shouldered the drudgery of exploration, and dogs were used less often in subsequent Antarctic expeditions. (In 1991, the Antarctic Treaty nations agreed to ban them outright from the continent by 1 April 1994, for fear of spreading disease among the seal populations.) Innes-Taylor's fate was to assume responsibility for Byrd's dogs just as the clanging of pistons spelled their eventual eclipse.

On his return to civilization, Innes-Taylor collected his second Congressional Medal for work on the expedition and lectured on the Antarctic throughout Canada and the United States.[76] In 1937 he was hired as Western Canada manager for New York–based Lederle Laboratories, in Winnipeg and Vancouver. The Canadian government hired him in 1942 to survey wooden vessels and shipbuilding yards for service in the Second World War. In July that year he joined the US Army Air Corps at the rank of captain (retaining his Canadian citizenship), rising to lieutenant-colonel by the time of his discharge in 1946. During these four years he specialized in Arctic training, stationed at Greenland, Washington, DC, Colorado and Alberta. As a de-mobbed civilian, he helped run an experimental beaver ranch near Entrance, Alberta, until 1948.

In 1948–9, Innes-Taylor became executive officer and project engineer for a Canada–US project to build a weather station and airstrip on Ellef Ringnes Island, eight hundred miles from the North Pole. He spent a year there with six others, taking observations and musing about how technology had sapped polar exploration of its excitment. With the outbreak of the Korean War in 1950, he rejoined the American military to teach survival techniques to US air force bomber crews. Innes-Taylor left the military in 1956, becoming a consultant to Air France, Royal Dutch Airlines and Scandinavian Airlines, which were then establishing transpolar passenger air routes. Much of his later life was devoted to preserving and documenting Yukon history, for which he was awarded an Order of Canada in 1977. Innes-Taylor died in his sleep at his home in Whitehorse on 14 January 1983. Mount Innes-Taylor in the Queen Maud Mountains, which he was never able to visit, was named to commemorate his two trips to Antarctica.

Jack Bursey became a proud American citizen and lived in the United States for the rest of his life.[77] He returned with Byrd to the Antarctic as a dog-driver and radio operator with the government-organized US Antarctic Service Expedition of 1939–41.

As part of a three-man team, he helped explore the Flood Range, where the easternmost peak was named Mount Bursey in his honour. On a third trip to Antarctica in 1955–7, Bursey was a technical adviser to Operation Deepfreeze I. In between, he was a member of the US Coast Guard, becoming navigating officer on the icebreaker *Northwind,* which toured the Arctic. His 1957 book, *Antarctic Night: One Man's Story of 28,224 Hours at the Bottom of the World,* became a minor classic of American polar literature. Bursey died on 23 March 1980 at his home in Montague, Michigan.

Frank Davies took unpaid leave from the Carnegie Institution in the summer of 1932 to lead an expedition to Chesterfield Inlet on Hudson Bay for the Canadian Meteorological Service.[78] With three others, Davies established an observation station that recorded weather, geomagnetism, and auroras until September 1933. 'It cost me money,' he later recalled, 'because by the time I got to Toronto the damn government there cut all these civil service salaries [by] 10 per cent.'[79] After spending a year in Toronto writing up the results, Davies returned to the Carnegie in Washington and analysed data. In 1936 he transferred to Huancayo, Peru, where the Carnegie operated an observatory eleven thousand feet up the Andes.

With Canada's declaration of war in September 1939, he became a civilian member of naval intelligence based in Ottawa and South America. After the war, Davies joined the Defence Research Board in Ottawa, remaining there until retirement in 1969. He played a key role in the development of *Alouette I,* Canada's first satellite launched in 1962. Davies also presided over numerous projects in the Arctic, including the establishment of Distant Early Warning stations and expeditions to northern Ellesmere Island. Cape Davies on Thurston Island, twelve hundred miles east of the Bay of Whales, was named to commemorate his service in Little America. In 1978 he was awarded an honorary PH D from McGill University, whose doctoral program in physics he had abandoned in 1928 to go south with Byrd.

Six years before his death in Ottawa on 23 September 1981, Davies mused about Byrd's leadership. 'Among Byrd's many credits was his selection of Larry [Gould] and Bernt [Balchen] as his main aid[e]s and the fact that he took big financial risks to see we all had proper grub, clothing and camp discipline,' he wrote. 'It can not be overemphasized that none of us in 1929 died – unusual in Antarctic expeditions and this must be among Byrd's credits.'[80] Davies later emulated Byrd's attention to the welfare of his men when he took charge of his own Arctic expeditions. Geoffrey Hattersley-Smith recalled Davies's last Arctic trip in 1968, when he visited Tanquary Camp on Ellesmere Island. 'He decided that our comfort in the camp called for a more spacious WC, and on his return to Ottawa put in hand design and construction of a splendid building to be sent in by icebreaker later in the season.'[81] Perhaps recalling the day almost forty years earlier when he was blown up in the latrine, Davies sought to ensure a measure of private dignity for his own men.

Among the eight new buildings Byrd left behind in February 1935 was the radio shack, 'the neatest, certainly the most comfortable building in Little America,' he wrote.[82] Fifteen by thirty-one feet, with an eight-foot ceiling, its hollow walls were stuffed with raw wool for insulation. The back half was partitioned as a living quarters for five men, while the front half contained radio equipment and a corner in which weekly live broadcasts were made to North America over the Columbia Broadcasting System. Just before Byrd's ships sailed north, the equipment was removed, the lights put out, and the shack abandoned to sink into oblivion. But barely ten months later, a shovel point pried open the shack's skylight and a rope was let down into the blackness. Like grave robbers at the Pyramids, two figures descended wearily into the icy chamber.

SEVEN

Across the Continent

WEDNESDAY, 27 NOVEMBER 1935, shortly after midnight. Pilot Herbert Hollick-Kenyon and navigator Lincoln Ellsworth climb stiffly out of their single-engine airplane onto the loneliest, most desolate spot on earth.

They are deep in the interior of Antarctica, high on an uncharted, wind-swept plateau. No mountains, no valleys, just broad undulations in the stone-hard ice. Their base at Dundee Island is some eighteen hundred miles to the north at the tip of the Antarctic Peninsula and well beyond range of their fuel tanks, which are now less than one-quarter full. The nearest coast where a rescue ship might penetrate the pack ice is over four hundred miles away. Their main radio transmitter failed four days earlier, and their trail set musters only weak signals, none of them acknowledged. Their receiver filters nothing intelligible from the jumbled transmissions out of Dundee, although dim time signals from Buenos Aires help to correct their timepieces.[1]

Hollick-Kenyon had managed a smooth landing on the

plane's broad skis, despite a thick fog that made it almost impossible to judge altitude. The fuselage, crumpled from a previous accident, looks no worse. With an easterly gale closing in, the two quickly pitch their tent and pull the entrance drawstring just as the blizzard hits. The temperature is –13° F. They huddle inside their caribou sleeping bags for three days while fifty-mile-an-hour winds blast the tiny outpost, which Hollick-Kenyon christens Camp Winnipeg after his home in Canada. The tent billows inward with such force that Hollick-Kenyon, bag and all, is repeatedly rolled on top of Ellsworth.

They soon discover a malfunction in their Primus cooking stove. The air-release valve is faulty, forcing them to cook and melt ice on a 'hot-pot' blow lamp normally used to pre-heat the aircraft engine before takeoff. The lamp spews out plumes of sooty smoke that blacken the tent walls and everything inside, including their faces. Three times each day they venture into the blinding snow and bitter cold to crank the trail radio ten minutes for their scheduled transmissions. They never get an acknowledgment, just gibberish larded with enough identifiable words to indicate the main base as the origin.

Three days after landing, with the storm subsiding, Hollick-Kenyon tries to repair the aircraft's radio in the hope of beaming a more powerful transmission. They drive three bamboo poles into the ice, string an antenna wire, and bring the radio set and a gas-powered generator inside the tent. The greasy exhaust fumes blacken further their bleak fabric home. Hollick-Kenyon makes a radio call at the appointed hour, then switches on the receiver only to have the magneto burn out, rendering the set useless.

Meanwhile, they have dipped dangerously into their dwindling supply of aircraft fuel to run the generator. Their calculations so far indicate that the plane, the *Polar Star*, is much more sluggish than the manufacturer's specifications. They had expected an air speed of 145 mph, but have been making a bare 92 mph. Many factors might account for the slow going, including increased drag from the skis and crumpled fuselage.

Whatever the explanation, they are not nearly as far along as hoped and the fuel tanks sound ominously hollow.

On 30 November, while gales continue to lash the tent, Hollick-Kenyon makes an even more startling discovery. The index on their sextant was not locked in place, casting doubts on all their previous sightings. That explains some variations in their calculations of longitude and latitude, readings that are vital in a region for which no maps could yet be drawn. But it also means they don't know their current location or whether the remaining gasoline can get them to safety. The storm blots out the sky, forestalling re-calculations.

The weather finally clears the next day, and the pair begin the long process of extricating the aircraft from a huge drift. As the slimmer man, Ellsworth has to worm into the cramped tail section to scoop out the sand-like snow crystals that pack the interior. Using a mug, he spends all day poised among the struts and cables to empty the machine, cup by cup. Hollick-Kenyon meanwhile cuts snow blocks and builds them into a wall around the tent to break the slamming wind. He also has to remove the tail section to get at the snow Ellsworth cannot reach.

The clouds clear several times, giving them a chance to take sun sightings with the sextant index now locked at a setting Hollick-Kenyon can only guess is correct. Pencilled jottings repeatedly produce the same disheartening figure: five hundred miles from their destination, Richard Byrd's abandoned Little America base at the edge of the Ross Sea. With so little aircraft fuel remaining, it is clear they will have to manhaul a sledge the final leg of the trip. That might prove dicey. Ellsworth earlier got a leather moccasin wet. It shrank as it dried, cutting off circulation so that his left foot has lost all sensation. It will soon become badly infected.

As they squirm into their bags that night, shots of pure grain alcohol lift their spirits. The plane is clear, ready for a fast take-off in the morning. Three months' emergency rations on board can help avert immediate disaster. Hollick-Kenyon has successfully fashioned a new valve for the Primus by carving down a lead valve taken from the precious supply of spare engine parts. And at least now they are more certain of their position. Their grand trans-Antarctic hop is nearing completion.

Fine, granular snow drifts back inside and around the *Polar Star* that night, forcing yet another exhausting round of shovelling and scooping. The weather remains unstable all day and they have little choice but to crawl back inside their bags, frustrated. More snow falls overnight. They have the aircraft cleared again by noon and are determined to get back into the skies that afternoon. The plane's skis sit in trenches, dug to keep the wings low to the ground and out of the gale. The two men unload the aircraft to make it light enough to taxi out of the depressions and away from the enveloping drift. A canvas hood is thrown over the engine, the fire-pot placed underneath to warm it. Forty-five minutes later, Hollick-Kenyon cranks the engine.

Silence.

Again he cranks.

Nothing.

Three more heart-stopping times. It simply will not start.

In the tiny lakeside community of Ewing's Landing, in British Columbia, Hollick-Kenyon's wife and mother busy themselves with daily chores, laying aside as best they can the nagging uncertainty. They have lived through this many times before. At least Hollick-Kenyon's two children, nine-year-old Marylea and six-year-old Tim, remain genuinely oblivious in their excitement over the approach of Christmas.[2] Newspaper reporters from as far as London and New York have been ringing up every day since radio contact with the aircraft was lost. But the only telephone among the village's ten households is at Bob Ewing's general store and post office. That's a good half-mile along a snowed-in footpath from the family's fruit farm in the heart of the Okanagan Valley.

The same week Herbert Hollick-Kenyon is struggling to pull

up stakes at Camp Winnipeg, a reporter finally gets his mother, Annie, on the other end of the line. Dark thoughts well up as she is prodded for comment. 'To have crashed in the waste areas en route to their destination would be an awful fate,' she says stiffly. 'I should prefer to think that the two men, in the event that they did not reach Little America, died instantly in a crash, than that they should be wandering in that awful territory slowly succumbing ... It may be that I'll have to wait a year or more before I learn if my son Berty is alive or dead.'[3]

Lincoln Ellsworth, born in 1880, was a rich and determined American.[4] His father was a Chicago businessman who began his career as a clerk and eventually made a fortune in coal mining. Young Lincoln quickly grew bored with the routine of managing the family business. Canada, he decided, offered real excitement. So he headed north at the turn of the century to become a civil engineer, surveying for the railways in Ontario, Saskatchewan, Alberta, and British Columbia. When he was just twenty-six he was chosen to lay out the town site for Prince Rupert, the Pacific terminus of the Grand Trunk Railway. Ellsworth also enjoyed hunting trips in Canada's wild northwest, and joined the Ottawa-sponsored buffalo round-up of 1911. He even considered becoming a Mountie.

Ellsworth's search for untamed frontiers led him to join several Arctic air expeditions with Roald Amundsen in the 1920s. By the 1930s he was drawn to the Antarctic, where the family money financed the last large private expeditions to Antarctica. Ellsworth took up the aviation challenge that had eluded both Byrd and Hubert Wilkins: a trans-Antarctic flight. Initially, Ellsworth envisioned a non-stop traverse from the Ross Sea to the Weddell Sea and back again, a round trip of thirty-four hundred miles. But he soon realized it would be foolhardy to assume good weather for the entire distance. Arctic pilots with ski-equipped aircraft often landed to wait out storms. Ellsworth would do the same in the Antarctic, a decision that also permitted ground-based corrections to in-flight navigation.

His first assault on the continent in January 1934 was to be from Byrd's abandoned Little America base at the Bay of Whales. Ellsworth hired Byrd's South Pole pilot, Bernt Balchen, and brought along Wilkins as expedition manager.

His aircraft was the first prototype built by the newly formed Northrup Corporation of California. Built entirely of metal, it was a two-cockpit, low-wing monoplane with flaps that could reduce the landing speed to 42 miles an hour. The *Polar Star*, as it was christened, was strictly state of the art. It cost $37,000, a small fortune at a time when middle-class salaries might reach $5,000. The single 600-horsepower engine gave it a top speed of 230 miles an hour. The wings stretched forty-eight feet, the fuselage thirty-one feet and the extreme range was estimated at about seven thousand miles. Ellsworth's expedition ship was a Norwegian herring trawler, built in 1919. Fitted with sails to augment the semi-diesel engine, the 400-ton oak-and-pine vessel might do nine knots. Wilkins had the 135-foot hull sheathed in extra layers of oak and three-quarter-inch steel armour plate for ice-ramming. She was named after Ellsworth's hero, Wyatt Earp, the American frontier lawman.

The expedition arrived at the Bay of Whales on 9 January 1934, and the men quickly unloaded the aircraft onto the bay ice. Ellsworth was concerned the frozen surface would not hold, but Balchen, exhausted from unloading, insisted the job of moving it onto more solid ice could be postponed until the morning. While they slept the ice broke up, dunking the *Polar Star* into the sea. They managed to haul it out after six desperate hours but damage to the wings and undercarriage put an abrupt end to the adventure. The *Polar Star* had to be shipped back to California for a complete overhaul.

Ellsworth was determined to return, but now revised his plans: he would make only a one-way hop that began near the northern tip of the Antarctic Peninsula and ended at Little America. This approach had several advantages. For one, the expedition could get into the field sooner since there was no pack ice impeding the ship's passage to Deception Island, where the men could bunk in an abandoned whaling sation. A one-way flight would also allow more emergency supplies to be carried by the *Polar Star* in case the two-man crew had to walk out from a mishap. And Byrd's base would provide shelter and supplies at the end of the flight until the *Wyatt Earp* could fetch them.

The ship reached Deception Island on 14 October 1934, but storms prevented unloading of the plane for two weeks. And when the crew tried to start the engine for a test flight, a connecting rod cracked. The expedition carried no spare, forcing the ship to return to South America for a new rod flown down from California. While they waited impatiently at Deception for the part, Ellsworth grew concerned about his pilot: 'Balchen was moody and temperamental ... subject to sudden fits of temper. Once, just as we were sitting down at table, Dr [Dana C.] Coman [the expedition doctor] let one of the cats into the dining room of the whaling-station cottage. Balchen picked up the animal and threw it against the wall.'[5]

The ship had returned by 26 November and the plane was repaired. But the intended snow runway on the shore of Deception Island had deteriorated in the weather. Ellsworth was forced to steam southeast in search of a runway, finally settling for a low rise on Snow Hill Island. Balchen and Ellsworth took to the air on 3 January headed for Little America, but Balchen's nerve failed him when the weather turned foul. He headed back to Snow Hill about an hour after departing. 'Ellsworth can commit suicide if he likes but he can't take me with him,' he told Wilkins on landing.[6] Ellsworth was furious. His assault on the continent had again ended in miserable failure. 'So at last I began to realize the truth,' Ellsworth wrote later. 'Balchen was not going to go through with this flight unless he found absolutely perfect flying conditions ... I shall always believe we could have gone through.'[7] Dispirited and angry, Ellsworth ordered the ship to steam north again.

Balchen was clearly the wrong man for the job so, after returning to New York, Ellsworth advertised with airlines and flying clubs in Canada and Alaska for a new pilot. Indeed, Ellsworth was so infuriated by his experience with Balchen that he determined to take two pilots, playing one off against the other. There would always be a backup should a pilot ever baulk at his instructions again. Dozens of applications arrived and by early May Ellsworth had found his men: Herbert Hollick-Kenyon and J.H. 'Red' Lymburner, both experienced northern pilots working for Canadian Airways.

Herbert Hollick-Kenyon was born to a storekeeper and his wife in London, England, on 17 April 1897.[8] His parents sent him to a school at Croydon, Surrey, where he excelled in mathematics and won a scholarship to the London Polytechnic Institute. But he could not complete the course because of a dispute in 1909 over management of a family business, prompting Herbert's parents to emigrate to Ewing's Landing, where they established an Okanagan Valley apple farm. There was as yet no school in the tiny community, so Herbert's formal education came to a halt. His mother, Annie, kept her three children and the village literate by operating a small lending library in a shed near Bob Ewing's general store, located at the pier which was a regular stop for the boat to Vernon.

In his mid-teens, Hollick-Kenyon worked at a local garage but with the outbreak of war in August 1914 he volunteered. He joined the British Columbia Light Horse (absorbed later into the 2nd Canadian Mounted Rifles) and was at the front by September. He saw action at Ypres and the Somme, and a bullet wound in his right arm in 1916 forced his return to Canada the following year. Within months he had joined the Royal Flying Corps in Canada, training at the University of Toronto and at a flying field in Fort Worth, Texas. He earned his wings at Camp Borden, Ontario, after his first solo flight in 1918. Hollick-Kenyon became an instructor at Borden for some months before heading back to Europe in October. While he was aboard ship, the armistice was signed.

Hollick-Kenyon became a flying instructor with the RAF in

May 1923, remaining until 1928. Mary Manning, a woman who drove officers to and from hangars in a side-car motorcycle, became his wife. A friend and fellow RAF pilot, Leigh Brintnell, had left the service to join Western Canadian Airways in March 1928. At his beckoning, Hollick-Kenyon also applied and was accepted after getting his Canadian pilot's licence in September. He, his wife, and their four-year-old daughter, Marylea, boarded a ship for Montreal, a train for Winnipeg, and flew seven hundred miles north to their new home, an isolated log cabin on Emma Lake, near The Pas, which was to be Hollick-Kenyon's base. Two years later they were transferred to Winnipeg, where Hollick-Kenyon flew for the newly established Prairie airmail service.

By 1935 Hollick-Kenyon had become superintendent of the northern division of Canadian Airways, the company that absorbed Western Canadian Airways. The firm's manager of operations, George Anson 'Tommy' Thompson, received Ellsworth's call for pilots that spring and recommended Hollick-Kenyon, partly because he had passed a rigorous navigation course in Britain and partly because he had over six thousand hours flying experience, many of them on ski-equipped aircraft, in addition to more than one thousand hours with the RAF. Thompson's recommendation for second pilot was a less-experienced company man flying in Quebec, James Harold 'Red' Lymburner. With only sixteen hundred hours flying experience, Lymburner was greener and knew only the basics about navigation. But unlike Hollick-Kenyon, he had come to flying after demonstrating a genius for keeping engines in good repair, an essential skill for Antarctic aviation.

Red got his nickname from the colour his face would turn after flying in open-cockpit aircraft.[9] He was born on 24 April 1904, on a farm in Caistor Township, in Ontario's fruit-growing Niagara Peninsula, east of Hamilton. His father, George Malcolm, recalled that Harold used to pore over aviation magazines after farm chores, and put down good money in 1925 to be a passenger in a plane at Hamilton's Beach Road airport.

Red took one year of business school in Hamilton, and in 1926 married a local girl, Jessie Tice. They lived with his parents on the farm while Red ran a garage nearby, still yearning to fly. They had their only child, Glenna, in 1927.

The following March they sold the farm and bought a house in Hamilton, where Red worked as a mechanic at a Chrysler dealership from 3 p.m. to 11 p.m. To fill up the early afternoon, Lymburner polished airplanes for free at Jack Elliot's air service. He happened to arrive at Elliot's office in July 1928 just as one of the mechanics was being fired in the heat of an argument. Said Lymburner to Elliot: 'I couldn't help hearing that you're looking for a mechanic.' He was hired on the spot and eventually was given company training as a pilot. The instructor on his first flight was unimpressed and refused to give any more lessons, calling Lymburner a washout. A second instructor took on Lymburner just to goad his rival, and over the next two days gave Red three training flights. On the second day, with less than two hours air time, Lymburner flew solo.

Lymburner was first tested by a federal inspector in July 1928 ('a very steady type of pilot')[10] but flunked the written meteorological and navigation tests. He was re-tested successfully in December, and by May the following year was granted a private pilot's licence. This was upgraded to a commercial licence in March 1930, and in February the following year he got his air engineer's licence.

Caught in the wave of mergers that swept the infant airline industry in the next few years, Lymburner was employed by International Airways of Canada, was transferred to Montreal, joined Canadian Airways and Inter-Provincial Airways, and worked out of various northern Quebec bases, including Lac St-Joseph, Oskelaneo, Chibougamau, Roberval, and Lac à la Tortue, specializing in aerial photography. In 1932, after the firm had been absorbed into Canadian Airways, Lymburner was appointed base manager at Noranda, Quebec, and in 1934 he was transferred to Oskelaneo. There, in the spring of 1935, he learned from one of his fellow pilots about Ellsworth's call

for experienced Arctic aviators and Thompson's recommendation. Lymburner had no particular interest in signing on,
though. He was looking forward to returning to southern
Ontario to visit his family.

Lymburner flew to Montreal, got his car out of storage and
started the long drive to Dunnville, where his wife and daughter were staying with family. At the fork with the road leading to
Ottawa, Lymburner stopped the car and debated whether to
drive to the capital where, he had been told, he could formally
apply for the Ellsworth expedition. 'I had just about made up
my mind to go home and forget about the expedition, and had
started to move when a car pulled out in front of me blocking
the road,' he recalled later. 'I had to wait till he moved on. I
considered that the turning point and drove to Ottawa.'[11] Two
days later he was interviewed by Wilkins, who offered him the
job. On 9 May Lymburner and Hollick-Kenyon converged on
New York City to sign contracts. They were to be paid $500
a month and all expenses. That by itself was good money,
but then Ellsworth added a big incentive to ensure a Balchen-
like episode didn't recur: a bonus of at least $2,000 if the trans-
Antarctic flight was successful.

That summer a crew member unexpectedly left the expedition and Wilkins decided to replace him with someone experienced in aircraft maintenance. Lymburner knew just the man:
Pat Howard, recently laid off after working alongside Lymburner in northern Quebec. Born on 14 February 1910 in Hast-
ings, Ontario, Howard moved with his family to Toronto in
1924.[12] In 1928 he joined the Ontario Provincial Air Service at
Sault Ste Marie and Sioux Lookout as a mechanic and returned
each spring until he was laid off in 1931. He eventually
obtained a commercial pilot's licence in September 1932 at
Toronto, and two years later met Lymburner at Rouyn, Quebec,
where Howard now worked for General Airways. He was laid
off in January 1935, then briefly (and unhappily) worked for a
Toronto life insurance company to help his widowed mother
pay the rent.

On 30 July 1935 Howard was playing in a tennis tournament in Toronto when Lymburner interrupted him in the middle of a match. How would he like to go to the Antarctic? Howard had no time to answer as his opponent was impatient to get on with the game. He lost the next point, but won the game, and after getting more details from Lymburner, Howard wired his acceptance to Wilkins in New York that night.

Eight days later, all three Canadians assembled in New York to board the *Wyatt Earp* for Montevideo, where they were to put the *Polar Star* through a month of tests at a nearby army airfield. Asked by a reporter why they wanted to go to the Antarctic, Hollick-Kenyon quipped: 'I have always wanted to winter in the south.' Lymburner and Howard added they were lured by 'the thought of being able to escape the rigors of a Canadian winter.'[13]

Lymburner was slightly injured in Montevideo during a test flight and the aircraft was laid up for six days for repairs to a wing. Ellsworth's decision to play two pilots off against one another was already working as Lymburner and Hollick-Kenyon vied for the job of flying the trans-Antarctic hop.

Kenyon goes for the publicity business like a fish for water [Lymburner wrote his wife in mid-October], and you would gather from what you read in the local papers (Spanish) that he was the only pilot in the expedition, and was certainly going to make the flight.

The other day I said to Wilkins, 'If Kenyon is going to make the flight, I suppose I do not need to have radio phones fitted in my helmet' and he said, 'We do not know who is going to make the flight yet,' so I do not know what to think. Kenyon does not do a bit of work in any way shape or form, and I cannot think that this goes over very big with Wilkins.[14]

Ellsworth joined the ship in Montevideo, and the expedition sailed on 18 October for a last refuelling stop in Magallanes, Chile, where a telegram from Richard Byrd indicated that gasoline and oil could be found at the Little America II base. (Byrd had not answered Ellsworth's inquiry about food supplies, saying only that he would respond later.) The *Wyatt Earp* sailed on 28 October for Deception Island, provisioned to remain in the Antarctic for two years if need be. Each man took a ninety-minute shift at the ship's wheel three times a day, including the Canadian trio, none of whom had ever piloted a vessel before. Lymburner wrote to his wife about the rolling seas: 'You climb in your bunk, get your back against one side and your knees braced against the other so that the motion of the ship can not throw you out, and sleep that way.'[15] Wilkins solved the problem by not sleeping at all.

Things got off to a bad start on the ship. During the voyage south, a simmering feud between the ship's doctor and the Norwegian crew finally boiled over when one of the crew landed a blow on the man's face. Rejecting all apologies, the sulking doctor posted a sign on his cabin door: 'During the rest of the voyage I will give no professional services to the members of this expedition.'[16]

On arriving at Deception Island, the *Polar Star* was re-assembled and lashed on deck. The ship then sailed in search of a flying field. During the previous expedition, Ellsworth had noted flat areas on Dundee Island, a readily accessible spot at the tip of the Antarctic Peninsula. (The island had been discovered by a whaling expedition that sailed from Dundee, Scotland, in 1892–3.) The *Wyatt Earp* nosed its way to the northeastern end of Dundee, 160 miles east of Deception, and made fast to the half-mile stretch of shore ice. Scrambling out of the ship, Ellsworth gazed upon a personal paradise: a broad, flat plain cemented with hard-packed snow. No matter that the crystalline field wasn't quite level. The experts, Hollick-Kenyon and Lymburner, shrugged it off as inconsequential. Wilkins could not conceal his jealousy about Ellsworth's good fortune, saying he would have made the trans-Antarctic hop seven years earlier had he known of this spot.

By 18 November Lymburner and Hollick-Kenyon each had test-flown the *Polar Star*, part of Ellworth's carefully orchestrated plan to keep his pilots in competition. The craft now sat waiting for the great leap across the continent, tanks topped up with 466 gallons of gas, cargo hold jammed with supplies, including Ellsworth's eccentric Americana: a 38-calibre revolver, Wyatt Earp's cartridge belt and a Mickey Mouse doll. They also carried 150 pounds of food for five weeks, a diet specially prepared by an American nutritionist to prevent diarrhoea, the bane of polar explorers.

Ellsworth had built in almost no room for manoeuvre. The flight path would take them over areas as much as 450 miles from the coast, where seal and penguin meat could sustain them. As inexperienced polar travellers, they were unlikely to manhaul the twelve miles a day necessary to ensure their food supplies did not run out before they could reach the coast, in the event of a forced landing. And if Byrd's men had cleaned out the food supply at Little America, a long stay at their destination could also be a hungry one. But at 7,600 pounds, the *Polar Star* was judged to be at its maximum load and unable to carry more food.

For reasons unrecorded, Ellsworth and Wilkins decided to let Hollick-Kenyon have first crack at the epic flight. A mid-morning attempt on 19 November failed because soft snow prevented the aircraft from building enough speed for take-off. The next flight was set for the following day at 7:44 a.m. Greenwich time (4 a.m. local time) to take advantage of the firmer, night snow surface. Good weather beckoned, and Hollick-Kenyon bounced the craft into the air less than half a mile from the starting point. But barely ninety minutes out, Hollick-Kenyon scribbled a quick note to Ellsworth in his flight log and passed it through an opening to the rear cockpit. It read: 'Sorry – we have to go back – I have a line leak which may give worse trouble.'[17]

After turning the aircraft about for Dundee, he jotted down a longer explanation. 'When we took off a fuel gauge broke its glass – and I find now that it is leaking more and more, and there iş only a thin celluloid film there – and a lot of pressure bulging it out – I will tell the ship we are headed back.'[18] Hollick-Kenyon faced a double danger. If the film broke, he'd be drenched in gasoline and the engine would shut down for lack of line pressure. Three hours and fifteen minutes after take-off they landed at Dundee for repairs. Ellsworth was incensed at his rotten luck. Lymburner, Howard and the rest of the ground crew began the drudgery of hauling steel drums of gas four miles from the ship and up a fourteen-hundred-foot slope.

The good weather held, and early the following morning, Hollick-Kenyon and Ellsworth climbed aboard once more. The engine, already warmed from the fire-pot, was started at 7:55 a.m. Greenwich time and five minutes later the skis of the *Polar Star* left the ground. After about three and a half hours in the air, they passed Wilkins's farthest south, at Stefansson Strait, and the weather ahead began to thicken. Hollick-Kenyon was forced to put the aircraft into a steady climb as they suddenly encountered a great mountain range never before seen. Its eleven-thousand-foot-plus peaks pierced the cloud cover. 'This was the greatest hour of my life,' Ellsworth wrote later. 'Obviously here was a mountain system of major importance, and our eyes were the first to behold it!'[19]

Ellsworth named the chain the Eternity Range, and its three highest peaks Mounts Faith, Hope, and Charity. Hollick-Kenyon, meanwhile, was struggling with more mundane matters. The ground was lost to view because of fog, clouds ahead obscured the horizon, and a rush of frigid air from the Antarctic plateau swept over the aircraft, making it extremely sluggish. They finally burst through the cloud cover, but ahead the cloud bank swept up like a wall, broken here and there by more peaks. Just at that moment, Hollick-Kenyon handed Ellsworth a note in his log: 'At 12000 ft – cannot see any end to cloud – am turning back – do you want to go look at Weddell Sea Coast.'[20]

Ellsworth's heart sank, his worst nightmare a numbing reality: another pilot was chickening out. As Hollick-Kenyon banked the aircraft east, Ellsworth was reduced to pleading: 'Cant you go to 80 degrees [latitude] so can drop flag.' The answer: 'Wait till I have time to get back to safety and figure it out – maybe.' Ellsworth did some more pleading but got only an abrupt reply: 'Let me work it out in peace. If we cant go now then we can another time.'[21] With a tail wind, the aircraft made it back to Stefansson Strait in short order but there ground fog put to rest Ellsworth's last hope, that they might sit out bad weather on the ground before taking another crack at the mountain range. He could do little more than suck vigorously on his pipe, scowling silently at his lily-livered companion.

'All the way back I tried to decide what I would do about this fiasco,' Ellsworth wrote later, 'scarcely observing anything from the plane, taking no pictures, entering no notes.' On landing back near the ship after ten hours and twenty-seven minutes in the air, he stormed off refusing even to acknowledge Wilkins's questions. Later, after brooding in his cabin, Ellsworth announced icily to Wilkins: 'Tomorrow I'm trying again, but I don't want Hollick-Kenyon. I'm going to take Lymburner.'[22]

Lymburner, however, was a physical wreck. He'd gone without sleep for thirty-six hours, checking the engine and hauling fuel. Wilkins interceded with Ellsworth, pointing out that not only was Hollick-Kenyon fresher but he now knew the route to the mountains. The decision to turn back, Wilkins argued, was perfectly reasonable. The aircraft had burned up too much fuel fighting the torrent of plateau air and a ready landing spot had not been available. Ellsworth finally relented after a face-to-face confrontation with Hollick-Kenyon. 'All right,' he said, 'but next time we won't turn back.'[23]

The next day Ellsworth and Hollick-Kenyon awoke in their cabins on the *Wyatt Earp* to find the weather still clear. Under Lymburner's direction, the men had refuelled the *Polar Star* and the machine was undergoing a final check and tune-up. The two explorers dressed – Hollick-Kenyon in trousers with a sharp crease – and after breakfast set off by snowshoe for the aircraft. There Wilkins had some hot pemmican waiting, and persuaded them to take more food supplies aboard since the *Polar Star* seemed to be getting into the air with little difficulty.

'We refrained from summing the total [weight] before we left for fear that, finding the load overweight, we might be inclined to reduce it,' Ellsworth wrote later.[24] Hollick-Kenyon's best guess was eight thousand pounds, which he dutifully recorded in his log. To compensate somewhat for the extra load, they would leave their skis at Dundee, relying only on snowshoes should they have to walk out.

The engine snapped to life at 8 a.m. and five minutes later they left the ground, the skies calm and clear. For the third time they cruised along the now-familiar spine of the Antarctic Peninsula. After about three and a half hours, they reached Stefansson Strait and began the ascent of the mountains. The winds were tame this time, the visibility so good they could gaze down on the broad sweep of the Eternity Range for 150 miles on either side. After about three hours of cruising at ten thousand feet, they crossed the last peaks to sail over the broad, nearly featureless plateau. The weather was so benign that Hollick-Kenyon could fly hands off.

During these long droning hours, both men studiously puffed on their pipes, which required a lot of breath to keep going at their oxygen-starved altitude. They also made frequent calculations for navigation corrections, trying to determine by how much the crosswinds were pushing them off course. Urination was accomplished by using small rubber balloons that were dropped overboard after filling. Ellsworth as photographer took thirty-one shots of the Eternity Range during their passage over it. Hollick-Kenyon was not a talkative man, but as they buzzed over the plateau he became briefly conversational. 'Well – so this is the Antarctic – how do you like it?' he jotted in his log, passing it to Ellsworth. 'Yes 100 per cent,' came the reply.[25]

At about 4:15 p.m., more than eight hours after leaving Dundee, the radio quit. The problem appeared to be a tangled aerial wire that trailed the aircraft. A weight on it now banged the fuselage. Their last slightly garbled message to the ship, however, was positive and another attempt to transmit at 4:30

p.m. was heard at Dundee although the signals could not be read. They passed near another small cluster of peaks, which Ellsworth named the Sentinel Range. The featureless ice plain below was christened James W. Ellsworth Land after his father (now Ellsworth Land), and that part above six thousand feet became Hollick-Kenyon Plateau. (He also named a spur of land discovered on this flight the Hollick-Kenyon Peninsula.) Ellsworth dropped a weighted American flag to claim the territory for his country.

More than ten hours after setting out, at 6:08 p.m., Hollick-Kenyon noted he saw a 'water sky.' This is a phenomenon in which the sky at the horizon reflects a darker body of water just beyond, in this case the Ross Sea, the goal of their journey. More than two hours later Hollick-Kenyon could still see the phenomenon, though there was still no sign of the sea. It was reasonable to assume they were now approaching Little America, since they calculated the flight would take about fifteen hours and they had been in the air thirteen hours. 'I really have no idea where we are,' Hollick-Kenyon finally confessed in his log.[26] Ellsworth then took a navigation reading that shook him up. His calculations indicated they were near the South Pole – more than six hundred miles off course.

Soon clear skies gave way to cloud. Both men agreed to land to wait out the poorer weather and to take ground readings to determine just where they were. At about 9:55 p.m. Hollick-Kenyon smacked the skis onto the hard, granular snow of the plateau. The aircraft was jolted and Ellsworth felt for a moment his teeth would go through his head from the impact. As they limbered stiff joints on the ground, Ellsworth noticed that part of the metal fuselage was crumpled and blamed the hard landing. Their altimeter read 6,400 feet, though in fact they were about one thousand feet lower. Ellsworth quickly took a navigational fix and got some mixed news: the pole was actually about 650 miles away, but so was their destination at the Bay of Whales. Something had gone wrong.

They quickly set up their temporary base – Camp Northrup,

Hollick-Kenyon called it, after the plane's manufacturer – and for the nineteen hours they were on the ground took repeated sextant readings to determine why things were amiss. They also tried the hand-cranked trail radio, but were unable to make contact with the *Wyatt Earp*. They dared not use up gas in the portable generator for transmissions from the aircraft radio, since they remained uncertain of how much farther they could fly on their dwindling supplies. The isolation preyed on Ellsworth's mind. 'I went out once to get exercise between the observations,' he recalled later, 'but the monotony of the terrible expanse of endless white got on my nerves, so that I was glad to get back into the four walls of the tent.'[27] Ellsworth rechristened the spot Camp Desolation.

They took off again the next day in fine weather at about 5 p.m., the lightened plane becoming airborne in less than fifty yards. Heading westward, they plunged into thick, low clouds and were forced to make another landing barely thirty minutes out. Here they remained for three days of sextant observations to determine finally their precise position, and to try the trail radio once more. Hollick-Kenyon was also determined to resolve a more personal problem. 'I always seemed to have the windy side of the tent where we camped,' he recalled later. 'One night I fooled Ellsworth by turning the whole tent around while he was out somewhere and he never noticed that wind until the middle of the night.'[28]

At this second camp they took thirty careful sun altitudes with the sextant. 'Nevertheless, in all thirty, each date, hour, and minute, when reduced to position, gave a hopelessly large spread,' Ellsworth wrote. 'Something was radically wrong ... [and] in great uncertainty we took off once more in what we hoped was the general direction of Little America.'[29] But the weather again turned against them, and after just fifty minutes in the air they made their third stop, Camp Winnipeg.

Wilkins had taken no alarm at the loss of the radio signal from the *Polar Star*, since there was no indication from the last messages that anything was wrong. On 26 November he ordered the ship back to Deception Island after leaving gasoline drums in a cairn at Dundee. The ship then made for Magallanes, Chile, where on 22 December the crew picked up another Northrop Gamma monoplane chartered from the Texaco company in case there was need to search for the missing aviators. The ship then steamed back towards the Antarctic Peninsula.

In the meantime, Prime Minister Joseph Lyons of Australia spearheaded a far more elaborate 'rescue' mission involving the New Zealand and British governments. The research ship *Discovery II* was ordered to Melbourne on 3 December to fit out for a search mission. Two aircraft, fuel, and supplies were taken aboard and the ship sailed for Dunedin, New Zealand, for last-minute supplies. This was an unsettling development for Wilkins who, in a radio message, advised the *Discovery II* that he believed Ellsworth and Hollick-Kenyon were safe and awaiting pickup at Little America as planned. This failed to dissuade the organizers, who wanted also to assert Commonwealth sovereignty in the Antarctic. *Discovery II* set sail for Antarctica on 2 January.

All their tribulations at Camp Winnipeg paled beside the realization the *Polar Star*'s engine might not start. Five times Hollick-Kenyon had tried to coax it to life. Fives times he failed. Finally he jury-rigged a jump start. The antenna wire became battery cables and the radio power cells were hooked in a parallel circuit with the aircraft's own battery. The extra burst of energy prodded the engine to a sputter and a roar.

Hollick-Kenyon taxied the *Polar Star* out of the drift with a tug on the throttle. They quickly loaded the plane, and took down the tent, as the last piece to go aboard. But before it was packed another thick snowstorm hit. In despair they unloaded again, pitched the tent and secured the plane. Inside the canvas walls they lightened their mental load with the last gulps of their grain alcohol. 'Maybe this is all meant to try us out,' Hollick-Kenyon said philosophically.[30]

The next day the weather remained ominous but they were determined to try again. The fire-pot was placed under the engine once more while they loaded the aircraft. Hollick-Kenyon started the engine at 7:07 p.m. and eight minutes later they were finally in the air, the snow walls of Camp Winnipeg quickly receding from view. As luck would have it, the thick skies were a local phenomenon. Within an hour the weather was perfect. The ice sheet of the Antarctic plateau began now to descend in smooth undulations, occasionally fracturing into great crevasses that would have made any landing suicidal. But when the surface bottomed out at one thousand feet, the ice plain was smooth again. After almost four hours in the air, Hollick-Kenyon set the aircraft gently down for a last ground check on their navigation. He christened this stop Camp Tranquille in recognition of the miraculous turnabout in their fortunes.

Three hours of sightings and calculations indicated they were now on the Ross Ice Shelf, not far from its juncture with the polar plateau and only about 125 miles from their goal. The day was windless, the sun rained warmth, melting the snow from the *Polar Star*. The tanks appeared to contain just enough fuel to make it to the coast. The only sour note was the failure of a last attempt to transmit with the plane's radio. Both men slept poorly in anticipation of the final dash.

The following morning they reloaded the plane and were in the air by 9 a.m. Almost immediately they sighted a 'water sky' ahead and after an hour the black ribbon of the Ross Sea sliced sky from snow. 'At such moments in the storybooks men are supposed to make memorable remarks,' Ellsworth wrote later, 'but in actual life behavior seems to be different. What happened was this: As soon as the open water appeared in the north, Hollick-Kenyon turned around and looked at me. I expected him to say something, but he did not. Nor could I think of anything to say. I stared back at him, that was all. Then we resumed our individual tasks. After all, what was there to say?'[31]

Still several miles short of the ocean edge, the engine sputtered and fell silent. The last drop of fuel had been spent and their sleek workhorse became a gliding chunk of metal sinking towards the ice. The twenty-hour, fifteen-minute powered flight had come to an end. The last minutes and yards would be in silence. At 10:05 a.m. Hollick-Kenyon gently made their final landing just beyond a heavily crevassed area in the north lee of ice-shrouded Roosevelt Island. They had discovered about 300,000 square miles of the earth's surface, an area larger than Hollick-Kenyon's home province of Manitoba. Their 2,200-mile line of flight was the equivalent of flying from Vancouver to Quebec City. Of that distance, 1,200 miles – the equivalent of flying from Winnipeg to Quebec City – was over virgin territory.

Hollick-Kenyon estimated that Byrd's abandoned Little America base was only about four miles off. But finding it would be no small task since there were no reliable maps, no landmarks, and the base was known to be completely buried in snow. The day they landed, they spotted a black object to the northeast estimated to be about three miles distant. The next day they donned snowshoes for a hike that turned out to be twice as far, and were prevented by a crevasse from visiting the object, which turned out to be a five-gallon empty gasoline drum. They were, however, able to make out the words 'Byrd Antarctic Expedition.' The following morning, 7 December, Hollick-Kenyon thought he could see Little America from the wing of the plane, about four miles away. They set out again on snowshoes, but after four miles the mysterious objects were no closer. They tromped back to put together their collapsible sledge for another attempt. That job took another thirty-six hours, but at last all was ready. So confident were they of finding Little America that they left the tent and sextant behind, carrying only food and sleeping bags on the sledge.

Manhauling two hundred pounds through soft snow proved nearly impossible. They had to rest every fifteen minutes to wipe sweat and unclog their snowshoes. After fifteen miles, the silhouette of Little America proved to be merely a jumble of ice-blocks. They cached the sledge, returned to the plane to pick up the tent and sextant, and trekked back after twenty-four hours and forty-five miles of manhauling. For ten hours they sank into a bottomless sleep. The next day they headed north again, and for days wandered about hoping only to reach the coast, find the Bay of Whales and double-back for Little America. Eventually they found the bay and followed a string of flags south until they reached a field of stovepipes, masts, and poles. Here was Little America at last, after one hundred exhausting miles of sledging. They calculated the base was a mere sixteen miles from the *Polar Star.*

The pair dug along a stovepipe until they reached a buried skylight, pried open the glass and let themselves down by rope into the abandoned radio shack. Ellsworth produced two bottles of Napoleon brandy from his knapsack to celebrate this final victory. The two exhausted men toasted one another while the drink softened the sharp, icy edges of their isolated world. But for Hollick-Kenyon, ever fastidious about his personal appearance, the happiest indulgence was a wash and a shave. He even talked Ellsworth into giving him a haircut.

Home at Little America consisted of a two-room shack, the main radio room bereft of its equipment, the other a bunk room. Hollick-Kenyon was official scavenger, and in the labyrinth of tunnels and buildings he collected coal to fire their stove and a variety of food to spin out their trail pemmican for three months if necessary. Ellsworth sank into melancholy. He had forgotten his glasses at the plane and thus was denied all reading while Hollick-Kenyon gorged on detective novels left by the Little America crewmen. 'By New Year's Day I would willingly have paid a thousand dollars for my reading glasses,' he wrote.[32] Ellsworth's foot became badly infected and for part of the time he was virtually bed-ridden. Hollick-Kenyon, meanwhile, bathed and shaved every day and clung to a routine of sleeping, cooking, scavenging and reading. So content was he with this uncomplicated existence that he remarked to Ellsworth after two weeks: 'I hope they won't bother us for at least another week.'[33] During their sedentary confinement, Hollick-Kenyon put on about five pounds.

Hollick-Kenyon was by nature a silent man. American journalist Lowell Thomas once said that getting information directly from him was 'like trying to write a history of the Civil War by interviewing the statue of General Sherman.'[34] On the trail or in flight, this trait was hardly noticeable. But in the quiet of an abandoned cabin, with nothing to distract, Hollick-Kenyon's manner grew oppressive. 'From my bunk I could not see, but I could hear,' Ellsworth wrote. 'The intermittent gurgling of his pipe. Thirty minutes of this, then a swipe to throw out the juice. Next, the lid of a candy tin coming off. Then the crunching of teeth on hard candy.'[35] For Ellsworth, now feverish because of his badly infected foot, this was the auditory equivalent of the Chinese water torture.

According to Ellsworth, Hollick-Kenyon broke the silence on only three or four occasions during the entire expedition. 'Have you any dogs at your home?' he muttered one evening, unprompted and without explanation. Ellsworth said he did not and Hollick-Kenyon fell silent once more. On another occasion, after Ellsworth had wasted two matches lighting his pipe, Hollick-Kenyon blurted out: 'You must be president of a match factory.' 'You use a good many more matches than I do,' was the hot retort. Then silence.[36] The last unprompted Hollick-Kenyon comment came late on 15 January, when he roused Ellsworth from a deep sleep by rustling a piece of paper before him. 'Read it. It's probably from Wilkins.'[37] Moments before, Hollick-Kenyon had scrambled outside after hearing the muffled roar of an airplane engine. He casually waved his arm and soon a parachute with food and a note came drifting down. It turned out to be from the commander of the *Discovery II*, which had beaten Wilkins to the 'rescue.'

Ellsworth was too ill to travel so he bid his companion make for the Bay of Whales alone to meet the ship. Hollick-Kenyon did so the following day on snowshoes. One of the British who welcomed him aboard recorded: 'He was shaved, washed and spruce and exuded an air of well-being which, we had to confess, was something of a disappointment to us. We had conjured up in our imagination thin features covered by a matted growth of beard and wasted by weeks of starvation diet in a twilight cell buried beneath the snow. But his cheeks shone from a recent shave and his stalwart frame in a check shirt showed no signs of anything but abundant health and vitality.'[38]

'Well, well! The *Discovery*, eh?,' Hollick-Kenyon said after sitting down with a pipe aboard ship. 'This is an affair. But, I say, it's awfully decent of you fellows to drop in on us like this. Thanks, I'll have a whiskey and soda.'[39] The men later told reporters that the dapper pilot's pants were creased, 'even his pocket handkerchief matching his necktie.'[40] Soon after he got aboard ship, Hollick-Kenyon sank into a hot tub and slipped into a fresh suit and camel's-hair coat he wrangled from the captain.

Eight men from *Discovery II* set out the next day to bring Ellsworth back to the ship, first availing themselves of the remaining grub in the radio shack as well as the food from their parachute drop. 'There was ... a kind of chill stuffiness in the room, a shivering airlessness denying all comfort and laying clammy fingers upon the spirit,' one of the men reported.[41] Despite his badly infected foot, Ellsworth insisted on dragging his own sledge the short distance to the icy quay. Soon all were back aboard and details of the flight were flashed to a fascinated and relieved world. The *New York Times* called it 'one of the great scientific achievements in the history of exploration ... The hazards were greater than in the old days. A crippled machine in an icy wilderness – what is a ship crushed in ice compared with this?'

Canada's Vilhjalmur Stefansson was equally effusive: 'It is the most spectacular and the most important flight ever made in the Antarctic. The most spectacular because the straight-away distance from the point of departure was much greater than in any previous flight in the area; most important because the amount of unknown territory covered is much greater than on any previous flight.'[42] Admiral Richard Byrd, himself an air pioneer, called the trans-Antarctic flight 'one of the greatest in the history of aviation.'[43]

Many of Hollick-Kenyon's relatives had by now given him up for dead. But when the first urgent dispatches reached New York and London on 16 January, the telephone at Bob Ewing's general store began to ring incessantly with word of the miraculous flight. Mary Hollick-Kenyon hastened through the snow drift to receive the good news and immediately cabled her husband: 'Delighted and relieved to hear of your safety and feel very proud of you. When will you be home? Love from all at Ewing's.'[44]

The frustrated crew of the *Wyatt Earp* finally nosed the ship into the Bay of Whales on 19 January, knowing they had lost the race. Three days earlier, the *Discovery II* had radioed Wilkins to tell him both explorers had been found safe and fit. The Commonwealth ship had performed no special service since Ellsworth and Hollick-Kenyon were exactly where they said they would be and the *Wyatt Earp* arrived three days ahead of schedule. Wilkins and Ellsworth felt awkward thanking the crew for the unnecessary search, but agreed for the sake of diplomacy that Ellsworth would accompany the *Discovery II* back to Australia to convey his personal appreciation to the organizers. That left the job of retrieving the *Polar Star* to Lymburner, Hollick-Kenyon, and Howard, a task that nearly killed them.

Over Lymburner's objections, they decided to haul gasoline to the *Polar Star* rather than fly out in the Northrup Gamma that had been lent to the expedition by Texaco.[45] They dug out three tractors left by the Byrd expedition before they could get one running properly, and connected a sled to it by rope to haul supplies. Howard sat amid the gasoline drums and crates on the sled, facing rear, while Lymburner, Hollick-Kenyon, and an airplane mechanic named Bill Klenke enjoyed the warmth of the tractor cab. Lymburner had not driven more than fifty feet when Howard heard the engine conk out and felt the sled jerk to a halt. He could see no sign of the tractor, just the tow rope which disappeared into the snow. He hopped off, covering the distance in a few seconds to discover the machine had become wedged in an eight-foot wide crevasse. A mere twenty-five feet below the dark waters of the Ross Sea lapped the icy walls.

Inside the cab, covered in broken glass, Lymburner fought furiously to free Klenke's legs, which had become jammed when the back of the cab was crumpled inward with the impact. Eventually he managed to cut off Klenke's rubber boots and fleece inner shoes and yank him free. No one was seriously hurt and the men calmed their frazzled nerves with a stiff drink all round. The next day they acquiesced in Lymburner's suggestion and flew out to the *Polar Star*, a nine-minute flight. In short order both aircraft were back at the ship, loaded on deck, and the *Wyatt Earp* departed the Bay of Whales on 30 January bound for New York and a rendezvous with Ellsworth.

The little ship arrived on 19 April to broad acclaim, all of which Ellsworth was determined to intercept. Four days earlier, President Franklin Roosevelt had pinned a medal to Ellsworth's chest in a ceremony at the White House marking the achievement. Ellsworth now decided to donate the *Polar Star* to the Smithsonian Institution, but a US Department of Commerce inspector refused to grant permission for this final flight from New York to Washington after viewing the crumpled fuselage. Eventually the objection was overruled and Hollick-Kenyon piloted the machine to the capital on 29 April, where it remains to this day on display.

The city fathers of Winnipeg, who claimed Hollick-Kenyon as their own, staged an enthusiastic homecoming for the Canadian trio ten days later.[46] The celebration included a motorcade, nationally broadcast speeches, an eleven-aircraft fly over, a Sheffield tea service for Hollick-Kenyon, a salver for Lymburner, and a banquet with five hundred invited guests. Even Al Cheesman showed up to make an impromptu speech, turning the event into an Antarctic reunion. The stack of congratulatory telegrams to be read out that evening included one from Prime Minister Mackenzie King. In addition to a few words of praise, King announced that Hollick-Kenyon was being given the honorary RCAF title of wing commander. Nothing was offered Lymburner. The Aviation League of Manitoba, official host of the banquet, regarded the message as an insult in view of the internationally recognized achievements of both men. The president of the league refused to read the cable to the assembly.

The federal cabinet had been placed in a difficult position by the trans-Antarctic flight. A memo from the head of civil aviation, J.A. Wilson, concluded 'the success of the flight is entirely due to the two Canadians'.[47] But King had recently abolished knighthoods in Canada and there was no ready state honour, such as the later Order of Canada, to mark the achievement. After dithering over the issue, cabinet finally came up with the honorary RCAF title for Hollick-Kenyon. But the defiance of the Aviation League of Manitoba forced Defence Minister Ian Mackenzie to fashion a high-sounding alternate.

By 26 May Mackenzie had a solution acceptable all round: Hollick-Kenyon would be given the honorary rank of air commodore, while Lymburner would become honorary group captain. 'The achievement of these two Canadian aviators was the fruit of unique experience gained in Canada,' Mackenzie said in making the announcement. 'It is recognized as a pioneer exploit, equivalent in its day to those of Alcock and Brown, Lindbergh and Kingsford-Smith.'[48]

Hollick-Kenyon returned to Canadian Airways, but left the following spring to join Skylines Express Limited, flying from Montreal to the Rouyn region. That fall he was picked by Wilkins to be chief pilot for the Levanevsky search with Cheesman as co-pilot. He later joined Trans-Canada Airlines (now Air Canada) and was based in Winnipeg, Toronto, and Lethbridge before defecting to Canadian Pacific Airlines in 1942, becoming the company's first chief pilot. By the time of his retirement from the company in May 1962, Hollick-Kenyon had been given charge of all pilot training. He spent the final years of retirement in Vancouver running a flower shop.

Honours for the Antarctic flight continued to accrue throughout Hollick-Kenyon's final years. He was named to Canada's Aviation Hall of Fame in 1973, for example, partly for the Ellsworth expedition. But 'Bertie,' as friends knew him, was always self-deprecating about his accomplishments. When his children asked why he had received some award, Hollick-Kenyon would answer: 'Brushing my teeth every day.'[49] A television interviewer who in 1972 asked about the naming of the Hollick-Kenyon Plateau was told: 'Since my return to Canada I've tried to sell lots there, but so far no one has bought one.'[50] Hollick-Kenyon died of cancer in Vancouver on 30 July 1975.

Pat Howard joined Wings Limited in Winnipeg on his return to Canada in 1936, and jumped to Trans-Canada Airlines the following year as a pilot instructor. Howard later became a test pilot, first for Canadian Associated Aircraft Limited, then in 1942 for Boeing Aircraft of Canada, based in Vancouver. Married in 1945, he was transferred to Seattle that same year where he test-flew B-29s. After the war, Howard tried unsuccessfully to establish his own airline in British Columbia. In 1947 he had a three-month stint with Canadian Pacific Airlines before becoming a businessman in the Toronto area. He resumed his aviation career in 1969 to set up an air ambulance service for the Ontario Ministry of Health. In late 1971 he had a heart attack and he died of complications in Toronto on 19 June 1972.

Lymburner was given another shot at polar glory. Buoyed by the success of his 1935 flight across the continent, Ellsworth hatched an even more daring plan in early 1938. He proposed another trans-Antarctic hop that would take him from Enderby Land, in the Indian Ocean sector of the continent, across the South Pole to the Bay of Whales, where his ship, the *Wyatt Earp*, would again pick up him and his pilot. The aircraft chosen was an all-metal Northrup Delta, powered by a 750-horsepower engine. With all but two seats removed from the passenger cabin, the low-winged aircraft had enough extra fuel tanks to push its cruising distance to two thousand miles, barely enough for the flight. Ellsworth's three previous expeditions had demonstrated the importance of finding a suitable flying field early in the season. To this end, he would bring along a small two-seater scouting plane built by the Aeronca company. Fitted with pontoons, the aircraft could direct the ship to the most promising starting point.

Although Ellsworth and Hollick-Kenyon respected one another, they never forged a friendship. Hollick-Kenyon's silent disposition was a lifelong obstacle to fellowship. And Ellsworth may have felt upstaged by this seasoned pilot whose skills with a sextant had saved their necks when Ellsworth failed to notice the index on the instrument had slipped. Hollick-Kenyon had been the real navigator as well as airplane mechanic when their machine failed, and their radio repairman when the transmission equipment died. As one aviation historian, John Grierson, has put it: 'Reading between the lines, Kenyon, apart from his high skill in piloting, was the man who pulled the flight through.'[51]

Weeks after the 'rescue' at Little America, Ellsworth decided that Lymburner, not Hollick-Kenyon, would be the pilot for his next Antarctic expedition. Reporting this by letter to his wife, Lymburner was game. 'He has plenty of money so why not get some of it?'[52] As it turned out, the formal offer was more than two years in coming. In the meantime, Lymburner rejoined Canadian Airways at Oskelaneo, living with his wife and daughter in a cabin at the base. In April 1938 he received a telegram from Wilkins finally inviting him to sign on the Ellsworth expedition. Lymburner, energized by another crack at adventure, bought a house in Montreal and then arranged a one-year leave of absence from Canadian Airways. He asked a fellow Quebec flyer, James Burton Trerice, to come along as mechanic and reserve pilot.

Trerice was born in Amherst, Nova Scotia, on 15 January 1913, and left home at the age of sixteen for Moncton, New

Brunswick.[53] He learned to fly at a nearby airfield and there joined Canadian Airways as a pilot and engineer. In the summer of 1936 he was transferred to Charlottetown and the following year he left Canadian Airways, bought a plane, and flew hunters and fishermen into the bush from St-Jovite in northern Quebec. He soon crossed paths with Lymburner, and signed on with the Ellsworth expedition when Lymburner made the offer. The two left for Floyd Bennett Field in New York that summer to fit pontoons and skis to the Northrup and Aeronca. The *Wyatt Earp*, meanwhile, was taken out of mothballs at Ålesund, Norway, and provisioned for the coming trip to the south, the ship's first voyage in two years.

The *Wyatt Earp* arrived in New York on 12 August, and over the next four days the planes were loaded and last-minute supplies placed in the hold.[54] The ship and crew left on 16 August bound for Cape Town, where Ellsworth joined them in October. The expedition got under way on 29 October and for the next sixty-five days ploughed through restless seas and hundreds of miles of pack ice. The *Wyatt Earp* became so wedged in at one point that the propeller was left idle for almost two weeks while they awaited benign winds and currents to unlock the ship. Lymburner took to the air twice in the Aeronca to scout an exit.

Once, when the crew was building steam to ram a path through the pack, a piece of glowing coal from the smokestack set the fabric wing of the Aeronca ablaze. Lymburner had placed a hose on the plane, fearing just such an accident, and had the flames out almost immediately. With five thousand gallons of gasoline aboard, a fire could be devastating. On another occasion, two oak sheaths were ripped from the ship and a hole in the main hull gouged because of ice-ramming. The crew shifted cargo and used block and tackle to tip the *Wyatt Earp* on its side so repairs could be made below the water line.

Finally, on the first day of 1939, the ship sighted the coast of Antarctica at the Amery Ice Shelf. For the next nine days they poked along the eastward coast, battling shore and pack ice and narrowly escaping rogue icebergs. Once again Ellsworth was plagued by bad luck. None of the ice-fields they encountered was suitable for take-off on skis by the fully loaded Northrup Delta. Lymburner went aloft for a one-hour, forty-minute reconnaissance flight in the Aeronca in a desperate bid to find an ice plain. His report was not encouraging; the best hope was a small fjord farther east, but even here conditions were difficult. The *Wyatt Earp* nudged its way past bergs, shore ice, and pack for the next five hours and moored to the fjord ice on 10 January. On closer inspection, the ice proved strong enough to permit only a short take-off, dashing Ellsworth's dream of a long flight towards the pole.

The weather cleared at about noon the next day, giving Lymburner his first chance to test the ski-equipped Northrup since it had been stowed for shipment. Unsure whether the bay ice would even take the dead weight of the aircraft, Lymburner managed to take off successfully and declared the machine and its radio equipment in working order. On landing again, he and Ellsworth decided to ignore the darkening sky to the north and attempt their first exploratory flight of the expedition. Only enough gas for a three-hour flight was siphoned into the tanks. Five weeks' worth of emergency supplies was loaded aboard and just before 1 p.m. Greenwich time Ellsworth and Lymburner left on the first journey into the interior of this side of Antarctica.

They rose quickly to 1,500 feet to mount the wall of ice rimming the edge of the continent and continued climbing to about 11,500 feet as they followed the gradual ascent of the plateau. The only discernible feature below was a heavily crevassed region for the first fifty miles south, which denied them an emergency landing area. After passing farther inland, a white expanse slipped by devoid of mountain, ridge, or nunatak. Cruising at 135 miles an hour to save fuel (the machine could do 170 miles an hour) they estimated their gas tanks were half empty after about 240 miles. At their farthest south,

Ellsworth dropped a brass cylinder claiming the territory for the United States. They had discovered about eighty thousand square miles, an area larger than all the Maritime provinces. The flight back was uneventful and after homing in precisely on the ship, they circled it a few times and landed safely on the ice. A storm threatened, so the aircraft was quickly hoisted aboard.

The ship steamed northeastward to outrun the storm but the expedition was cut short days later when one of the crew members crushed his kneecap in an accident and had to be rushed back to civilization for surgery. The *Wyatt Earp* again fought desperately with the pack ice before finally making Hobart, Tasmania, on 4 February.

Lymburner and Trerice took a commercial steamer from Sydney, Australia, to Honolulu, where Lymburner disembarked to double-back to take the Suez route to Montreal. Trerice arrived in Victoria on 10 March and resumed his job in St-Jovite briefly before joining Trans-Canada Airlines. He remained with the airline until his retirement, and died on 28 August 1987, at his home in Crescent Beach, British Columbia.

Lymburner became chief test pilot for Fairchild Limited at Longueuil, Quebec, on his return to Canada. He flew the first Canadian-built Hampden bomber in 1940, and the firm's first Helldiver bomber in 1943. After the war, he organized a small airline based first in Mont Laurier, then in Roberval, Quebec. In 1953 he was managing airlines out of Mont Joli, Quebec, and Ottawa. He became a base manager at Churchill, Manitoba, in 1955 to help build the Distant Early Warning line. From 1958 until his retirement from aviation in 1964, Lymburner joined firms in Dorval, Quebec, and Frobisher Bay in the Northwest Territories. Beginning in 1964 he lived in Florida, managing a ranch and two hotels for a time before retiring for good in the early 1970s. He died on 5 August 1990 in Orange Park, Florida. Mount Lymburner, a 6,360-foot peak in Antarctica's Sentinel Range, commemorates his two trips south with Ellsworth.

EIGHT

A Secret
Military Mission

Aﾠ FTER TWO AND A HALF YEARS of grinding war, with men and equipment in short supply, the British cabinet decided in early 1943 to launch an unlikely geopolitical adventure on the other side of the world. A handful of men would be sent on a secret military mission to the barren shores of Antarctica's Graham Land, part of the narrow, arching peninsula that stretches towards the tip of South America. There they were to erect a permanent base, the first on the continent to be manned year round. Secondary bases would be established in the area and a program of meteorology and surveying begun. A special series of half-penny postage stamps would be issued bearing the names of territories claimed by Britain, and token postmasters appointed. One man would become a regional magistrate. Scientists were to accompany the mission, but science was of only secondary interest. Even as the European conflict was snipping the slender bonds between Britain and her once-mighty empire, the British war cabinet seized a chance to control a chunk of the planet's last freely available territory.

The glory days of empire may have passed, but Britain's world-conquering spirit was to flicker alive once more on the ice-battered beaches of Graham Land.[1]

Unlike its predecessor, the Second World War was a truly global conflict, sparing not even the south polar regions. At least twice in 1941, German raiding ships found harbour at Gazelle Basin in the Kerguelen Islands where they rendezvoused with a supply ship and took on freshwater. And much of the Norwegian whaling fleet – two factory ships, eleven whale catchers, and a supply vessel – had been captured in Antarctic waters by German raiders on 14 January 1941. The two principal German raiding vessels that operated in sub-Antarctic waters had by war's end destroyed almost 200,000 tons of Allied shipping and captured 22,500 tons of valuable whale oil. The Royal Navy had accordingly stepped up sea and air patrols in the South Atlantic. At least four waterways in the Kerguelen Islands were mined by the Australians, and in March 1941 the HMS *Queen of Bermuda* dropped anchor at Deception Island to destroy a cache of coal and some oil tanks depoted there before the war by whalers.[2]

But the British war cabinet was little concerned about military strategy when it made the decision in 1943 to establish a permanent base in Graham Land. The Royal Navy was adequately equipped to counter the threat to commerce and shipping. Instead, wartime leaders in Westminster were annoyed by fresh territorial challenges to Britain's interests in Antarctica.

On 6 November 1940 Chile had issued a declaration claiming a wedge of Antarctic territory that encompassed the Antarctic Peninsula and which extended to the South Pole. And in November 1941 Argentina opened a post office at its meteorological station at South Orkney Island, a legally significant move under international conventions regarding territorial claims. Then in 1942 the Argentine naval transport *Primero de Mayo* stopped at several sites in and around Graham Land to raise the flag, leave an official territorial claim, and destroy previous British marks of sovereignty. The HMS *Carnarvon Castle* discovered these claims in January 1943 during a routine patrol to ferret out German raiders. The crew obliterated the Argentinian marks of sovereignty and restored the British equivalents. A few weeks later the *Primero de Mayo* returned and changed things back again. This sandlot diplomacy marked the first serious rivalry for territory in Antarctica. Although most expeditions until then had made competing territorial claims on behalf of supporting countries, the British-Argentine dispute was the first that threatened to deteriorate into a show of arms. Indeed, warning shots were actually fired in 1952 over this very territory, although there were no deaths or injuries.[3] The ten-week Falkland Islands war in 1982 demonstrated the persistence of this dangerous rivalry.

In the early 1940s it was clear that both Chile and Argentina believed Britain's war-weary state offered an opportunity finally to satisfy their claims on Antarctica. But Britain's own view as to her territorial rights in the south polar region remained steadfast, and was given credibility by the many Antarctic expeditions that left her shores and planted her flag on the ice. Indeed, at the 1926 Imperial Conference, Canada and other delegates had ratified British policy on Antarctica, made formal in 1920, that 'the whole of the Antarctic should ultimately be included within the British Empire.' The European war beginning in 1939 may have diverted scientific resources from the Antarctic, but it also clarified the geopolitical importance of certain outposts of the old empire.

And so in May 1943 the British war cabinet decided it had been pushed too far; a military unit would occupy strategic points in the region to assert more forcefully Britain's claims. Naval Party 475, its official name, was hastily assembled in the autumn of 1943, its fourteen men under strict orders not to reveal to anyone the purpose or destination of their mission lest it prompt a pre-emptive strike by the Argentines. The expedition was told to begin 'a more or less continuous occupation'[4] in the region. As fate would have it, this bold assertion of

British sovereignty was eventually to be led by a Canadian colonial, Captain Andrew Taylor of Winnipeg.

In its earliest planning stages, the mission was assigned the code name Operation Tabarin, after the Bal Tabarin night club in occupied Paris. One story has it the name was chosen simply because the shore party would spend a long winter night in the Antarctic. Yet another account says the name referred to the chaotic and sometimes burlesque preparations for the mission. Some who witnessed the anarchy first hand had yet a third explanation: like a night-club audience, the expedition members were kept continually in the dark by the organizers.[5]

The operation[6] was overseen by a three-man advisory committee, each of them Antarctic veterans: James Wordie, a Shackleton man, ornithologist Brian Roberts, a graduate of a British expedition of the 1930s, and Neil Mackintosh, once head of a series of scientific voyages in the south polar seas. But day-to-day preparations fell to the expedition leader, Lieutenant-Commander James Marr. Marr got his start as a polar explorer with Shackleton when he was picked as a representative boy scout to sail on the *Quest* on what would be Shackleton's last voyage. When called back to England to lead Operation Tabarin, Marr was serving in a Royal Navy minesweeper in the Far East. Finding qualified men during the war was a tall order, and Marr may have seemed the best choice under the circumstances. He had never actually led a polar expedition and his Antarctic experience was restricted to sea-going rather than land-based ventures.

Andrew Taylor at the time was a surveyor with the Royal Canadian Engineers, stationed in Leatherhead, about sixty miles southwest of London.[7] Born on 2 November 1907 at Edinburgh, Taylor, along with his younger sister, had been taken by his parents, Robert and Jane Ann, to Winnipeg in April 1911. Robert Taylor was a plumber and had seen an advertisement extolling Moose Jaw, Saskatchewan, as Canada's next industrial centre. After a sea voyage and a rough five-day train trip from Halifax to Winnipeg, Jane Ann steadfastly refused to go any farther, so the family settled in Winnipeg, where Robert started a plumbing business.

In the late 1920s Andrew Taylor worked as a department store clerk and in threshing gangs when he was not helping in his father's shop. He graduated from the University of Manitoba in 1931 with a B SC in civil engineering and the next year became a dominion land surveyor working in northern Manitoba. In 1935 Taylor was hired as municipal engineer with the mining community of Flin Flon, Manitoba. There he met and married the local schoolteacher, Martha Jane Porter, in September 1939, and signed on with the Royal Canadian Engineers a year later. In April 1941 he was sent to Britain and by June 1943 he had been posted to Leatherhead, where his primary task was to train soldiers in the use of maps for the coming cross-channel invasion of Europe.

One Saturday morning in late September 1943 Taylor had started for London with a three-day pass in hand when his commanding officer caught him on the way out. 'They had had a request from the British for someone who was accustomed to surveying in very cold climates,' Taylor recalled.[8] Taylor had plenty of cold-weather field experience from surveying in Manitoba, including dog-driving. Told only that the Antarctic was his next posting, Taylor was ordered to report immediately to Marr at the fashionable Park Lane Hotel in London's west end. 'I knew almost nothing about the Antarctic – I barely knew where it was,' Taylor said later. His only previous exposure to the south polar regions was as a boy, when his father took him to lectures by Shackleton and Wilkins at Winnipeg's Walker Theatre.

Taylor was warned by his commanding officer to keep all information about the expedition in the strictest confidence. 'In my own experience in the army, the more secrecy there is about an operation, it generally indicates the incompetence of somebody running it who does not want that discovered,' Taylor said in an interview years later. That awkward maxim was borne out over the next few weeks.

The expedition's prefabricated hut, for example, was designed at Cambridge University using mortice-and-tendon joints, a construction technique entirely unsuited to Antarctic conditions and quickly abandoned when the expedition arrived in the south. Each specialist for the expedition was given a free hand to order his own supplies, whether or not he had any polar experience. As a result, much of the equipment proved useless and lay idle during the mission. A 250-ton wooden sailing vessel, the *Godthaab*, was refitted and rechristened the HMS *Bransfield* to become the expedition ship. The new name was politically essential, since the ship was owned and provided by the government-in-exile of Norway, the victor over Britain in the race to the South Pole thirty years before. Lieutenant Edward Bransfield of the Royal Navy had for the first time charted part of the Antarctic mainland in the early nineteenth century, and therefore was a useful historical figure for asserting primacy in the region.

During a raucous party aboard ship late one night in September 1943, a bulkhead was smashed, with consequent damage to the freshwater tanks, which in turn flooded the hold, delaying the departure by two months. Taylor used the time to visit his wife and newborn son in Winnipeg while the rest of the expedition members continued to order supplies. By the time the ship was finally ready to sail it was so perilously overloaded that Taylor and another member, Sub-Lieutenant Gordon Howkins, were ordered to travel south independently. Ironically, the only berth they could find was aboard an Argentine meat boat, the *Marquesa*, which was leaving Liverpool for Buenos Aires.

Neither ship managed to make the voyage. Soon after its midnight departure, the *Marquesa* struck a submerged wreck and took on twenty-six feet of water as it hobbled back to port. The *Bransfield*, meanwhile, left Tilbury in November but soon sprang a leak because of the enormous load. The ship limped into Portsmouth using auxiliary engines, somehow skirting submerged mines. With all the guns of the harbour trained on the suspicious-looking visitor, the *Bransfield* then ignominiously sank. Because it was so late in the season – the Antarctic summer lasting only from November to March – plans were hastily redrawn. There would be no expedition ship after all; instead, supplies would be sent by a military troop ship heading for the Falkland Islands as well as by a pair of vessels headed for Montevideo. Men and supplies would rendezvous at the Falklands, where two ships, the HMS *William Scoresby* and a private vessel, the SS *Fitzroy*, would ferry them to the Antarctic Peninsula.

The men sailed south in December on the *Highland Monarch*, part of a convoy that left Glasgow for Gibraltar, Dakar, and eventually Montevideo. At this last stop, Taylor spent six agonizing days in hospital after suffering a severe allergic reaction to the quinine in a glass of tonic water. Men and supplies rendezvoused at Port Stanley in the Falkland Islands on 26 January and the *Scoresby* and *Fitzroy* sailed south three days later with lights out and radios silent to thwart German raiders. On 3 February they sailed with some apprehension through the narrow entrance to the harbour at Deception Island.

The Argentinian flag had been painted on an abandoned fuel tank at the old whaling station, but neither Germans nor Argentinians were to be found anywhere in the harbour. Underground volcanic processes warmed the beach sand, steam from hot springs drifted across bleached whalebones, while sulphurous gases gurgled occasionally around the ship. The Union Jack was promptly raised after some quick repairs to the station flagpole, and the expedition's first base established in one of the still-serviceable whaler dormitories. Here four men would winter, led by geologist W.R. Flett, who was also appointed postmaster, magistrate, and coroner.

The two ships then pressed on towards Hope Bay, near the tip of the Antarctic Peninsula, to establish the critical mainland base. The *raison d'être* of the mission was to gain a toehold on the continent itself, as all previous British expeditions to the area had been located on islands. The ships arrived at the mouth of Antarctic Sound on 6 February and found a belt of pack ice barring the way to Hope Bay. The *Scoresby* proceeded through the ice and landed Marr and his team to pick a site for the hut while the thin-hulled *Fitzroy* dropped anchor a dozen miles off. As Marr dutifully scouted the terrain, the captain of the *Fitzroy* got cold feet, fearing the ice and wind would trap or destroy his vessel. He withdrew to safer waters with half the expedition's supplies, including the prefabricated hut, thus forcing Marr to abandon Hope Bay in favour of some less ice-choked spot on the western side of the peninsula.

With the season growing late and the captain of the *Fitzroy* spooked by the ice, Marr eventually was forced to settle for Port Lockroy at tiny Goudier Island, adjacent to Wiencke Island, as the main base. The locale, about two hundred miles from Deception Island, was a well-known anchorage and in fact had been visited by the Argentine ship *Primero de Mayo* the year before. But the site did nothing to advance the geopolitical goal of Operation Tabarin. For one, it was on yet another island. For another, the sea ice girding the bleak outcrop was so unreliable that the expedition would never be able to travel onto the mainland.

Supplies for the base had to be hauled up a steep rock face forty feet above the shore – Heartbreak Hill it was soon dubbed – and setting up took many weeks. 'The hard, awkward outside work, and often the foul weather, induced an excess of swearing,' Sir Vivian Fuchs wrote in *Of Ice and Men*, an official account of the expedition and its aftermath. 'To counter this it was decreed that anyone using bad language at the dinner table should carry up an extra sack of coal from the beach. Soon their anxiety was lest the hut entrance become totally obstructed by the accumulation of sacks.'[9]

Even exploring the island heights was a daunting task. There were no dogs on the expedition to help haul bulging sledges, so manhauling was the order of the day. Taylor thought the omission of dogs yet another example of fuzzy planning by Tabarin's trio of advisers, or the 'block-and-tackle brigade,' as they were dubbed by one of the frustrated men. After all, Wordie, the most senior of the three, was a graduate of the so-called heroic age of Scott and Shackleton, when the dismal chore of dragging a sledge was thought noble. Worse still, Tabarin's men had been provided with skis but no training in their use, forcing them to learn as best they could while on the trail.

The two supply ships departed for Port Stanley on 17 February and the eight men settled in for the long polar night. They were north of the Antarctic circle so they never lost the sun entirely, although the mountain range to the east cast them in deep shadow when the sun hung low in the sky. The *Scoresby* made two more short visits to Port Lockroy with supplies, but by the end of April they were on their own. Contact with the outside world was maintained with their second-hand army radio, although everything had to be sent in code to keep confidential the aims of the mission. Transmissions were kept to a minimum.

The official history of Operation Tabarin and its immediate successor, the Falkland Islands Dependencies Survey, paints a picture of Marr as a gregarious, inspiring leader during this first winter of isolation. 'On special occasions after the day's labours they held a party,' writes Fuchs, 'Marr reciting his most recently composed monologue, or accompanying their songs on his mouth-organ as alternatives to gramophone music.' But in reality, Marr was withdrawn, pensive, and fretful. His black moods became worrisome to some of the men who detected signs of a mental breakdown.

The main purpose of being there was to get on the mainland, not to occupy a little island a couple of hundred feet long like we were at Port Lockroy [Taylor said years later]. If you're going to claim a continent, you want to be on it, not 10 miles away from it.

And in that sense he (Marr) probably realized more than any of us how ... the first year had been a failure, and I think it likely preyed on his mind ... He was a very, very introverted man. He was a nice chap, a kindly person, but he didn't have the experience that a man should have had to do what was going to be done down there. He would find the hardest way of doing things to show how tough he was.[10]

Daily life during the winter was anything but military, and each man was free to take up his special responsibilities without direction. The easy-going attitude towards research reflected the secondary importance of science to the expedition. However, surveying – Taylor's profession – was essential to their geopolitical aims. Among the first tasks was to establish their precise latitude and longitude. Taylor did so with such skill that the numbers have not been altered since his reports. Taylor also struggled with a clockwork camera, dating from 1903, to take six-foot-long panoramic photographs of the area from the heights of Wiencke Island. They had no distance-measuring meters for their army sledges, which themselves had to be greatly modified to suit conditions in Antarctica.

Recreation in the hut consisted mainly of card-playing, listening to the gramophone and reading. The *Port Lockroy Prattler*, the limited-circulation expedition paper, appeared occasionally, its unsigned articles usually spoofing some mundane aspect of the daily routine. The expedition also had an excellent polar library and Taylor used much of his spare time to bone up on Antarctica's thin history. The men drank alcohol almost every evening, partly because the expedition was being run by naval veterans, but excess drinking never became a problem.

By spring, a four-man team with two sledges ventured out to explore the confined territory of neighbouring Wiencke Island. It was during this month-long trip that inexperience nearly cost them their lives. The four – Marr and another man hauling one sledge, Taylor and botanist Mackenzie Lamb hauling the other – were crossing a glacier at the base of a two-thousand-foot cliff. 'Nobody down there had had any experience in the Antarctic except Marr, and his experience was aboard ship,' Taylor recalled in an interview. 'And what was needed at this point was someone who knew about mountaineering. There wasn't anyone to tell us we were going too close to the face of this mountain.'[11]

Each sledge was packed with 650 pounds of gear and supplies, far more than necessary for the trip. They soon came to an area strewn with blue-ice blocks that barred the way. 'I don't know any more soul-destroying task than pulling the dead weight of a sledge like that for hour after hour,' Taylor said. 'And you get kind of stupid at that stage and you make stupid remarks and you ask stupid questions. So I said to Lamb, "I wonder where these ice blocks came from?" And he gave me a withering look. He said, "There's only one place they can come from – up there." And whether it was the vibration of his voice that triggered it, it started to fall.'

The avalanche began with a gunshot sound, then turned into a deep rumbling as tons of snow and huge blocks of ice hurtled like a deadly curtain down the face of the cliff. 'For some time, probably only a second or two, we stood still in our harness, terrified, and watching in a kind of fascination the huge blocks that seemed to overwhelm us,' Marr wrote in the official account. 'Even as we hesitated the avalanche had reached the level of the glacier and was now churning up before it a dense white cloud of powdered snow which rolled towards us with the speed of an express train.'[12] Before the avalanche, Taylor and Lamb had veered towards the edge of the glacier to skirt a depression in the ice. 'But suddenly, the depression that we'd been trying to avoid took on all the appearance of the Garden of Eden,' Taylor said years later. 'We went down towards it as fast as we could. Then this great thud took place behind us and pieces of ice [were] rolling past on either side of us. Lamb lost his hat and his mitts from the force of the blast.

'And then it was all quiet. A little bit of snow dust in the air and that gradually settled. And absolute silence in the end.'[13] To the surprise of all, there were no injuries and all of their equipment survived the deluge intact. Marr's report conceded that the team had 'approached rather more closely to the precipitous North Wall than perhaps was wise.'[14] Taylor dubbed the spot Thunder Glacier, and so it remains today.

The *Scoresby* returned in mid-November with fresh supplies, including soil and plants for a gardening experiment and a young pig named Gertrude who ate table scraps for months before she herself became a main course. Marr, clearly eager for the opportunity for escape, left Port Lockroy for passage to the Falkland Islands, where he planned to ask the governor to be relieved of duties. 'He walked out the door and looked over his shoulder, saying "By the way Taylor, I'm leaving you in charge",' Taylor recalled.[15] The group was unclear about Marr's intentions, and in fact it would be several months before Marr was able to persuade the governor of the seriousness of his mental condition. In the meantime, Taylor was given only the barest outline of what was expected of him.

The plan now was to replace the Port Lockroy men with a smaller team of four to continue weather reports from Bransfield House, as the Port Lockroy hut was now called. All efforts would then be concentrated on finally establishing a base at Hope Bay to start an occupation of the continental land mass. On 3 February 1945 Taylor and crew were taken back to Deception Island. Four days later, while hauling bags of coal for the next winter's supplies, Taylor was called into the base headquarters, where the governor waited with Marr at his side. Taylor was asked formally to take charge of Operation Tabarin and to be leader of the proposed Hope Bay base. 'I didn't have very much time to make up my mind, so I said yes,' Taylor remembered. Tough, methodical, thrifty, and with a flair for numbers, the new leader would inject some belated direction into the sputtering enterprise.

Even though he was relieved of responsibility, Marr did not improve. 'The next day, Marr's physical and mental condition seemed to have deteriorated and, in consultation with [Surgeon-Lieutenant Eric] Back, we became most apprehensive he might do himself some permanent harm,' Taylor wrote to the governor in confidence. 'One could sense and sympathize with the tremendous mental and emotional struggle which he was attempting to cope with in this decision which he had made.'[16] (Published accounts of Marr's relinquished command all carefully refer to his problems as entirely physical.) Taylor made immediate arrangements to have Marr evacuated by ship lest he create unnecessary chaos just when the expedition was attempting to redeem itself. As for the promotion of a Canadian to the head of a British team, Taylor said later: 'I often wondered why a colonial was put in charge. But I never felt any sense of resentment [from the men] – we were all good friends.'[17]

A spirited Newfoundlander was to provide Taylor with some critical help. Captain Robert C. Sheppard had been lured from his job as harbour master at St John's, Newfoundland, to command a ship that would take the men to Hope Bay. At London's request, Sheppard had commissioned the ss *Eagle*, a steam-powered wooden sealer built in Norway in 1902 and among the last of her kind. Although the 550-ton ship leaked badly and devoured coal, it was the only one of the expedition's vessels that had a fighting chance against the ice floes. Sheppard's skill and tenacity won him quick and lifelong admiration from Taylor and the others. On the voyage south, for instance, Sheppard had slipped on a ladder during a vicious storm and cracked two ribs but, realizing he was the only qualified officer aboard, endured considerable pain to carry on. The *Eagle* and her crew of Newfoundlanders would prove to be as spirited as her captain.

Another boon was the arrival of twenty-three sledge dogs. The Colonial Office, apparently having twigged to the folly of manhauling, had sent a zoologist to Labrador to obtain huskies. These were put under the care of Lieutenant David James, newly appointed for the season though with no dog-driving experience. Her decks groaning with supplies, huskies tethered in every free spot, the *Eagle* finally steamed out of Deception Island on 11 February. Less than a day later, she sighted the deep waters of Hope Bay, three miles long and a mile wide.

Despite its reputation as ice-choked, the bay was miraculously free of floes this season. Only a strong wind prevented the *Eagle* from dropping anchor immediately.

While the ship plied the harbour, Taylor took charge. He called the fourteen-member shore party together to announce they would take an entire day to chose the hut site. The men were divided into six pairs and given quadrants to explore. They were to look for a level spot in the gravel away from the stench and noise of the nearby penguin rookery, with access to a freshwater glacier stream. The site must also be close enough to the sea for landing supplies and ideally would give year-round access to the interior via a glacier at the head of the bay.

Meanwhile, Lamb the botanist was ordered to take the camera and record the remains of the first and only previous dwelling erected at Hope Bay. It was an emergency stone hut built in 1903 by three stranded members of a Swedish expedition led by Otto Nordenskjold. The trio had been landed at the spot on 29 December 1902, by the *Antarctic,* a former Norwegian whaler, after the ship was unable to relieve the main shore party at a hut on nearby Snow Hill Island. The three were to sledge the distance from Hope Bay to the island but found the sea ice unreliable. They returned to Hope Bay but to their horror soon realized that the ship was unable to reach them again, forcing them to overwinter with few supplies.

In one of the great survival sagas of the Antarctic, they built a stone hut and dined on seals, penguins, and fish until they finally met an astonished Nordenskjold on the trail on 12 October 1903. 'Never before have I seen such a mixture of civilization and the extreme degree of barbarousness,' Nordenskjold wrote in describing the moment he stumbled across the three, who were black with blubber soot from head to toe. 'My powers of guessing fail me when I endeavour to imagine to what race of men these creatures belong.'[18] Nordenskjold's companion advised getting a revolver at the ready in case these Antarctic aborigines proved violent. But the strange visitors simply held out their hands and said 'How do you do?' and the mystery was quickly solved. In 1945 the stone-hut walls were still standing but the place was covered in guano from the tens of thousands of penguins that breed in the area. In the muck, Lamb found a rusted stove, pieces of canvas, a crowbar, and an old shoe.

Another relic retrieved from the stone hut was a tall wooden pole, which was then mounted upright on a corrugated-iron hut that was Operation Tabarin's first building at Hope Bay. By mid-afternoon on 15 February the Union Jack was hoisted, saluted, and photographed. Taylor's men spent more than a month landing supplies and constructing two other buildings, the main living hut, and a separate Nissen hut for storage. A constant menace was the high winds, which sometimes hit two hundred miles per hour and continually knocked away building materials. The roof of the corrugated-iron hut, which was used temporarily as a galley, had to be weighed down with three and a half tons of coal in sacks because the gusts would lift the structure right off the rocky beach. 'Every night after our labours, there were unbelievable winds,' Taylor recalled. 'I get the shakes even now when a big wind comes up.'[19]

Accidents threatened constantly but never blossomed into disaster. Taylor damaged his back trying to transport pieces of a large cook stove from the shore to the main hut, now called Eagle House after the ship. He was in pain for three weeks. The frames of the main building and the Nissen hut collapsed in the fierce winds on separate occasions during construction, forcing the men to begin again. On the *Eagle*, a careless smoker had tossed a match onto some boxes of gunpowder, causing an explosion that sent a barrel of beef masthigh. The ship was undamaged, though some briefly airborne supplies had to be fished out of the bay. The *Eagle* was also caught in a furious gale on 17 March that snapped an anchor line. An iceberg then gored the bow, and as the ship took on water, its remaining anchor was lost. Captain Sheppard radioed he would have to beach the ship on the rocky shore in a desperate attempt to save lives. But just as the moment approached the ship's pumps began to work again and the *Eagle* headed back out to sea. The crew managed to limp back safely to Port Stanley for repairs, though the incident denied the expedition many supplies that remained in the *Eagle*'s hold. No supply vessel managed to reach them again before winter, so without fanfare – or a final mail pick-up – the men were on their own.

Each evening Taylor tapped out yet another report on his typewriter, determined to record every minutia of the expedition. 'Quadruplicate Taylor,' the men called him. Unlike many of his British predecessors in the Antarctic, Taylor placed little faith in muddling through. Rather, he tried to build in margins of safety that in retrospect were sometimes excessive. The hut, for instance, was placed well back from the sea edge to keep it safe from ice and flooding but the choice also increased the distance for hauling supplies. Nevertheless, Taylor quickly earned the respect of the men for his tact, for his methodical and rational approach to decision-making, and for his care in gathering and weighing everyone's opinion.

Eight days after their arrival at Hope Bay, Taylor made a point of showing all the men the tentative drawings for the hut and asking their advice. 'Now that we are beginning to feel a bit cramped and cold in the tin galley, it is comforting to hear of such spacious accommodation,' David James wrote in his diary. 'It was a sound psychological move on Taylor's part to bring it up at this juncture.'[20] Taylor also won fast friends for his liberal liquor policy: rum served every night, with port, sherry and whiskey available Saturday nights. As at Port Lockroy, excessive drinking never became a problem.

On 8 May having learned by radio of VE Day, Taylor sent a message to the governor of the Falkland Islands: 'In these lonely outposts His Majesty's loyal subjects from England, Scotland, Wales, Ireland, the Falkland Islands, New Zealand and Canada join with the Empire to celebrate this historic day.'[21] Few of the men could have anticipated in 1939 that this moment would arrive while they were stationed on the desolate shores of Antarctica, about as far removed from the hostilities as one could imagine.

Their winter sojourn was brightened a bit by the appearance on 21 June of the first issue of the *Hope Bay Howler*, 'Guaranteed Circulation, 100 copies.' This illustrated monthly newsletter was the immediate successor to the *Port Lockroy Prattler*. It never attained the sophistication of the grandfather of Antarctic expedition papers, Scott's *South Polar Times*, though it offered the novelty of correspondents' reports from other Tabarin bases, thanks to the magic of radio. The humour was often sophomoric. Perhaps the most common theme was resentment towards the expedition organizers in London for keeping everybody in the dark about plans. Typical was the following:

PUBLIC NOTICE
Rumours have been circulating recently that we are likely to receive some news in the near future. The Government wish to make it quite clear that these rumours are entirely without foundation. There is no intention whatsoever of giving us any information.

Any person who knows the originator of these rumours must report at once to the nearest police station. It cannot be emphasized often enough that security is one of the chief pillars of democracy.[22]

An editorial in another issue noted:

The Hope Bay Signwriters Ltd. have been very busy lately making a sign for Eagle House and another for the Hope Bay Post Office. Readers should not jump to conclusions and assume that the presence of a post office indicates the prospect of mail ... insignificant persons such as they have no right to expect either information or mail.[23]

Fuchs, the chronicler of Operation Tabarin, identifies this phenomenon as the 'No one ever tells me anything syndrome,'[24] common on Antarctic expeditions, where isolation can breed resentment. However, wartime circumstances made this operation more secretive than most and the men were often denied the simplest information despite the opportunities that radio offered. For example, Taylor had the greatest difficulty obtaining the instructions that had been given to Marr for the command of the expedition. He eventually located the documents tucked away at the bottom of a box full of Marr's dirty socks and underwear.[25] To counter the sluggish flow of information at the top, Taylor vowed to make Tabarin Antarctica's best-documented expedition and made special efforts to pass on what he knew to the men.

The 21st of June the *Hope Bay Howler*'s debut, was also midwinter day, traditionally an occasion for celebration. The highlight was a thirteen-course dinner followed by plenty of spirits. In the weeks following, the men struggled to learn the rudiments of dog-driving. Bad weather in March had forced the *Eagle* to cache about twenty-five tons of supplies at a cove about three-quarters of a mile from the base. The men set about retrieving it, using dogs and sledges. They also made brief forays into the immediate surroundings to survey the local topography, to measure the flow of glaciers, and to collect fossils, especially on Mount Flora, the tallest nearby peak. The men even indulged in some ice-fishing, catching hundreds of edible notothenia of about half a pound each.

By spring, preparations for the first field trip of the season were well advanced. The number of dogs had been reduced to fourteen, or two teams of seven (some pups born in the winter would later replace the losses). Taylor had planned a three-man team for the modest thirty-day journey south along the east coast of the Antarctic Peninsula. 'However, James was so enthusiastic to go, and had looked after the dogs for most of their time here so had virtually assumed that he was going; so I was reluctant to leave him out,' Taylor wrote in a report explaining why he decided upon a four-man team.[26] The men were to survey and geologize, all the while acquiring sledging skills. Taylor also intended that two of the men should occupy Nordenskjold's 1902 hut on Snow Hill Island, depending on whether Ellsworth's expedition had left sufficient supplies during its visit there ten years before.

The proposed departure on 1 August was delayed for a week by incessant blizzards and a case of mange among the dogs. The weather cleared, the dogs improved, and they set out, soon discovering that temperatures on the Weddell Sea side of the peninsula were much colder than at Hope Bay.[27] On the second night out the thermometer plunged to –35° F, one of the lowest temperatures recorded on the trip. Their sledges were overloaded and made the going slow at the outset. Taylor chose to snowshoe for much of the way while the rest of the men used skis. Six days after setting out they made a depot to lighten their sledges, leaving behind three of four sets of skis and a rifle that refused to fire.

Taylor ordered stricter rationing the next day when it was discovered they had used two-fifths of their cooking paraffin though they had been out just one-quarter of their intended time. On 20 August, James stumbled upon some welcome news. While trying in vain to contact the other bases on an inadequate field radio, he managed to catch a 6:45 p.m. newscast from overseas. 'Not having heard anything for a fortnight, it was a wonderful surprise to learn that the Japanese war was just ending,' James wrote in his diary. 'Down here in this remote and silent land, one's own little problems assume such importance that there is hardly time to think of the outside world and, until this moment, we had not given the news a single thought.'[28]

They made their farthest-south camp on 23 August, near Cape Longing, then headed almost due east to round James Ross Island for the run home. A few days later they located a small Swedish food depot left there forty-three years before. Tea, sugar, biscuits, sardines, and a tin of pâté were duly added to their own dwindling supplies. But the most exciting prospect was Nordenskjold's hut, which Ellsworth had reported was in good condition when he paid it a visit in 1935. 'So often had we read about it that there was a touch of unreality about actually visiting the spot – rather as if one were taken to have tea with Sherlock Holmes in Baker Street,' James wrote in his diary. 'And apart from this aspect, we were looking foward to the good eats and comforts which we were sure awaited us.'[29]

Taylor and Lamb were the first to arrive. 'We found the building there structurally sound, but with no windows, many leakages in its walls and roof, and full of ice and snow to a depth of two feet, ice which holds everything in its relentless clamp,' Taylor wrote. 'It might be repaired if this ice was melted out, but this would be quite a task. We found no food stuffs, but came away with some relics and candles.'[30] There was also no obvious sign of Ellsworth's visit. James arrived some time later: 'It was as though one had been invited to a wedding and gone to a funeral by mistake,' he wrote in his diary that night. 'Over everything hung an air of indescribable gloom, and in probing about I was filled with a feeling of desecration.'[31] A few days later they located another depot left by Nordenskjold's Argentine rescue ship, the *Uruguay*. After scraping away the guano and ice, they discovered corned beef, rice, beans, and sugar, which were loaded onto the sledge. 'In the ruins they discovered a case of booze that was intact,' one of them later recorded in the *Howler*; 'it did not remain so for long.'[32] The discovery of this cache was thick with irony. Here was a British team, inadequately provisioned, attempting to establish sovereignty while relying on food and drink from a rescue depot laid down four decades before by the rival Argentines.

The trip back to Hope Bay was stymied by soft, deep snow. They had only one pair of skis among them, in addition to Taylor's snowshoes, having rashly left the other three pairs near the start. Dog pemmican and paraffin were also running dangerously low, and the weather got worse. Slush lurked under the soft snow, which soaked their boots and then froze. 'I remember trying to take my moccasin off (or whatever I was wearing at the time) and it was frozen securely to the sock underneath it,' Taylor recalled. 'And then when I went to try to take the sock off, the sole of my [left] foot was coming off with it so I slapped them back together and put the moccasin back on and went to bed. I didn't have any bandaids big enough to replace the sole of my foot.'[33]

Desperate, they made an emergency depot of unneeded equipment and geological specimens on 4 September and ploughed ahead in snow that came up to their hips. 'We are fortunate indeed to be under the leadership of Taylor, whose considerable experience of sledging in Northern Canada is invaluable at this sort of juncture,' James wrote in his diary.[34] The dogs flagged on their half-rations, and on 7 September Taylor ordered the weakest one shot in order to feed the stronger companions. The next day the animals pulled with vigour and the surfaces improved. Wearily they arrived at base four days later, having been out five days longer than intended and travelled a total distance of 271 miles. 'Since their return they have amazed the population by the apparently limitless capacity of their stomachs which have been working overtime for this past week,' the *Howler* reported 21 September. Taylor acknowledged in his final report that taking James along was a mistake: 'In the light of subsequent events, three would have made a much more efficient, homogeneous and harmonious party.'[35] They had also learned the importance of having skis always at the ready for soft surfaces.

The November 1945 edition of the *Howler* had carried the following advertisment: 'The Mayor and Aldermen of Hope Bay give notice that, following the custom on the St Lawrence [River], they will present a cigarette holder mounted in silver to the captain of the first vessel entering Hope Bay in the 1945–6 season. This offer holds until January 1st, 1946.' But the only thing to arrive by New Year's Day was a heat wave, which eventually pushed the temperature to 49° F and created flooding around Eagle House. Finally on 14 January, without warning, HMS *William Scoresby* sailed into Hope Bay to relieve the men.

With the war ended, Taylor chose to return home after five years away from his family. He had succeeded in carrying out the primary goal of establishing a base on the mainland. Others would assume the less glamorous chore of making the occupation continuous. Operation Tabarin, the secretive wartime mission, had become the prosaic Falkland Islands Dependencies Survey as the Royal Navy passed the baton to bureaucrats at the Colonial Office.

Meanwhile, another ship sailing out of St John's, Newfoundland, had been commissioned for the expedition from the Canadian government, the MV *Trepassey*, one of ten 325-ton wooden vessels built in Newfoundland during the war. To the men's delight, she was placed under the command of Captain Sheppard. On board was another group of huskies collected along the Labrador coast that, with the Hope Bay pack, were to be the patriarchs of a dog colony that survived for decades.

The Hope Bay region itself gained a kind of cinematic immortality shortly after the war. In early 1947 James returned to Eagle House with two cameramen to film background scenes for *Scott of the Antarctic*, the meticulously presented British film about Scott's fateful expedition. The following year tragedy struck: Eagle House burned to the ground in an accident that killed two men. The British abandoned the site until 1952, when a team sent to rebuild the base discovered that the Argentines had set up their own base nearby. The Argentine commander ordered his men to fire over the heads of the British to prevent their occupation. After a toughly worded diplomatic protest by the British in Buenos Aires, the Argentines relented and a new British base was soon built.

Taylor returned to London via the Falkland Islands aboard HMS *Ajax* in February 1946. For four months, he borrowed a study at an estate in Sussex, where he completed his sledging reports and other paperwork. In June, Taylor travelled by troop ship to Halifax, reporting at Ottawa before returning home to Winnipeg. A short trip back to Flin Flon persuaded him that all the best postwar civilian jobs in Canada had been taken, so he accepted an offer to remain in the Canadian army, stationed in Ottawa. Taylor continued his military career for the next seven years, and was promoted to the rank of major. In 1947 he was Canadian observer in a US task force that established a weather station at Resolute Bay, Cornwallis Island, in the High Arctic. While there, Taylor discovered some relics from Captain Henry Kellett's 1852–4 expedition to search for the lost Franklin expedition.

Taylor attended McGill University's summer school in geography in 1948 at Stanstead, Quebec, and a year later began work on an MA at the Université de Montréal. All courses were taught in French. Taylor spoke not a word, but less than two years later he had absorbed the language, completed his master's thesis (on the history of arctic exploration in Canada), and finished the coursework for his PH D, which was awarded in May 1957. Both his theses were later published and remain standard reference works for the study of Canada's Arctic.

Taylor was also involved in siting the radar stations for the Distant Early Warning Line in northern Canada. And he helped his faithful sledging companion, Ivan Mackenzie Lamb, land a job at the Victoria Museum in Ottawa, where he became Canada's foremost botanist. 'I think he named some miserable little lichen after me,'[36] Taylor recalled. Eventually returning to private survey work in Winnipeg, Taylor lives there alone in retirement 'burning food,' as he likes to say. He never returned to the Antarctic, which nevertheless set him upon a lifelong course of polar studies.

Taylor had mixed emotions about his Hope Bay experience. In 1953 Britain awarded the prestigious Polar Medal to the men who helped build the mainland base – to all except their Canadian commander. Taylor never learned whether the British government simply forgot, or did not want it widely known that the base was established by a Canadian, which might have undermined the geopolitical purpose of the mission. Taylor reluctantly accepted when he was awarded the medal a year later. The British also failed to notify the Canadian army of Taylor's increased responsibility in the Antarctic during 1945–6. He was given a promotion in due course, but it was not made retroactive, and he was thus deprived of much-needed pay. His many friends and admirers in Canada, however, were keen for

Ottawa to make amends and launched a campaign in 1985 for formal recognition of his polar achievements. Taylor was duly appointed an officer of the Order of Canada on 23 June 1986, and other honours soon followed. About two miles from the head of Hope Bay lies a flat-topped mountain about 3,200 feet high. Though it was discovered in the early 1900s by the Swedes, it has been christened Mount Taylor for the Canadian who gave Britain a toehold on the Antarctic continent.

NINE

Science over Politics

Halff A CENTURY after Hugh Evans was flattened
by a storm as he checked scientific instruments at Cape Adare,
another young explorer found himself in the same predica-
ment on the other side of the Antarctic.

Fred Roots, a geologist from Western Canada, left his base
hut in Queen Maud Land on the morning of 16 May 1950,
headed for a small igloo containing instruments to measure the
earth's magnetic field.[1] The igloo, about five hundred yards
from the main hut, kept off the wind while Roots took notes in
the sputtering light of a candle. The short trip out had been
uneventful. Though the sky was like pitch, the route was well
marked by stakes and the winter breezes moderate. Back by
about one o'clock, Roots had told his colleagues.

But shortly after noon the weather deteriorated into a near-
hurricane. A sleeping bag and food supplies in the igloo could
sustain him for days, but Roots was determined to keep his
promise to return by one o'clock lest a search party place more
lives at risk. He grabbed a spade on his way out into the swirling

Antarctic darkness. The wind made walking impossible. Roots had to hug the ground lest the gusts get under and carry him off. As he bellied forward, the blasts shoved him back, so he used the spade to chip toeholds in the ice surface. All the while the gale whipped the breath from his lungs and the snow blinded him. Slowly he gained ground, laboriously digging toeholds, crawling ahead, locating the next stake, eyes sealed shut against the stinging snow. Often he had to stop to rest. Part way along this horizontal stairway, the gale grew fiercer still. 'I might just as well crawl forward as crawl back,' Roots thought, and continued to inch towards safety like a half-frozen caterpillar.

As one o'clock passed, the men in the hut grew uneasy. 'Now, Fred is a tough and experienced mountaineer from the Rockies,' expedition leader John Giaever recalled later. 'We were just beginning to know this silent Canadian, and we suspected that nothing less than a violent gale could keep him. Besides he had remarked that he would be back by one o'clock. When one o'clock came we were on the verge of a hurricane, and there was no sign of Fred; but we had to allow for the possibility that he was already on the way.' Two of the men donned furs and grabbed some rope to begin the search. But just before they headed out, Roots staggered through the doorway exhausted, his face crusted over with ice. 'Oh, I am so sorry,' he said faintly, trying to catch his breath.

Queen Maud Land, an ill-defined stretch of Antarctica that faces Africa, was little explored when Roots and his colleagues established the first base there. The only previous comprehensive exploration in the region was a photo-reconnaissance by Germany in 1938–9, ostensibly to build territorial legitimacy for a small German whaling fleet in the Antarctic. The expedition used a so-called catapult ship, the *Schwabenland*, originally used to refuel Lufthansa mail planes travelling between Africa and South America. Aircraft would land on their bellies in the sea, get hoisted aboard ship for refuelling, and then be launched at about ninety miles an hour by an elaborate sling-shot.

The expedition, led by Captain Alfred Ritscher, used two

planes to photograph vast stretches of Queen Maud Land without establishing a mainland base. The aircraft were Dornier Super Wals, with two propellers, one pulling, the other pushing. Luftwaffe chief Hermann Göring was especially keen to know how the planes would function in cold weather, such as might be encountered in a military campaign against the Soviet Union. The ship sailed from Hamburg on 17 December 1938 without fanfare but the Norwegian government soon became aware of its destination. A month later, on 14 January 1939, Oslo declared sovereignty over the whole of Queen Maud Land based on coastal exploration carried out earlier by Norwegian nationals. Undaunted, the Germans launched their first flight less than a week later. In addition to hundreds of photographs of the interior, they dropped five-foot aluminum markers every twelve to eighteen miles along their flight paths to support any subsequent claim Germany might make in the region. In all, seven lengthy flights were completed by 23 January covering almost one hundred thousand square miles. The Nazi government officially acknowledged the expedition on 9 March and announced the results.

By far the most important discoveries were ranges of mountains about two hundred miles in the interior. Nestled among some of the peaks were frozen blue lakes, one of them encircling an iceberg within its five-mile width. But because the air photos were not supplemented by land-based surveying, the maps produced by the Germans proved wildly inaccurate. Plans for a second German expedition were scuttled because of the Second World War and almost twelve thousand negatives perished with the fall of the Third Reich.

The first published photographs of the Queen Maud Land mountains caught the attention of a Stockholm glaciologist, Hans Ahlmann.[2] In 1943 he wrote to J.M. Wordie – who was then planning Operation Tabarin – to propose a Swedish-British expedition to the region when the war ended. With Wordie's support, the Norwegians were consulted after the war, they being the sole claimants of that Antarctic sector. A detailed proposal was subsequently drawn up in 1948 for an international assault on the continent, the first time independent countries supported an Antarctic expedition as equal partners. 'Scientists in the three countries ... welcomed [the plans] with enthusiasm. The very idea of an international expedition in the Antarctic was in itself enticing and new,' Giaever, a Norwegian national, wrote later.[3]

Ahlmann's chief interest in Queen Maud Land was the German discovery of mountain peaks poking through the Antarctic ice sheet. Studies of glaciers in the northern hemisphere had suggested a recent warming trend. Retreating ice left bare rock patches on which no life forms, such as lichens, had yet had an opportunity to grow. Was this a uniquely Arctic phenomenon, or were both polar regions becoming warmer. The mysterious reports of blue-ice lakes among the mountains suggested temperatures had risen enough in recent times to cause melting. Perhaps the Queen Maud Land peaks would exhibit bare patches at their intersection with the Antarctic ice sheet? Such a phenomenon would clearly indicate a global warming trend. Of the many scientific questions posed by the expedition planners, this was perhaps the most intriguing.

Under arrangements worked out between the three countries, Norway would supply the ship, the expedition commander, half the dogs, and all the ski equipment, and be responsible for meteorology; Sweden would provide glaciology expertise, the buildings, medical equipment, and most of the provisions; and Britain was to organize the geological research and provide tents, the rest of the dogs and radio equipment. Hundreds of letters from unskilled adventure-seekers poured in, including some from men who had been with the *Schwabenland* expedition. But finding qualified young scientists, especially those with cold-weather field experience, proved difficult. As they often did when filling Antarctic posts, the British scoured the Commonwealth. In Australia they eventually recruited a physicist, Gordon Robin. And in Canada they found an energetic young geologist.

Fred Roots, born in Salmon Arm, British Columbia, on 5 July 1923, was the son of an engineer who looked after hotels owned by the Canadian Pacific railway.[4] In 1924 the family moved to Banff, where Roots's father died five years later in a typhus epidemic. Living in the mountains gave Roots a taste for the outdoors. He worked at the Canadian government weather station in Banff from 1936 to 1938; joined a lumber camp at Squamish, British Columbia, in 1938-9; prospected for a Kelowna mining company in 1940; and helped survey sections of the Rocky Mountains for the Canadian government in 1941-2. Fascinated by the mountaineering work, Roots took up geology at the University of British Columbia during the war and became an instructor there; later he received his PH D in geology at Princeton. Beginning in 1943, he worked with the Canadian Geological Survey until a fateful day in 1949, when he received an invitation from the Royal Geographical Society.

'It was out of the blue at that stage,' Roots recalled. His mountaineering and published geology reports, as well as his work at Princeton, had become known to the expedition planners in London. 'I had just been busy organizing a rather extensive Arctic journey at that time and I had hoped to get the [Canadian Geological] Survey to sponsor it. And this other thing came along, and I had to decide which way to go, north or south.'

The proposed Maudheim expedition offered living expenses but only a token salary – a serious financial hurdle for someone who was then the sole support for his mother. 'We did some calculations to see if we could make ends meet with no wages for three years, and that was a gamble.' In addition, the geological survey did not second its staff to other work. Roots would have to quit his secure government post and hope to get rehired on his return from the south. 'I thought I had a chance probably to come back and work in Northern Canada again but I might not have a chance to get to the Antarctic.'[5] Roots accepted the offer. His assistant would be Alan Reece, a Briton who had been in charge of the Deception Island base in 1945-6 while Andrew Taylor established Operation Tabarin's Hope Bay base.

Because it drew on the resources and polar expertise of three countries, the Maudheim expedition was among the best equipped ever to sail for Antarctic waters. The expedition ship, the *Norsel*, was built as an icebreaking tug during the Second World War under orders from the Nazi occupation force in Norway. The hull, completed in 1945, was hauled to Flensburg, Germany, in 1949 for fitting out as a modern expedition ship. The Royal Air Force contributed two Auster reconnaissance aircraft for scouting the ice floes. Three caterpillar-tracked snow vehicles called 'weasels' were obtained from Britain. And Canadian Longyear Limited of North Bay, Ontario, supplied a two-ton ice-boring machine using relatively new technology that the company had tested in Alaska and Spitsbergen.

The heavily laden *Norsel* left Oslo on 17 November 1949, less than a month after her delivery from Flensburg. The ship docked at London six days later to pick up Roots, Robin and the RAF crews, along with more equipment, then continued to Cape Town to take on more supplies during a Christmas break. Final loading was carried out among the Antarctic ice floes when the *Norsel* rendezvoused with the Norwegian factory whaler *Thorshovdi* on 12 January. Without even sighting the whaler, the men knew by the smell of blood and whale offal that the ship was near. Using two dead fin whales inflated as bumpers, the *Norsel* drew alongside the whaler and used cables to transfer forty-seven dogs, five men, three weasels, the ice-boring machine, and two tons of dripping, bloody whale meat that spattered the crew and deck. 'We did need the meat, but this way of dealing it out struck some of us as unusually violent and overpowering after so many years of [war] rationing,' Giaever wrote.[6] As Roots put it: 'What had once been merely a cargo-cluttered sealer took on the gory appearance of a mediaeval slaughter-house.'[7]

The British dogs supplied to the expedition were recent descendants of the Labrador huskies that had begun their Antarctic career at Hope Bay under Andrew Taylor. Through some botched planning, these dogs were shipped from bases in the Antarctic Peninsula through the tropics to England, where many of them contracted hard-pad, a contagious disease in which the foot-pads swell and stink, the nails grow long, and hair falls off the tail. Veterinarians could provide neither remedy nor ready explanation. The British dogs were sent on to Oslo, transfered to the *Thorshovdi*, then shipped through the tropics again practically back to their starting point near the Antarctic Peninsula for transfer to the *Norsel*. More than a dozen of the worst-infected dogs had to be shot on the whalers' voyage south, while the remainder recovered only slowly once in Queen Maud Land.

After frustrating weeks spent dodging the pack ice of the Weddell Sea, the *Norsel* finally located a suitable landing spot near Cape Norvegia on 10 February. Here, in a sheltered bay, the ice front dipped low enough to unload supplies directly from the ship. The slope also rose gently enough, and without crevasses, to ease the transfer of supplies inland about one and three-quarter miles to a secure spot on the ice shelf. This base site was christened Maudheim. The unloading of materials and stores took less than ten days, and with two main huts nearly complete, the *Norsel* steamed off on 20 February. The fifteen men of the wintering party would be on their own for a year, though radio technology had so improved that by 13 March they were able to contact Oslo directly and be patched into the Norwegian telephone network. Later, they would even transmit photographs via radio. Snow began to drift over all of the base buildings. Stacked packing cases and canvas provided covered corridors between the structures.

Roald Amundsen had demonstrated forty years before that a base built on an ice shelf – the Ross Ice Shelf for his expedition – would be secure if placed far enough from the water's edge. Richard Byrd had also successfully established Little America in the same area as Amundsen. Even so, there was nagging fear among Maudheim's inhabitants that a chunk of the floating shelf might break away, turning the expedition into a sea-going venture. This concern 'found expression in flashes here and there – for instance, when the stove gave a jolt for no obvious reason or when the windows suddenly rattled,' Giaever noted. 'Sometimes, too, an air bubble in a firmly placed theodolite would move in the horizontal glass tube, thereby showing that the substratum was shaking – just a little. Or again, we would hear dull noises out to sea at night.'[8] As their subsequent observations were to show, the base actually rose and fell more than a yard because of tides. The ice shelf, they learned later, moved on a hinge of crevasses that lay several miles south.

A four-man team, including Roots, set out on 3 April on a reconnaissance of the immediate vicinity of Maudheim, partly to test equipment and become familiar with dog-driving. There was little for the science specialists to examine; no coastal mountains for Roots, and mere floating ice rather than inland ice for the glaciologists. In addition, Maudheim was altogether too west for field parties to reach the highest peaks of the mountain chain discovered by the Germans. After twelve days on the trail, the party and its two dog-teams pulled back into base and the men settled in for the long winter night.

Each expedition member was assigned a cubicle measuring just 6.5 by 4.5 feet, ill-heated and separated from the main living area by only a curtain. Giaever, who suffered from insomnia throughout his stay in the south, did not insist on a rigid schedule for the men and often wandered to the breakfast table late and bleary-eyed. Alcohol was used often to break the winter monotony. 'Every man must work out his own salvation in this matter: I find my own is best achieved with one or more drinks,' Giaever admitted. 'In the tiringly overcrowded conditions of Maudheim, cut off as we were from civilization, under the constant pressure of monotonous work, some opportunity must be provided for relaxation such as a festive evening brings.'[9] For their Antarctic cocktails, the ice-boring machine provided ice-cubes that had been formed from snowfall of the year 1800.

Expedition members, with three mother tongues, soon developed their own language, dubbed Maudheimsk. A patchwork of Norwegian and English, with some German and Swedish, it came so naturally that on the expedition's return to England the group's rapid-fire discussions befuddled friends, family, and reporters. English-speaking members studied Norwegian from phrase-books during the passage south. 'All of the technical people and all the scientists could speak English,' Roots recalled. 'Like all European scientists, they learned English as a scientific language. So the erudite talk was easiest in English and the small talk about whether the cookies were burnt or not was easiest in Norwegian.'[10]

Roots saw the pursuit of science rather than geographical discovery as the great adventure ahead. 'Exploration now offers its greatest attraction, and its most permanent rewards, not when undertaken for its own sake, but when used as a medium to meet the more indirect and much wider challenge of general scientific investigation,' he wrote, distancing the expedition from the slapdash approach of expeditions past. 'From the start, it was intended that the success of the expedition should be judged solely on what was brought back in its notebooks and specimen boxes.'[11] To some of the other non-scientists, though, Roots seemed rather too puritan. 'There may, in fact, be many so constituted that, like Fred Roots, they deny the romance of adventure under God's blue, frosty sky,' Giaever wrote, 'and devote themselves simply and solely to concrete and undreaming research.'[12] But Roots's mastery of geology, cold-weather travel, dog-driving, and mountaineering was essential to the survival and success of the expedition. These skills, combined with an even temperament, made him a natural leader in the field. Giaever spoke for others when he called his geologist a 'quiet, experienced and unfailingly helpful Canadian, whose sensible advice and instructions – precise but given in a modest and friendly way – came to mean so much for so many of the most difficult enterprises of the expedition.'[13]

As spring approached, Roots was assigned prime responsi-

bility for establishing the southern trail depots that would provide them a head start on their treks into the mountains some
two hundred miles towards the pole. He and Réece took two
teams of dogs on 8 September for a six-day route-finding
excursion. About forty-five miles south of Maudheim, they
staked out 'departure depot,' the main starting point for the
weasel trips to lay depots to the south. The route from Maudheim was marked with numbered flags. On 25 September,
Roots led a five-man party in two weasels for a depot-laying
trip back along this route.

Roots joined a second reconnaissance team to stake out a
route from departure depot to advanced base, the main depot
that would supply field parties working in the southern mountains. This trip, ending in the middle of November, included
the first landfall since the expedition had set out from Cape
Town nine months before.

In our explorations we came to a rocky hill which we found irresistible [one of the men recorded]. How wonderful it was to bask in the
hot sun! Even the rock felt warm, and the birds had left their traces all
around. The geologist Fred was like a calf let loose in a spring-time
pasture. Rock, after all, is his chosen work and his passion; and until
that day his only treasure trove had been a few pebbles from the
stomach of a penguin.[14]

With the route to the mountains now well marked, Roots led
a six-man, three-weasel party to advance base to deposit eighty
days' of supplies for the summer field parties. Less than a week
after setting out, the caravan encountered a heavily crevassed
area through which earlier parties had worked out a rough
route. Glaciologist Charles Swithinbank was given the task of
negotiating the first weasel through the area.

According to Roots, on his machine he had devised a curious steering
contrivance out of spikes and rope, so that with long reins he was in
fact able to steer the vehicle from where he skied along in the rear of

the loaded sledge ... Everything went splendidly over the critical area, but then the weasel broke free from its driver and proceeded on its own account, and quite blindly, across a very wide crevasse with an unusually sagging bridge. Luckily this held. Charles got hold of the reins again and steered the runaway machine on to safe ground.[15]

On the morning of 24 November the party arrived at their destination, the foot of a pyramid-shaped mountain that was to mark advance base. Here, in celebration, the 'weasel was driven right on to the rocks of Queen Maud Land, in a grand pageant with the flag flying, a large surveying parasol over the passengers, and a thermos of hot chocolat providing the toasts,' Roots wrote. Later he climbed the Pyramiden, as the mountain was dubbed.

Despite the gusty wind, at times of gale force, on the summit of the nunatak, the scene was peaceful, and perhaps typical of that entrancing quality of Antarctica – the combination of serenity and space, the furious storms, beautiful scenery and treacherous country that blends harmoniously to make a land which is completely indifferent to human activities and yet possesses an almost irresistible attraction for many men.[16]

Four days later, the weasel teams pulled back into Maudheim. So well had the journey gone that Roots soon led another weasel run to load the advance base with yet more provisions.

With trail depots bursting with supplies, it was high time for some exploration. A four-man glaciological party with two dog teams set out early on 19 December. About fifteen hours later, Roots led a four-man geological party with three dog teams toward Pyramiden and the mountains beyond. The departure was worthy of the Keystone Cops. Roots's report noted that while the merits of the fan hitch for connecting dogs to a sledge were debatable, the hitch was 'undeniably superior for entangling spectators. One driver carried his research a step further, and found his whip to be more effective in controlling the bystanders than his [dog] team. When the air cleared, Reece was standing forlornly, out of breath, several hundred yards away from Maudheim, watching his team and sledge disappear towards the Advanced Base, doggedly determined to get on with the field work, driver or no.'[17]

Roots's party reached advanced base on 6 January, and he and Reece immediately set out for a mountain chain eighteen miles farther south, while the surveyors began triangulation and photography.[18] So began months of continuous field-work, travelling from peak to peak, nunatak to nunatak, picking up specimens, and making extensive notes and detailed maps. One memorable moment occurred at a newly visited mountain on 29 January:

At the little col on the north ridge [surveyor Nils] Roer and Roots stepped from their skis on to dry gravelly ground where orange, white and black lichens and clumps of brilliant green moss nestled between the stones. ... In the moment of that first glimpse of greenness, Roer and Roots could not deny a feeling of kinship with these other representatives of the organic world; both men and plants seemed to be strangers and trespassers in an indifferent, implacable, inorganic land. One felt a real admiration for the adventurous pioneer spirit of a clump of moss.[19]

Elsewhere, the glaciology team had determined by the location of lichens on the exposed rock that the Antarctic ice sheet was not receding. Further exploration of the so-called frozen lakes determined that persistent local winds, which swept away snow cover, had exposed the underlying ice. There was no evidence in the 'lakes' or on the mountain tops of any warming trend to parallel the Arctic phenomenon. Indeed, they estimated that the ice levels had remained stable for one hundred years or more. The glaciologists, however, did make the unexpected discovery of two kinds of tiny spiderlike creatures clinging to pebbles in an ice-locked patch of rock. These creatures had apparently been frozen in the ice sheet when it first covered the once-lush continent and were freed when some patches of rock became exposed once again. Their tenacity in a desperately hostile environment made a deep impression on the men.

Ironically, the discovery of life in the interior of Queen Maud Land coincided with the tragic deaths of three men. In late February, after the *Norsel* had arrived with supplies and left again, four of the men from Maudheim took a newly overhauled weasel on a test run towards the sea. A sudden fog obscured the coastline, along which a well-travelled section of ice had broken away unknown to the men. The machine plummeted over the edge and into the sea. All four aboard jumped free only to plunge into the frigid coastal waters. Three were sucked to their deaths by sea currents under the ice edge while a fourth managed to scramble onto a small floe. There he shivered for thirteen hours before being discovered and rescued.[20]

The loss of men at Maudheim forced the return of some members of the field parties to take on routine repair and maintenance duties at the base. Accordingly, a member of Roots's team turned back to Maudheim, reducing the survey and geology party to three. Then barely two weeks after the three drownings came another tragedy. On 11 March Alan Reece was struck in the eye by a fingernail-size rock chip while he was hammering at a specimen. Despite searing pain, he managed to return to the field camp. He lost his sight completely in the damaged eye. With the little medication available, Roots tried to stop any infection. After consulting with Ove Wilson, a medical specialist travelling with the glaciology party, Roots allowed Reece to carry on in the field. Although occasionally painful, the now useless eye did not seem to worsen.

By a strange quirk of fate, Roots's brother Walter was leading a similarly bedevilled field party that same month on the island of South Georgia, about sixteen hundred miles to the northwest. Walter Roots was the only Canadian member of a six-man British expedition to the poorly charted island.[21] The team was led by Duncan Carse, and its chief goal was to produce the first accurate map of South Georgia. Existing charts were based largely on a quick sketch made by Captain James Cook when he discovered the mountainous island in 1775. Despite its long use as a base for whaling, South Georgia had become a geographical anachronism – 'a paradox of the inhabited unknown,' as Carse put it – for remaining unmapped. Describing himself as a freelance explorer, Carse secured the backing of the Royal Geographical Society and the Scott Polar Research Institute for the venture.

Born at Banff on 17 July 1927, Walter Roots graduated from the University of British Columbia in 1950 with a degree in physical education.[22] He left Canada to become a mountaineering instructor at an Outward Bound school in Eskdale, Cumberland, England, that same year and was recruited by Carse the following summer. The team arrived at South Georgia on 1 November 1951. A few weeks later the men completed the first crossing of the island since 1916, when Ernest Shackleton made a forced march to bring aid to his shipwrecked crew.

Walter led a four-man team into the interior again on 18 March. They had hoped to locate a depot left earlier that would allow them to stretch the trip out to three weeks of surveying. But after three days of travel to the depot site, they failed to find the crucial supplies under a heavy snowfall. Forced to retreat, they camped on 26 March just as the wind was rising. Their overturned sledge was weighed down with supplies and staked with skis driven into the ground. Each of the two tents was battened down with snow on the curtain. Guy lines anchored with ice-axes held the canvas fast.

Walter Roots and Gordon Smillie, a surveyor, were resting in one of the tents at about noon. Smillie was reading, Walter dozing, when a hurricane hit, packing winds estimated at 140 miles per hour. 'Suddenly I was out in the cold,' Walter recalled. 'There was no sign of the tent, but various boxes and a full 5-

gallon tin of fuel were bounding across the ice. Poor Gordon had been sitting up reading and had nothing but a few pages of his book, and the clothes he slept in.' The pair scrambled inside the other tent. 'Soon flying stones began to tear holes in the sides. These we tried unsuccessfully to patch with adhesive tape, but ended up just holding our hands over the largest holes.'[23] A loud crash indicated that the sledge had become airborne, and at least four skis had been broken in the process.

The wind died down after about fifteen hours, and the next day the men collected what gear they could find strewn over several miles. They hastily returned to the main base to discover that the hurricane had knocked down two buildings and beached several ships. The men set sail for England on 18 April after more than five months and five hundred miles of surveying.

Deep in Queen Maud Land, Fred Roots and his men were well fed and productive thanks to hard-working dogs and ample supplies. Reece's freak accident was their only setback. Indeed, the men were still out on the trail on 19 May, the beginning of winter darkness, when the sun disappears below the horizon for weeks. No precise date for their return had been agreed upon with Giaever, but by late May he was growing uneasy that another tragedy might be in the works. A relief team was soon dispatched only to discover Roots and company in good health and already on their way back to Maudheim. 'We felt it a little humiliating to be "rescued", just when we thought we were doing quite well,' Roots recorded.[24] Both groups pulled back into base on 30 May. Roots's team had been on the trail continuously for 189 days without support or resupply. By comparison, Scott's doomed manhauling march in 1911–12 had lasted only 150 days. The weasel-laid depots and dogs had made all the difference.

Reece's eye continued to deteriorate until it threatened to infect his remaining eye. Ove Wilson had never even observed an eye operation, yet it was clear he would have to perform one. Roots was appointed his assistant, and they set about creating surgical instruments from found materials at the base, such as iron scraps and welding rods. Wilson, meanwhile, radioed a former professor in Sweden for instructions on how to carry out the delicate procedure. Rehearsals were dutifully staged in the radio shack. On 21 July, in a makeshift operating theatre, Reece's eye was successfully removed during a two-hour and forty-minute procedure. According to Giaever,

among all the capable assistants [at the operation] it was Fred Roots who impressed me most. Smiling and evidently engrossed, he acted as assistant to the operating surgeon, carrying out the orders of the latter with precision and complete imperturbability ... He is one of the most congenial among all the people I have met on expeditions; this was due to his being so profoundly considerate for others and at the same time so sure of himself.[25]

With the return of the sun on 26 July, planning began in earnest for the final summer of sledging. Because the *Norsel* was to return in late December or early January, the field trips would of necessity be much shorter than those of the year before. The ice-boring machine had reached its farthest depth of 330 feet that August, thanks to infinite patience and improvisation. Among the results, the glaciologists determined for the first time that fallen snow developed into solid blue ice only at a depth of about 230 feet. But the biggest questions, the depth of the ice-sheet and the contours of the land beneath could be answered only through a program of ice seismology – that is, drilling holes, exploding dynamite, listening for and timing the echoes, and then calculating the distance of solid rock under the ice. This became the next major project, to be carried out over terrain already surveyed.

Roots and others left Maudheim on 27 September with dog sledges to begin the second season's geology in the mountains. The glaciologists, meanwhile, took the two remaining weasels and on 18 October began a three-month seismological journey, living in a caboose dragged by one of the vehicles. Penetrating south 375 miles, they recorded the ice sheet as 7,800 feet thick. And as they laboriously calculated the topography, they confirmed something only hinted at previously: under the ice, Queen Maud Land closely resembled the coastline of Norway with its irregular fjords and deep valleys.

The *Norsel* returned unexpectedly early on 22 December. Roots's party arrived back at Maudheim on 6 January. The ship had brought down a Swedish air crew, which eventually covered some one hundred thousand square miles of air reconnaissance and photography. Roots was aboard for one of these flights to view from the air the southern mountains he had so laboriously explored from the ground. On 12 January, amid frantic packing, Giaever ordered all but four of the loyal huskies shot. British authorities would not allow them to return home because of the risk of disease, but wanted four to examine. On 15 January the flags at Maudheim were lowered and the *Norsel* set sail for Britain. 'We came back with a lot of information ... established the basis for a sound, careful scientific study of the polar regions rather than an expeditionary exploration,' Roots recalled. 'Also, it was a good step forward in international cooperation. It had a strong influence on the ideas that led to the International Geophysical Year [1957–8] and from that to the Antarctic Treaty. So I think it was an influential expedition.'[26]

In Britain, Roots became a research fellow at Cambridge University in the Department of Mineralogy and Petrology and began the task of writing up his expedition work. Beginning in September 1953, he taught geology at Princeton for a year, then returned to Cambridge until January 1955, when the Geological Survey asked him to head an expedition to some remote Arctic islands. Three years later he was asked to establish the Polar Continental Shelf Project, intended to bolster Canadian claims to the Arctic by surveying and studying the Queen Elizabeth Islands right to the North Pole. He remained with the project until 1971, returning to the Arctic every year but one.

Norwegian authorities gave the name Rootshorga (Roots

Heights) to a small chain of peaks in Queen Maud Land to mark the work of Maudheim's energetic geologist. Fred Roots's labours were also honoured when the Norwegians gave his name to a basin on the west flank of Rootshorga, Fredbotnen (Fred Cirque) – a rare example of an Antarctic feature given an explorer's first name.

Fred Roots has returned to the Antarctic at least half a dozen times. Just before Christmas 1967 he visited the American South Pole station, and three and a half months later he stood at the North Pole as part of a survey for the Polar Continental Shelf Project. In 1973, he became chief science adviser for the federal Environment Department and in 1991 he was made adviser emeritus. Today Roots is one of Canada's reigning experts in polar matters, and has been a guest at Chilean, American and New Zealand bases in the south. His career has been so hectic that he is still trying to find the time to write up his geological reports from the Maudheim expedition.

Sharing Tales

10 December 1985: Three hardy skiers begin ascending a snowy slope leading to the Beardmore Glacier, the ice highway to the South Pole discovered seventy-seven years earlier by Ernest Shackleton. It is a historic moment for the three, two Britons and a Canadian, Gareth Wood. They are commemorating Robert Scott's death march to the pole,[1] and the geography suddenly resonates with the past. For near this spot, Scott ordered his ponies shot, sent his dogs back to base, and began manhauling in earnest. Like Scott, the modern adventurers are without radios or air support, using compasses for navigation, dragging every ounce of food and equipment behind them on sledges. They are almost half-way to their goal.

One of the three, Roger Mear, rushes far ahead of the others to drink in the breathtaking sweep of glacier that confronted Scott and Shackleton more than two generations past. But in just a few seconds, the spell of history dissolves like fog before bright sunshine. 'My eye was attracted to an unexpected movement at the base of the red cliffs on my left,' Mear later writes.

'It was – I was sure, there was no doubt – a figure, 800 yards away, and its significance exploded into our isolation. It disappeared from sight over the horizon, and I was left alone again to wonder if I had imagined it. Yet I knew it was not a fancy and, as I continued, I pondered what this awful event might mean.'[2] Mear presses ahead and spots a cluster of yellow tents and three men, an American field party doing geology in the mountains that channel the Beardmore south. He skies on and dutifully introduces himself with a handshake.

Wood, Mear, and Robert Swan have spent more than two years planning a traverse to the pole that will surmount the same challenges Scott faced. But bumping into the geologists ends their splendid isolation and effectively chops the 873-mile journey in two. The unexpected camp is like a supply depot and emergency back-up en route. In spite of his disappointment, Mear grabs his movie camera and turns back to record his companions' reaction to the discovery. As the two pull up, their gaze settles uncomfortably on the encampment ahead. The realization stuns them. Wood is in tears, swearing, while Swan falls despairing to his knees. Their independence has been snatched away in the blink of an eye.

'Can we invite you in for something hot?' says geologist John Goodge.[3] The hungry trio do not refuse. Soon they all gorge on lobster tails, steak, and broccoli, washed down with coffee, Earl Grey tea, and Amaretto. Over the next two days, they idle about the geologists' camp, washing themselves and their clothes and enjoying meals so vast that two of them suffer bouts of vomiting. 'It is 5:00 a.m. on the morning of the 11th and have not slept a wink,' Wood writes in his diary the day after meeting the Beardmore party. 'The trip objective is gone forever and can never be restored.'[4]

As if to confirm their bad luck, the three set off again for the pole on Friday the 13th. A month later, as they pull to within a day or two of their goal, Swan changes his underwear and socks, and smears on deodorant. Wood decides to put off changing into fresh clothes until after an expected hot shower at the end of the trip. The next day, they sight a line of flags marking the trail into the Amundsen-Scott Station at the South Pole, a collection of structures dominated by a broad geodesic dome sheltering the main buildings. They are soon inside the world's most southerly community, shaking hands with the residents. Hot food and tea are served.

'The Pole. Yes, but under very different circumstances ... ,' Scott had written on 17 January 1911.

Nothing highlights so clearly the end of the golden age in Antarctic exploration as the Footsteps of Scott expedition. No unexplored landmarks, no great science, no untried transport technique beckoned these modern adventurers. Instead, the field of inquiry had shifted to the human psyche. The trio set out to explore themselves by testing their limits against the performance of a cultural icon. Their path to the pole had been traversed hundreds of times by scientific field parties or by giant Hercules aircraft on their way between McMurdo Station and Amundsen-Scott Station. The peaks along the route had been visited and photographed by land and air many times. All that remained for them to discover was the *terra incognita* of their own personalities and of their relationships to one another. They hoped in the process to peer into the mind of Scott.

Wood, Mear, and Swan deliberately eschewed proven technology, such as field radios, in their attempt to resurrect a bygone era. Scott and Shackleton, on the other hand, had brought experimental snow-tractors, Wilkins and Byrd added planes, all to try the cutting edge of technology. Even Amundsen, with a healthy respect for native techniques, installed a modern diesel engine on his ship and used a theodolite, hypsometers and aneroids to calculate positions. Oddly, in trying to recreate the past, the Footsteps of Scott expedition broke faith with it. Their journey to the pole, despite its personal triumphs, demonstrated that the Antarctica of the golden age is simply unrecoverable.

How crowded the continent had become. The three modern adventurers set forth on 25 October from their hut at Cape Evans on McMurdo Sound, but within a day were tucked into two warm rooms at McMurdo Station, fifteen miles south. Hundreds of people swarmed about the US base, with regular shuttle buses taking them to and from the nearby airfield where dozens more scientists arrived daily from New Zealand. The night before the three resumed their march south, they attended a jammed Halloween costume party at McMurdo.

Politics always follows men to Antarctica, but politics had never seemed so petty as during this walk to the pole. American officials were openly hostile to the Footsteps of Scott expedition, considering it an amateur exercise that was destined to founder and require rescue. (In fact, the expedition ship was crushed by pack ice and members were evacuated back to New Zealand by US aircraft, though they did not require it.) Even within the expedition, politics percolated into daily life on the ice. Wood had somehow forgotten to bring a Canadian flag to carry to the South Pole, and began to sew one at their base hut. Swan was vexed, forbidding anything but a Union Jack to flutter at the end of their trek. This was to be a British expedition, pure and undiluted. (Wood barely qualified for the trip, having been born in 1951 in Edinburgh, though raised in British Columbia from age one. He has dual citizenship.)

Fearing for his safety on the trail, where teamwork was essential, Wood compromised by sewing a Canadian flag onto the shoulder of his jacket. To twit Swan, the photographer taped the initials CDN – for Canadian – onto the back of Wood's sledge.[5] Swan's sensitivity was another break with the past. Antarctic expedition leaders of the golden era were often proud of the varied nationalities of members. Mixed rosters gave these ventures an international cachet, proclaiming their world importance and helping to broaden the fund-raising base. Scott, the hero Swan wanted to emulate, took along Charles Wright, a Canadian who flew his flag on the trail and who named a glacier after his country.

Antarctica has always lured adventurers seeking thrills and fame, but in the golden age they were also compelled by duty and conviction to extend the boundaries of knowledge. No longer. In the modern age, the continent has become a kind of park where, for some, adventure can be pursued for its own sake. Typical of this new breed is Pat Morrow, a native of Kimberley, British Columbia. Then thirty-three, he climbed Antarctica's Vinson Massif in November 1985 to complete a fifteen-year quest to conquer the highest mountains on the seven continents. Indeed, a Vancouver-based company, Adventure Network International, was founded by Morrow in 1984 as a blue-chip Antarctic tourist agency. Its tours for the well-heeled have included one-day flights to the pole or ski traverses across the Antarctic plateau. In the 1991–2 season, Adventure Network ferried eighty-eight passengers on its aircraft in the Antarctic, including some scientists, making it the largest private air carrier operating on the continent.

But if some have snubbed Antarctic science for pure adventure, others, including many Canadians, continue to nibble away at the frontiers of knowledge. Ian Whillans, a Toronto-born glaciologist, has visited Antarctica many times and is currently a professor at Ohio State University. Stephen Morris, a geophysicist from Calgary, was head of science at the South Pole station in 1984. Indeed, one of the scientists who greeted Gareth Wood at the South Pole on 11 January 1986 was Greg Crocker, a Canadian glaciologist.

Canadian companies have also prospered from sales of specialized equipment to support scientific expeditions to Antarctica. Among the earliest was a Sioux Lookout, Ontario, firm run by the brothers Carmen and Warner Elliott. In the 1920s they expanded their production of toboggans and sleighs to include sturdy aircraft skis. Most bush planes in the Canadian north were soon equipped with Elliott skis and they became standard equipment on aircraft taken south by Byrd and others.[6] Beginning in the 1950s, Toronto-based de Havilland of Canada became a steady supplier of rugged aircraft to Antarctic expeditions. In the International Geophysical Year of 1957–8, at least twenty-two de Havilland Beavers and Otters were in operation on the continent. Users included the US navy, Australia, New Zealand, Chile, and Japan. Among the most dramatic flights was a non-stop trip across the continent in a single-engine Otter on 6 January 1958. De Havilland's Twin Otter, introduced in 1965, quickly became a new standard for small, reliable aircraft in Antarctica. Among the high-profile users was Sir Ranulph Fiennes, who acquired a Twin Otter to supply his trek around the world via the poles between 1979 and 1982.[7]

A few tracked vehicles developed in the 1950s by Bruce Nodwell and his son Jack were sold for Antarctic use. The company they incorporated in 1965, Canadian Foremost Limited of Calgary, shipped the first of several dozen modern tracked vehicles to the Antarctic in 1977.[8] Another Calgary-based company, Atco Limited, has been a steady provider of prefabricated buildings to Antarctic bases. Their Antarctic customers include the Chilean government, for whom they constructed an eighty-man housing complex in 1981 on the Antarctic Peninsula. In 1970–1, Atco completed a contract for the US navy and National Science Foundation to provide a sixty-foot tower and living and working quarters for the South Pole station. The buildings were completed under the geodesic dome at the pole in January 1975, eleven years before they gave shelter to Gareth Wood and his two companions.[9]

But Canada's most enduring legacy to the Antarctic has been the handful of early explorers who opened up the mysterious continent with frozen fingers, aching backs, and pounding hearts. Fifteen of them have been chronicled here, and despite some diversity they shared many common traits. Almost all were professionals – a doctor, two physicists, two geologists, a civil engineer, five aviators. Even the so-called non-professionals had unique skills: Innes-Taylor and Bursey were experienced dog-drivers, Walter Roots was a trained mountaineer, and Evans had conducted previous zoological studies in Antarctic waters.

About one-third were born outside Canada, all of them in the United Kingdom, which dominated Antarctic exploration for the first two decades of the century. All were men, for women were allowed no role in Antarctica's golden era. And all were young. Their average age was twenty-eight at the time of arrival in Antarctica; pilot Herbert Hollick-Kenyon was the oldest, at thirty-eight, physicist Charles Wright the youngest at twenty-three. Many went on to careers with a strong military connection, as Canadian and US forces sought cold-weather survival skills to help defend and control the Arctic. Five returned to the Antarctic at least once. Eleven of the fifteen made contributions considered of such lasting importance that they were commemorated in names given to Antarctic geographical features.

Their personalities were also suited to exploration in a hostile land, having the right mix of daring and caution. Many put their lives at risk – expedition deaths were not uncommon, from Hugh Evans's first wintering party in 1899 to Fred Roots's international venture of the early 1950s. But fellow expedition members remarked on the even temperaments of their Canadian colleagues. Though not averse to danger, they never made rash decisions, and it is significant that no Canadian died or even suffered serious injury on these expeditions. The harsh climates and vastness of Canada seem to have bred in them powerful instincts for survival. These men were also quiet, hard-working professionals intent on getting the job done with a minimum of fuss. They tended to blend well with their fellows, defusing conflicts with humour and compromise. Most worked in obscurity and did not seek out public honours for their accomplishments. Only one of them published a book about Antarctic adventures, Jack Bursey, and it is perhaps significant that he had become an American citizen by the 1930s. Most were quick to deflate any notion that they were heroes. Many might have been amused that someone decades later would chronicle their adventures in the south.

Inside the cramped canvas womb of a tent, with a blizzard

battering the walls, or around a mess table in a stuffy winter hut, men told each other tales to ward off the gloom. Some shamelessly embellished their stories, recasting them from one telling to the next. A few plucked their narratives out of the thin Antarctic air. Laughs, groans, and hot arguments would punctuate these sessions, but every man clung to the camaraderie. Sharing tales was as much a part of survival as a well-built sledge, a properly stocked depot or a boot that did not pinch. Their stories bound them more closely to one another and kept their sometimes rickety enterprises together. Sharing tales helped make them one.

Notes

INTRODUCTION AND ACKNOWLEDGMENTS

1 The CSS *Hudson*, based at the Bedford Institute of Oceanography in Dartmouth, Nova Scotia, undertook the first circumnavigation of the Americas in 1969–70. During the course of this voyage, in February 1970, several landings were made in the South Shetland Islands, north of the Antarctic Peninsula. This portion of the voyage was the nearest Canada has come to mounting an Antarctic expedition. See P. Wadhams, '"Hudson-70" Canadian Oceanographic Expedition, 1969–70,' *Polar Record* 15, no. 97 (1971), 524–6.
2 See Peter J. Beck, 'Canada as a bi-polar power: Canada's Antarctic dimension,' Lakehead University Centre for Northern Studies, occasional paper 7 (1990) for a summary of Canada's recent interest in the continent.
3 W.P. Adams et al., *Canada and Polar Science* (Ottawa 1987), 17
4 Dean Beeby, 'Canada under pressure to set a clear position on Antarctica,' *Ottawa Citizen*, 13 December 1984, A9

5 Canada, Secretary of State for External Affairs, 'Canada accedes to the Antarctic Treaty,' news release 96, 4 May 1988
6 Ibid., 'Canada signs protocol to protect Antarctic environment,' news release 222, 7 October 1991
7 Canada's first contacts with Antarctica may be traced to sealing and whaling voyages from Nova Scotia and Newfoundland in the late nineteenth and early twentieth century. I have chosen not to chronicle these in this study as they were primarily commercial rather than exploratory ventures. My thanks are due to Robert Headland of the Scott Polar Research Institute in Cambridge, England, for kindly providing background on these voyages. See entries in Robert K. Headland, *Chronological List of Antarctic Expeditions and Related Historical Events* (Cambridge 1990).

ONE: WINTER AT CAPE ADARE

1 Description of this incident is from C.E. Borchgrevink, *First on the Antarctic Continent* (London 1901; Montreal, 1980), 130–1; Louis Bernacchi, *To the South Polar Regions* (London 1901), 127–8; Hugh B. Evans, 'The *Southern Cross* expedition, 1898–1900: a personal account,' *Polar Record* 17, no. 106 (1974), 25–6; author's transcript of OECA interview (*c.* 1971) with Evans, from videotape copy at Film, Television and Sound Archives of the National Archives of Canada.
2 Bernacchi, *To the South Polar Regions*, 127
3 Biographical information about Evans's early life from 'Hugh Blackwall Evans,' *Geographical Journal* 139, pt. 1 (February, 1973), 192–3; A.G.E. Jones, 'Obituary [of Hugh Blackwall Evans],' *Polar Record* 17, no. 110 (1975), 573–4; transcript of OECA interview with Evans
4 *Qu'Appelle: Footprints to Progress* (Qu'Appelle, Sask. 1980), 156–62
5 Hugh B. Evans, 'A voyage to Kerguelen in the sealer *Edward* in 1897–98,' *Polar Record* 16, no. 105 (1973), 789–91
6 Evans, 'The *Southern Cross* expedition,' 23
7 For a brief biography of Borchgrevink, see Hugh B. Evans and

A.G.E. Jones, 'A Forgotten Explorer: Carsten Egeberg Borchgrevink,' *Polar Record* 17, no. 108 (1975), 221–35.

8 The following section is based on the two standard accounts of the *Southern Cross* expedition, Borchgrevink, *First on the Antarctic Continent*, and Bernacchi, *To the South Polar Regions*; and on Evans's own account in 'The *Southern Cross* expedition.'

9 Evans, 'The *Southern Cross* expedition,' 24

10 Bernacchi, *To the South Polar Regions*, 78

11 Borchgrevink, *First on the Antarctic Continent*, 91

12 *Antarctica: Great Stories from the Frozen Continent* (London 1985), 133. Frederick A. Cook, *Through the First Antarctic Night, 1898–1899* (London 1900; rpr. Montreal 1980), is an account in English of the *Belgica* expedition.

13 Bernacchi, *To the South Polar Regions*, 93

14 Borchgrevink, *First on the Antarctic Continent*, 128–9

15 Transcript of OECA interview with Evans

16 Borchgrevink, *First on the Antarctic Continent*, 154

17 Ibid., 112–15

18 Transcript of OECA interview with Evans

19 Bernacchi, *To the South Polar Regions*, 140

20 Evans, 'The *Southern Cross* expedition,' 26

21 Transcript of OECA interview with Evans

22 Ibid.

23 Borchgrevink, *First on the Antarctic Continent*, 279

24 Bernacchi, *To the South Polar Regions*, 266

25 See introduction by Tore Gjelsvik to the 1980 edition of Borchgrevink, *First on the Antarctic Continent*; Evans and Jones, 'A forgotten explorer,' 227.

26 Raymond E. Priestley, *Antarctic Adventure: Scott's Northern Party* (London 1914; repr. Toronto 1974), 102–3

27 Ibid., 87

28 Ibid., 88

29 Ibid., 22

30 'Hugh Blackwall Evans,' 193; Jones, 'Obituary,' 573; transcript of

OECA interview tape with Evans; Eleanor F. Evans to author, 8
October 1987
31 Jones, 'Obituary,' 573; transcript of OECA interview with Evans;
'Hugh Blackwall Evans,' 193
32 Eleanor F. Evans to author, 8 October 1987; Jones, 'Obituary,' 573
33 Eleanor F. Evans to author, 13 January 1986
34 'A voyage to Kerguelen'; 'The *Southern Cross* expedition'; and with
A.G.E. Jones, 'A forgotten explorer'

TWO: SHACKLETON'S BROKEN DOCTOR

1 Roland Huntford, *Shackleton* (London 1985); Margery and James
Fisher, *Shackleton* (London 1957); Ernest Henry Shackleton, *The
Heart of the Antarctic* (London 1909); Stanley Newman, ed.,
Shackleton's Lieutenant: The Nimrod *Diary of A.L.A. Mackintosh,
British Antarctic Expedition 1907–09* (Auckland, NZ 1990). These
were drawn on for the following account of the expedition.
2 Michell's early life from James Kinlock, 'The Collegiate Institute,'
in *Perth Remembered* ([Perth, Ont.] 1967), 151–3; Canada, 1891
Census; *Perth Courier*, 6 January 1928, 5; M. Eisenberg, College of
Physicians and Surgeons of Ontario, to author, 1 December 1987;
National Archives of Canada (NAC) MG30, B90, 'Toronto doctor
back from the Antarctic expedition,' undated newspaper clipping
c. 1910; W.A.R. Michell, 'With Shackleton to the Antarctic,' *Canadian Numismatic Journal* 3, no. 4 (April 1958), 96
3 NAC, MG30, B90, corrected typescript of 'With Shackleton to the
Antarctic'
4 Michell, 'With Shackleton,' 96
5 G. Hattersley-Smith, 'The Michell MS,' typescript appraisal of
Michell papers, 15 March 1970, for Scott Polar Research Institute
(author's files)
6 Michell, 'With Shackleton,' 97
7 Shackleton, *Heart of the Antarctic*, 26
8 Michell, 'With Shackleton,' 98
9 Ibid., 100

10 Ibid.
11 NAC, MG30, B90, England to Michell, 27 April 1908
12 Michell, 'With Shackleton,' 101
13 Ibid.
14 A.G.E. Jones to author, 4 March 1985; NAC, MG30, B90, 'Toronto doctor back from the Antarctic expedition,' undated newspaper clipping c. 1910
15 Based on Michell personnel file in Archives of Ontario, Civil Service Commission, Personnel Records 1920–56
16 Interview with Alfred E.H. Petrie, 11 August 1986
17 Section based on interview with Alfred E.H. Petrie, 11 August 1986; Petrie's notes and corrected version of section, 1988 (author's files)
18 Ibid.

THREE: THE MAN WHO FOUND THE BODIES

1 Patricia Wright, ed., 'Leaves from an Antarctic diary,' Introduction, 14 (author's files). The following section is also based on this memoir of Wright's early life.
2 Ibid., 1
3 Ibid., 7
4 'Note on an improvement in the method of determining visibility curves,' *Bulletin of the Royal Society of Canada* 2 (1908); 'On variations in the conductivity of air enclosed in metallic receivers,' *Bulletin of the Royal Society of Canada* 8 (1908)
5 'On the susceptibility of mixtures of salt solutions' (Toronto 1907)
6 Author's transcript of OECA interview (c. 1972) with Wright, from videotape copy at Film, Television and Sound Archives of the NAC.
7 Wright, ed., 'Leaves from an Antarctic diary,' Prologue, 1; Marie Sanderson, *Griffith Taylor: Antarctic Scientist and Pioneer Geographer* (Ottawa 1988), 23, 30; Charles Neider, *Edge of the World: Ross Island, Antarctica* (New York 1974), 274–5; Griffith Taylor, *With Scott: The Silver Lining* (London 1916), 7–8
8 Neider, *Edge of the World,* 274

9 Reginald Pound, *Scott of the Antarctic* (London 1968), 198; Wright's measurements given in Taylor, *With Scott,* 225

10 C.S. Wright and R.E. Priestley, *Glaciology* (London 1922). See also Colin Bull to author, 26 January 1987.

11 Wright, ed., 'Leaves from an Antarctic diary,' Departure, 3

12 Ibid., 2

13 G.C. Simpson and C.S. Wright, 'Atmospheric electricity over the ocean,' *Proceedings of the Royal Society of Australia* 85 (1911)

14 H.G.R. King, 'Obituary [of Sir Charles Seymour Wright],' *Polar Record* 18, no. 114 (September 1976), 313; transcript of OECA interview with Wright; Bowers quote cited in Wright, ed., 'Leaves from an Antarctic diary,' Reference notes, 15

15 Transcript of OECA interview with Wright

16 Wright, ed., 'Leaves from an Antarctic diary,' Reference notes, 17

17 Ibid., Departure, 16

18 Ibid., Reference notes, 25

19 Ibid., 26

20 Charles S. Wright, 'General Physics,' in R.F. Scott, *Scott's Last Expedition* (Toronto 1913), II: 314

21 Herbert G. Ponting, *The Great White South,* 4th ed. (London 1923), 153–4

22 Ibid.; Taylor, *With Scott,* 272–3

23 Wright, ed., 'Leaves from an Antarctic diary,' Departure, 24

24 Taylor, *With Scott,* 96

25 Ibid., 105

26 The following account of trip is based on Taylor, *With Scott,* 118–98; T. Griffith Taylor, 'The western journeys,' in R.F. Scott, *Scott's Last Expedition,* II: 124ff; Wright, ed., 'Leaves from an Antarctic diary,' Exploring the Western Mountains.

27 Taylor, 'The western journeys,' 130

28 Scott, *Scott's Last Expedition,* I: 159

29 Ibid., 213

30 Wright, ed., 'Leaves from an Antarctic diary,' Night, 74; ibid., 220

31 Scott, *Scott's Last Expedition,* I: 220

32 Ibid., 338

33 Neider, *Edge of the World,* 279

34 Taylor, *With Scott*, 269
35 Ibid., 274
36 Wright, ed., 'Leaves from an Antarctic diary,' Reference notes, 62
37 Ibid., 69, 75–6. See also Neider, *Edge of the World*, 285.
38 Wright, ed, 'Leaves from an Antarctic diary,' Barrier journey, 101
39 Ibid., 102
40 Ibid., 104
41 Ibid., 106, 108–9
42 Taylor, *With Scott*, 441
43 Scott, *Scott's Last Expedition*, I: 341
44 Ibid., 352
45 Wright, ed., 'Leaves from an Antarctic diary,' The Beardmore, 109
46 Apsley Cherry-Garrard, *The Worst Journey in the World* (Harmondsworth, England 1970), 439
47 Wright, ed., 'Leaves from an Antarctic diary,' The Beardmore, 113
48 Ibid., 120
49 Ibid., 124
50 E.L. Atkinson, 'The last year at Cape Evans,' in Scott, *Scott's Last Expedition*, II: 215
51 This section is based on Wright, ed., 'Leaves from an Antarctic diary,' Search journey, 144–6; Reference notes, 96–8; Neider, *Edge of the World*, 283–4; E.L. Atkinson, 'The finding of the dead,' in R.F. Scott, *Scott's Last Expedition* (London 1923), 466–9.
52 Wright, ed., 'Leaves from an Antarctic diary,' Reference notes, 96; transcript of OECA interview with Wright
53 Cited in Elspeth Huxley, *Scott of the Antarctic* (London 1979), 305
54 Ibid., 305–6; and Roland Huntford, *Scott and Amundsen* (London 1979), 555
55 *News* (Toronto), 10 February 1913, 1; *Toronto Daily Star*, 19 February 1913, 1
56 *Toronto Daily Star*, 11 February 1913, 15
57 This account of Wright's return to civilization is based on Wright, ed., 'Leaves from an Antarctic diary,' Aftermath, 156–7.
58 Manitoba Archives, Canadian Club of Winnipeg Collection, Box P2752, Canadian Club (Winnipeg), *Annual Report 1913*, 37
59 *Winnipeg Free Press*, 9 June 1913

60 *Toronto Daily Star*, 10 June 1913, 1; 11 June 1913, 1
61 *Toronto Daily Star*, 11 June 1913, 1; *News*, 11 June 1913, 1
62 *Toronto Daily Star*, 17 June 1913, 1
63 The account of Wright's later life is based on Wright, ed., 'Leaves from an Antarctic diary,' 156–7; King, 'Obituary [of Sir Charles Seymour Wright],' 313–15; Charles Wright, 'Sir Raymond Priestley: an appreciation,' *Polar Record* 17, no. 108 (1974), 215–20; 'Sir Charles S. Wright, KCB, OBE, MA, MC,' *Journal of the Naval Service*, 2, no. 1.
64 Wright, ed., 'Leaves from an Antarctic diary,' Search journey, 150
65 Neider, *Edge of the World*, 294
66 Wright, ed., 'Leaves from an Antarctic diary,' Epilogue, 158–9
67 Neider, *Edge of the World*, 294

FOUR: A GEOLOGIST ADRIFT

1 NAC, MG26, I, vol. 13, file 7, Memorandum, 'Plan of the expedition'
2 On Canadian claims, see Morris Zaslow, *The Northward Expansion of Canada, 1914–1967* (Toronto 1988), 12–21; Kenneth C. Eyre, 'Canadian sovereignty 1922 style,' *North/nord* 23, no. 3 (May–June 1976), 2–5.
3 NAC, MG26, I, vol. 13, file 7, L.C. Christie to the prime minister, 28 October 1920
4 Eyre, 'Canadian sovereignty 1922 style,' 3
5 NAC, MG26, I, vol. 13, file 7, L.C. Christie to the prime minister, 28 October 1920
6 Ibid., Stefansson to the prime minister, 30 October 1920
7 NAC, MG26, I, vol. 13, file 7
8 Margery and James Fisher, *Shackleton* (London 1957), 442; Roland Huntford, *Shackleton* (London 1985), 680–1
9 NAC, MG26, I, vol. 13, file 7, Stefansson to Sir Robert Borden, 8 January 1921; Stefansson to the prime minister, 8 January 1921
10 Zaslow, *The Northward Expansion of Canada*, 17–19
11 NAC, MG26, I, vol. 13, file 7, Arthur Meighen to Sir James Lougheed, 5 February 1921; Lougheed to Meighen, 14 February 1921
12 Ibid., Shackleton to the prime minister, 5 April 1921

13 Scott Polar Research Institute Archives (SPRI), Fisher Papers MS 1456/78 [Douglas] George Vibert Douglas to Marjorie Fisher, 29 November 1955

14 NAC, MG26, I, vol. 13, file 7, Shackleton cablegram to John Bassett, 20 April 1921

15 Ibid., governor general draft telegram to colonial secretary, 25 April 1921

16 Ibid., Shackleton cable to Meighen, 6 May 1921; Meighen cable to Shackleton, 9 May 1921; Shackleton cable to Meighen, 12 May 1921; Meighen cable to Shackleton, 16 May 1921

17 Ibid., memorandum to London, 8 June 1921

18 This account of Douglas's early life is based on Pat Douglas letters to author, 21 March 1988, 21 April 1988; A. Vibert Douglas to P.F. Wright, 27 January 1978; author's interview with Pat Douglas, 16 February 1986; L.J. Weeks, 'George Vibert Douglas,' *Proceedings and Transactions of the Royal Society of Canada*, 3rd ser., vol. 53 (1959), 93–4.

19 SPRI Fisher Papers MS 1456/78 [Douglas] George Vibert Douglas to Marjorie Fisher, 29 November 1955

20 Ibid.

21 Ibid.; Fisher, *Shackleton*, 453; Douglas family papers, Toronto, agreement dated 16 September 1921 between Captain G.V. Douglas and Sir Ernest H. Shackleton

22 Lowell Thomas, *Sir Hubert Wilkins: His World of Adventure* (New York 1961), 141

23 Douglas family papers, Toronto, Douglas *Quest* diary, 17 September 1921

24 J.W.S. Marr, *Into the Frozen South* (New York n.d.), 44–5

25 Thomas, *Sir Hubert Wilkins*, 144

26 Frank Wild, *Shackleton's Last Voyage: The Story of the Quest* (London 1923), 59

27 Douglas *Quest* diary, 9 January 1922

28 Marr, *Into the Frozen South*, 99–100

29 Wild, *Shackleton's Last Voyage*, 80–2

30 Ibid., 94; Marr, *Into the Frozen South*, 124

31 Wild, *Shackleton's Last Voyage*, 95

32 Ibid., 117
33 Douglas *Quest* diary, 19 February 1922
34 Ibid., 21 February 1921; 22 February 1922
35 Wild, *Shackleton's Last Voyage*, 139
36 Douglas *Quest* diary, 27 February 1922
37 Ibid., 3 May 1922
38 SPRI, Fisher Papers MS 1456/78 [Douglas] George Vibert Douglas to Marjorie Fisher, 29 November 1955
39 Wild, *Shackleton's Last Voyage*, 314
40 *Report on the Geological Collections Made during the Voyage of the Quest* (London 1930)
41 This account of Douglas's later life is taken from Weeks, 'George Vibert Douglas,' 93–4; author's interview with Pat Douglas, 16 February 1986; A. Vibert Douglas to P.F. Wright, 27 January 1978; Douglas personnel file at Dalhousie University, Halifax; Pat Douglas to author, 21 March 1988.
42 SPRI Fisher Papers MS 1456/78 [Douglas] George Vibert Douglas to Marjorie Fisher, 29 November 1955
43 G. Vibert Douglas, 'The Antarctic and the spirit of discovery,' *McGill News*, September 1934, 44–6

FIVE: A WAYWARD BUSH PILOT

1 'Obituaries,' *Polar Record* 4, no. 29 (January 1945), 243
2 Canadian Press Library, Toronto, Canadian Press report dateline Halifax, 1 February 1943; Frank Lowe, 'Jaunty Cheesman "never worried" about rescue,' Canadian Press report in *Fort William Times-Journal* (Ontario), 2 February 1943, 1–2
3 The account of Cheesman's early life is from NAC, RG12, vol. 16, 5802–1191; NAC, Personnel Records Centre, Cheesman files 2506, C–2001; 'Al Cheesman pioneer pilot in NWO,' *Thunder Bay Chronicle-Journal* (Ontario), 26 July 1983, 28; Ken A. Cheesman scrapbook, Sault Ste. Marie, Ontario; biographical notes provided by Ken A. Cheesman; Charles Whitney Gilchrist, '"Al" Cheesman,' *MacLean's* Magazine, 1 August 1930, 16, 38, 40; 'Death-cheating pilot yields life to sickness,' Canadian Press report in *Globe and*

Mail, 4 April 1958; K.M. Molson, *Pioneering in Canadian Air Transport* (Winnipeg, 1974), passim; '"Al" Cheeseman [*sic*] home from Antarctic,' *Saint John Times-Globe* (New Brunswick), 22 March 1930, 1, 5.

4 NAC, Personnel Records Centre, Cheesman files 2506, C-2001 'Proceedings on discharge'

5 NAC, RG12, vol. 16, file 5802–1991, 'Camp Borden flying report'

6 Gilchrist, '"Al" Cheesman,' 16; Molson, *Pioneering in Canadian Air Transport,* 23–4

7 NAC, RG12, vol. 16, file 5802–1991, 'A.T. Cowley report'

8 Bernt Balchen, *Come North with Me* (Norwich, England 1959), 85; Molson, *Pioneering in Canadian Air Transport,* 25

9 On Wilkins's career, see Lowell Thomas, *Sir Hubert Wilkins: His World of Adventure* (New York 1961); John Grierson, *Sir Hubert Wilkins: Enigma of Exploration* (London 1960).

10 Thomas, *Sir Hubert Wilkins,* 249–50

11 On Wilkins's second Antarctic expedition, see Hubert Wilkins, 'Further Antarctic explorations,' *Geographical Review* 20, no. 3 (July 1930), 357–88; Grierson, *Sir Hubert Wilkins,* 120–34; Thomas, *Sir Hubert Wilkins,* 248–57; Gilchrist, '"Al" Cheesman,' 16, 38, 40.

12 Wilkins, 'Further Antarctic explorations,' 366

13 Gilchrist, '"Al" Cheesman,' 38

14 Wilkins, 'Further Antarctic explorations,' 370

15 Ibid., 382

16 Ibid., 383

17 '"Al" Cheeseman [*sic*] home from Antarctic,' *Saint John Times-Globe* (New Brunswick), 22 March 1930, 5

18 This account of Cheesman's later life is taken from NAC, RG12, vol. 16, file 5802–1191; NAC, Personnel Records Centre, Cheesman files 2506, C-2001; Ken A. Cheesman scrapbook, Sault Ste Marie, Ontario; biographical notes provided by Ken A. Cheesman; 'Airman killed, Cheesman injured in plane crash,' Canadian Press report in *Fort William Daily Times-Journal* (Ontario), 25 May 1940, 1; 'Al Cheesman pioneer pilot in NWO,' *Thunder Bay Chronicle-Journal* (Ontario), 26 July 1983, 28; 'Death-cheating pilot

yields life to sickness,' Canadian Press report in *Globe and Mail,* 4 April 1958.

SIX: BYRD'S MEN

1 Paul Siple, *90 Degrees South: The Story of the American South Pole Conquest* (New York 1959), 319–20; author's transcript of US National Archives, 13 March 1972, interview with Davies, from copy at Film, Television and Sound Archives of NAC; Eugene Rodgers, *Beyond the Barrier: The Story of Byrd's First Expedition to Antarctica* (Annapolis, Maryland 1990), 134
2 Background for Byrd's first expedition is based partly on Rodgers's excellent study, *Beyond the Barrier,* as well as Richard Evelyn Byrd, *Little America* (New York 1930).
3 Harry Adams, *Beyond the Barrier with Byrd* (Chicago 1932), 102
4 Transcript of US National Archives, 13 March 1972, interview with Davies
5 This account of Davies's early life is taken from ibid.; Geoffrey Hattersley-Smith, 'Obituary [of Dr. Frank T. Davies],' *Polar Record* 21, no. 130 (1982), 80–1; Frank T. Davies curriculum vitae in family papers; Frank T. Davies to Pat Wright, 26 September 1977.
6 Jack Bursey, *Antarctic Night: One Man's Story of 28,224 Hours at the Bottom of the World* (New York 1957), 27. The account of Bursey's early life based on *Antarctic Night,* 27–36; 'Obituary [of Commander Jacob Bursey],' *Polar Record* 20, no. 127 (1981), 382; 'Bursey, Jacob (Jack),' in Smallwood, ed., *Encyclopedia of Newfoundland and Labrador* 1 (1981), 299; 'Newfoundland Antarctic explorer, Cmdr. Jack Bursey dies at 76,' *St. John's Evening Telegram,* 27 March 1980; 'Jack Bursey recalls his polar expeditions,' ibid., 26 September 1978.
7 Bursey, *Antarctic Night,* 31
8 Ibid., 38
9 Byrd's early life is based on Rodgers, *Beyond the Barrier.*
10 Ibid., 181
11 Transcript of US National Archives, 13 March 1972, interview with Davies

12 Russell Owen, *South of the Sun* (New York 1934), 11–12
13 Rodgers, *Beyond the Barrier*, 47
14 Laurence McKinley Gould, *Cold: The Record of an Antarctic Sledge Journey* (New York 1931), 161–2
15 Paul Siple, *A Boy Scout with Byrd* (New York 1931), 20
16 Bernt Balchen, *Come North with Me* (Norwich, England 1959), 163
17 For the following section, see Norman D. Vaughan with Cecil B. Murphy, *With Byrd at the Bottom of the World: The South Pole Expedition of 1928-30* (Harrisburg, Pa. 1990).
18 Bursey, *Antarctic Night*, 43
19 Vaughan, *With Byrd at the Bottom of the World*, 50
20 Transcript of US National Archives, 13 March 1972, interview with Davies
21 Owen, *South of the Sun*, 67
22 Alan Innes-Taylor, 'Empty boots – a whaling story,' edited by Philip S. Marshall, *Arctic* 37, no. 1 (March 1984), 87
23 This account of Innes-Taylor's early life is taken from Philip S. Marshall, 'Charles Alan Kenneth Innes-Taylor, 1900–1983,' *Arctic* 37, no. 1 (March 1984), 84–6; 'Obituary [of Alan Innes-Taylor],' *Polar Record* 21, no. 135 (1983), 622; 'Innes-Taylor dead at 83,' *Whitehorse Star*, 14 January 1983; Innes-Taylor curricula vitae in family papers; 'Northerner Allan [*sic*] Innes-Taylor's life reflects a half-century of global travel, exploration,' *White Pass Container Route News* 16, no. 9 (February 1971), 1–2.
24 Innes-Taylor, 'Empty boots,' 87
25 Rodgers, *Beyond the Barrier*, 81
26 Owen, *South of the Sun*, 63–4
27 Equipment described in Frank T. Davies, 'Byrd scientists study Earth's magnetism,' *New York Times*, 24 November 1929, Section 11, 4; Byrd, *Little America*, 264–7; transcript of US National Archives 13 March 1972, interview with Davies
28 Davies, 'Byrd scientists study Earth's magnetism,' 4
29 Owen, *South of the Sun*, 182
30 Siple, *A Boy Scout with Byrd*, 86–7
31 Owen, *South of the Sun*, 180
32 Byrd, *Little America*, 224–5

33 *New York Times,* 12 May 1929, 3
34 Owen, *South of the Sun,* 124
35 Byrd, *Little America,* 263
36 Gould, *Cold,* 110
37 Byrd, *Little America,* 266–7
38 Transcript of us National Archives, 13 March 1972, interview with Davies
39 Byrd, *Little America,* 212
40 Ibid., 237
41 Owen, *South of the Sun,* 100
42 Rodgers, *Beyond the Barrier,* 131
43 Bursey, *Antarctic Night,* 79–80
44 Byrd, *Little America,* 203–4
45 Rodgers, *Beyond the Barrier,* 130
46 Transcript of us National Archives, 13 March 1972, interview with Davies
47 Byrd, *Little America,* 221
48 Ibid., 167
49 Owen, *South of the Sun,* 109, 112; Byrd, *Little America,* 272
50 The account of Innes-Taylor's voyage aboard *Kosmos* is based on 'Empty boots,' 87–90.
51 Ibid., 89
52 Ibid., 90
53 Ibid.
54 Bursey, *Antarctic Night,* 88–9
55 Balchen, *Come North with Me,* 191
56 Vaughan, *With Byrd at the Bottom of the World,* 177
57 Glenbow Museum Archives, Calgary, M564, Alan Innes-Taylor, 'Kings of the Polar Trail,' reprint of *American Kennel Gazette,* December 1935, by Lederle Laboratories, Inc.; Richard E. Byrd, *Discovery: The Story of the Second Byrd Antarctic Expedition* (New York 1935), 18
58 Byrd, *Discovery,* 47
59 Ibid., 73
60 Ibid., 83
61 Ibid., 189

62 Ibid., 132–50, 156, 164–5
63 Glenbow Museum Archives, Calgary, M564, 'The fall southern journey - base laying,' 9 March 1934 entry
64 Ibid., 10 March 1934 entry
65 Byrd, *Discovery*, 143
66 Glenbow Museum Archives, Calgary, M564, 'The fall southern journey,' 16 March 1934 entry
67 Ibid., 22 March 1934 entry
68 Richard E. Byrd, *Alone* (New York 1968), 38
69 Paul A. Carter, *Little America: Town at the End of the World* (New York 1979), 189
70 Glenbow Museum Archives, Calgary, M564, 'The fall southern journey,' 25 March 1934 entry
71 Ibid., 9 March 1934 entry
72 Byrd, *Discovery*, 171
73 Ibid.
74 Glenbow Museum Archives, Calgary, M564, 'The fall southern journey,' section entitled 'Purpose of southern fall journey'
75 Byrd, *Discovery*, 262
76 The account of Innes-Taylor's later life is based on Philip S. Marshall, 'Charles Alan Kenneth Innes-Taylor, 1900–1983,' *Arctic*, 84–6; 'Obituary [of Alan Innes-Taylor],' *Polar Record*, 622; 'Innes-Taylor dead at 83,' *Whitehorse Star*, 14 January 1983; Innes-Taylor curricula vitae in family papers; 'Northerner Allan [*sic*] Innes-Taylor's life reflects a half-century of global travel, exploration,' *White Pass Container Route News*, 1–2.
77 The account of Bursey's later life is based on Bursey, *Antarctic Night*; 'Obituary [of Commander Jacob Bursey],' *Polar Record*, 382; 'Bursey, Jacob (Jack),' in Smallwood, ed., *Encyclopedia of Newfoundland and Labrador*, vol. 1 (1981), 299; 'Newfoundland Antarctic explorer, Cmdr. Jack Bursey dies at 76,' *St. John's Evening Telegram* (Newfoundland), March 27, 1980; 'Jack Bursey recalls his polar expeditions,' *St. John's Evening Telegram*, September 26, 1978.
78 The account of Davies's later life is based on transcript of US National Archives, 13 March 1972, interview with Davies;

Hattersley-Smith, 'Obituary [of Dr Frank T. Davies],' *Polar Record*,
80–1; Frank T. Davies curriculum vitae in family papers.
79 Transcript of US National Archives, 13 March 1972, interview with
Davies
80 US National Archives, Harry T. Harrison papers, 'Byrd Antarctic
Expedition I News' 2, no. 1 (29 November 1975), 9
81 Hattersley-Smith, 'Obituary,' *Polar Record*, 81
82 Byrd, *Discovery*, 189

SEVEN: ACROSS THE CONTINENT

1 The account of 'Camp Winnipeg' is based on Lincoln Ellsworth,
Beyond Horizons (New York 1938), 328–32, 373–81; John Grierson,
Sir Hubert Wilkins: Enigma of Exploration (London 1960), 163–4;
John Grierson, *Challenge to the Poles: Highlights of Arctic and Antarctic Aviation* (Hamden, Connecticut, 1964), 367–9, 656–7; Kenneth J. Bertrand, *Americans in Antarctica, 1775–1948* (New York
1971), 383–8; author's transcript of OECA interview with Hollick-
Kenyon from copy at Film, Television and Sound Archives of the
NAC; Hollick-Kenyon family papers, Hollick-Kenyon Antarctic
flight logbook; US National Archives, RG 401–36, Antarctic Expedition 1935–6, Notebook; Lincoln Ellsworth, 'My flight across Antarctica,' *National Geographic* 70, no. 1 (July 1936), 24ff; Canadian
Press clipping files, Toronto.
2 M.R. Gemie to author, 25 June 1986; Tim Hollick-Kenyon to
author, 24 March 1986; Hollick-Kenyon family papers, scrapbook.
3 Hollick-Kenyon family papers, scrapbook; *Vancouver Province*, 5
December 1936, dispatch from Vernon, British Columbia
4 Ellsworth's early life is based on *Beyond Horizons*.
5 Ibid., 278
6 Ibid., 294
7 Ibid., 293–4
8 Details of Hollick-Kenyon's life and career are from NAC, RG12,
vol. 1794, file 5802–4019; 'H. Hollick-Kenyon,' in *Canada's Aviation Hall of Fame* (Calgary, Alta., c. 1974), 35; K.M. Molson, *Pioneering in Canadian Air Transport* (Winnipeg 1974), passim;

Hollick-Kenyon family papers, scrapbook; author's correspondence with family; Canadian Press clipping files, Toronto; Ellsworth, *Beyond Horizons*, 299–300.

9 Lymburner's life and career are taken from NAC, RG12, vol. 1794, file 5802-4530; Jessie Lymburner to author, 14 September 1988; author's interview with Red Lymburner, 4 July 1986; with Glenna Tisshaw, 23 February 1986; West Lincoln Historical Society, *Our Links With the Past*; Canadian Press clipping files, Toronto; Lymburner family papers, scrapbook; Lymburner curriculum vitae in family papers.

10 NAC, RG12, vol. 1794, file 5802-4530, 12 July 1928 report on flight

11 'Proceedings of [May 9, 1936] dinner to H. Hollick-Kenyon and J.H. Lymburner,' 35, copy obtained from Ken Molson, Toronto

12 Details of Howard's life and career are taken from W.J. Wheeler, 'Editorial,' *Canadian Aviation Historical Society Journal* 5, no. 3 (fall 1967), 63; Pat Howard scrapbooks; R.G. Halford, 'Patrick Matthew Howard,' *Canadian Aviation Historical Society Journal*, vol. 10, no. 3 (fall 1972), 93; 'Was with '35 Antarctic expedition; early TCA pilot Pat Howard dies,' *Canadian Aircraft Operator* 9, no. 5 (17 July 1972), 1–2; NAC, RG12, vol. 937, file 5802-3657; interview with Marjorie Howard, 19 April 1986; Howard family papers; Pat Howard Antarctic diary.

13 Unidentified newspaper clipping dateline New York, 7 August [1935], in Howard family papers, scrapbook

14 Red Lymburner to Jessie Lymburner, 15 October 1935, Lymburner family papers

15 Ibid., Red Lymburner to Jessie and Glenna Lymburner, 25 October 1935

16 Ellsworth, *Beyond Horizons*, 302–3

17 Hollick-Kenyon family papers; Hollick-Kenyon Antarctic flight logbook, 3

18 Ibid., 4

19 Ellsworth, *Beyond Horizons*, 313

20 US National Archives, RG 401–36, Ellsworth Papers, Antarctic Expedition 1935–6, Notebook

21 Ibid.

22 Ellsworth, *Beyond Horizons*, 315
23 Ibid., 316
24 Unidentified newspaper clipping from *New York Times*, 18 January 1936 in Hollick-Kenyon family papers, scrapbook
25 Hollick-Kenyon family papers; Hollick-Kenyon Antarctic flight logbook, 20
26 Ibid., 26
27 Ellsworth, *Beyond Horizons*, 376
28 Unidentified newspaper clipping dateline New York, 20 April [1936], Lymburner family papers, scrapbook
29 Ellsworth, *Beyond Horizons*, 327
30 Ibid., 332
31 Ibid., 335
32 Ibid., 350
33 Ellsworth, 'My flight across Antarctica,' 32
34 Lowell Thomas, 'Pilot of adventure,' unidentified clipping dated 6 March 1938 in Canadian Press clippings files, Toronto
35 Ellsworth, *Beyond Horizons*, 350
36 Ibid., 351
37 Ibid., 352
38 F.D. Ommanney, *South Latitude* (London 1938), 202–3
39 Ibid., 203
40 *New York Times*, 18 February 1936
41 Ommanney, *South Latitude*, 204
42 Associated Press dispatch from London, 17 January [1936], Lymburner family papers, scrapbook
43 Richard Byrd to Herbert Hollick-Kenyon, 29 November 1954, Hollick-Kenyon family papers
44 Unidentified 17 January [1936] clipping in Hollick-Kenyon family papers, scrapbook
45 Details of tractor incident in Red Lymburner to Jessie and Glenna Lymburner, 25 February 1936, Lymburner family papers; Montreal *Standard*, 11 June 1938; 'Proceedings of [May 9, 1936] dinner to H. Hollick-Kenyon and J.H. Lymburner,' 9; Howard family papers; Pat Howard Antarctic diary, 25 January [1936] entry
46 On the Winnipeg reception, dinner and awards, see 'Proceedings of [9 May 1936] dinner to H. Hollick-Kenyon and J.H. Lymburner';

Winnipeg Free Press, 9 and 11 May 1936; Lymburner scrapbook.
47 NAC, RG12, vol. 1794, file 5802-4019, J.A. Wilson memo 29 April
1936
48 Canadian Press dispatch from Ottawa, 27 May [1936], Lymburner
family papers, scrapbook
49 M.R. Gemie to author, 25 June 1986
50 Transcript of OECA interview with Hollick-Kenyon
51 Grierson, *Challenge to the Poles,* 374
52 Red Lymburner to Jessie and Glenna Lymburner, 4 March 1936,
Lymburner family papers
53 Details of Trerice's life and career are taken from Canadian Press
clippings file, Toronto; 'Canadian pilots return from Antarctic
expedition,' *Canadian Aviation,* May 1939, 42.
54 The narrative of the 1938–9 expedition is taken from Lincoln
Ellsworth, 'My four Antarctic expeditions,' *National Geographic,*
76, no. 1 (July 1939), 136–8; Bertrand, *Americans in Antarctica,*
395–406; Lymburner scrapbook.

EIGHT: A SECRET MILITARY MISSION

1 On the political background to this expedition, see Peter J. Beck,
'A cold war: Britain, Argentina and Antarctica,' *History Today* 37
(June 1987), 16–23.
2 'German raiders in the Antarctic during the war,' *Polar Record* 4,
no. 32 (July 1946), 402–3; 'German raiders in the Antarctic during
the Second World War,' *Polar Record* 6, no. 43 (January 1952),
399–403
3 Beck, 'A cold war,' 16–19
4 Ibid., 21
5 Vivian Fuchs, *Of Ice and Men* (Shropshire, England 1982), 22;
Beck, 'A cold war,' 21; interview with Andrew Taylor, 6 November
1987
6 Expedition background is taken from Fuchs, *Of Ice and Men,* 22–
58; J.M. Wordie, 'The Falkland Islands Dependencies Survey,
1943–46,' *Polar Record* 4, no. 32 (July 1946), 372–84; David James,
That Frozen Land (London 1949); Harold Squires, *S.S. Eagle: The
Secret Mission, 1944–45* (St. John's, Newfoundland 1992).

7 Details of the life and career of Andrew Taylor are taken from interviews, 19 January 1984, 7 November 1986, 6 November 1987; Andrew Taylor file at Chancellery of Canadian Orders and Decorations, Rideau Hall, Ottawa; author's correspondence with Andrew Taylor.
8 Interview, 6 November 1987
9 Fuchs, *Of Ice and Men*, 34
10 Interview, 6 November 1987
11 Ibid.
12 Wordie, 'The Falkland Islands Dependencies Survey, 1943–46,' 376
13 Interview, 6 November 1987
14 Wordie, 'The Falkland Islands Dependencies Survey,' 374
15 Interview, 6 November 1987
16 British Antarctic Survey Archives, AD6/2D/1945/A, Captain Andrew Taylor's report to the governor, December 1944–March 1945, 2
17 Interview, 7 November 1986
18 Otto Nordenskjold, *Antarctica, or Two Years amongst the Ice of the South Pole* (London 1905; repr. Toronto 1977), 308
19 Interview, 7 November 1986
20 James, *That Frozen Land*, 82
21 Fuchs, *Of Ice and Men*, 47
22 *Hope Bay Howler*, 21 October 1945 (author's files)
23 Ibid., 21 November 1945
24 Fuchs, *Of Ice and Men*, 54
25 Interview, 6 November 1987
26 British Antarctic Survey Archives, AD6/2D/1945/K1, First sledge journey, 1945, 2
27 The account of the sledge journey is based on ibid.; Fuchs, *Of Ice and Men*, 49–53; James, *That Frozen Land*, 121–69.
28 James, *That Frozen Land*, 131
29 Ibid., 142
30 British Antarctic Survey Archives, AD6/2D/1945/K1, First sledge journey, 1945, 8
31 James, *That Frozen Land*, 143

32 *Hope Bay Howler*, 21 October 1945
33 Interview, 6 November 1987
34 James, *That Frozen Land*, 159
35 British Antarctic Survey Archives, AD6/2D/1945/K1, First sledge journey, 1945, 2
36 Interview, 6 November 1987

NINE: SCIENCE OVER POLITICS

1 The following account is based on John Giaever, *The White Desert: The Official Account of the Norwegian-British-Swedish Antarctic Expedition*, trans. by E.M. Huggard (London 1954), 107–8.
2 The account of the expedition is based on Giaever, *The White Desert*; E.F. Roots, 'An international expedition to Antarctica: the voyage to Queen Maud Land,' *Geographical Magazine* 23, no. 3 (July 1950), 85–100; E.F. Roots, 'The Norwegian-British-Swedish Antarctic expedition, 1949–52,' *Science News* 26 (1952), 9–32; author's interviews with E.F. Roots, 8 January 1984 and 29 October 1990.
3 Giaever, *The White Desert*, 15
4 The account of Roots's life and career is based on Giaever, *The White Desert*, 303; interviews, 8 January 1984 and 29 October 1990.
5 Interviews, 8 January 1984 and 29 October 1990
6 Giaever, *The White Desert*, 48
7 Roots, 'An international expedition to Antarctica,' 90
8 Giaever, *The White Desert*, 97
9 Ibid., 123
10 Interview, 29 October 1990
11 Roots, 'The Norwegian-British-Swedish Antarctic Expedition, 1949–52,' 9
12 Giaever, *The White Desert*, 99
13 Ibid., 137
14 Ibid., 146
15 Ibid., 154. A similar technique was developed on Richard Byrd's second Antarctic expedition; see Richard Evelyn Byrd, *Discovery:*

The Story of the Second Byrd Antarctic Expedition (New York 1935), 152.

16 Giaever, *The White Desert*, 156

17 Ibid., 245

18 For this sledging trip, see Roots's account, 'Journeys of the topographical-geological party, 1950–51,' Appendix 3 of Giaever, *The White Desert*, 245–80.

19 Ibid., 251

20 Ibid., 176–81

21 The following account is based on Duncan Carse, 'The survey of South Georgia, 1951–7,' *Geographical Journal* 125, pt. 1 (March 1959), 20–37; and Walter Roots, 'South Georgia,' *Canadian Alpine Journal* 36 (May 1953), 5–19.

22 Walter Roots's life and career is based on a letter to the author, 16 January 1986.

23 Roots, 'South Georgia,' 18

24 Giaever, *The White Desert*, 280

25 Ibid., 195

26 Interview, 28 January 1984

CONCLUSION

1 This account is based on Roger Mear and Robert Swan, *A Walk to the Pole: To the Heart of Antarctica in the Footsteps of Scott* (New York 1987), 168–229.

2 Ibid., 169

3 Ibid., 172

4 Cited in Mark Hume, 'Antarctic diary: a Canadian's trek to the South Pole,' *Ottawa Citizen*, 30 January 1988, F2

5 Transcript of author's interview with Gareth Wood, 19 November 1991

6 Timothy Dube, 'Arctic aviation,' *Archivist* 15, no. 5 (September–October, 1988), 5

7 Fred W. Hotson, *The de Havilland Canada Story* (Toronto 1983), 134–6, 224–6; J.E. Grimshaw, 'Assault on Antarctica,' *Canadian Aviation* 30 (September 1957), 46–7, 56

8 Jan McKillop, Canadian Foremost Limited, to author, 27 September 1984
9 Paul Friggens, 'They build houses from pole to pole,' *Reader's Digest*, January 1972; 'Trip to the bottom of the world,' *Time*, 5 January 1976, 58–9; company annual reports

Picture Credits

Index

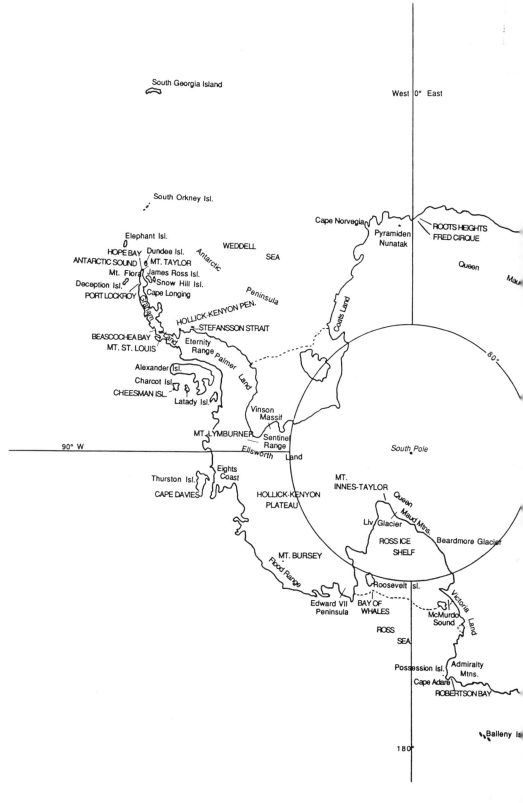